Talking It Over

George Sweeting

1 Cor. 13:13

Talking It Over

Fifty-two Inspiring Devotionals
with Daily Bible Readings
for People on the Move

By
George Sweeting

ISBN 0-8024-8529- 4

DEDICATION

To my four sons
George David
James Douglas
Donald William
Robert Bruce

with whom I have spent many
hours TALKING IT OVER

CONTENTS

BEGINNING

1

God's Favorite Word

Sunday—*Jesus' invitation (Matthew 11:25-30)*

²⁵At that time Jesus answered and said, "I praise Thee, O Father, Lord of heaven and earth, that Thou didst hide these things from the wise and intelligent and didst reveal them to babes. ²⁶"Yes, Father, for thus it was well-pleasing in Thy sight. ²⁷"All things have been handed over to Me by My Father; and no one knows the Son, except the Father; nor does anyone know the Father, except the Son, and anyone to whom the Son wills to reveal Him. ²⁸"Come to Me, all who are weary and heavy-laden, and I will give you rest. ²⁹"Take My yoke upon you, and learn from Me, for I am gentle and humble in heart; and YOU SHALL FIND REST FOR YOUR SOULS. ³⁰"For My yoke is easy, and My load is light."

Do you have a favorite word? A word you find yourself using over and over again? Does some noun or adjective have a particular ring that you enjoy?

Although no one fully knows the mind of God, I have a feeling that God must have some very special words. One word, the word given to man before God judged the earth with the Flood, echoes in every part of the Bible.

This same word changed Peter from a rugged, rough, coarse fisherman into a devoted and beloved disciple of Christ.

It is the word that Jesus spoke to the little children who gathered about Him, and to the sick and burdened multitudes. What is that word? It is the word *come*. The word *come* is one of the greatest words of the Bible.

"Good words," said the English poet George Herbert, "are worth much but cost little." That may be true in writing or speaking, but the beautiful word *come* was infinitely costly for Christ. Jesus left His dwelling place in eternity to come to earth to be crucified for our sin that we might come into a personal relationship with Almighty God.

Yes, *come* is the great word of the gospel. *Go* was the great word of the Law. The Law pointed out the gulf between God and man, but the gospel of Jesus Christ bridges that great gulf. It calls us to be reconciled to God; it provides a way to escape judgment for our sins.

Throughout the entire Bible, we find God's invitation to come for forgiveness and salvation. To the weary, Jesus offers rest and comfort. "Come unto me, all ye that labour," said Jesus, "and I will give you rest" (Matthew 11:28, KJV).*

The hands of Jesus were open to lift the fallen, to bless the little children, to touch the sick. On the cross, the hands of Jesus were wide open. Those very hands reach out lovingly to you, saying, "Come with your fears, your frustrations, your emptiness, and your sin."

*Unless noted otherwise, Scriptures quoted in the meditations are from the King James Version.

12

When David Brainerd, a great missionary statesman, was seventeen, he was confused about God's plan of salvation. He knew that the Bible told him to come to Christ, but he did not know how to come. He said, "I thought I would gladly come to Jesus, but I had no directions as to getting through."

As he prayed, Brainerd thought, *"When a mother tells her child to come to her, she does not tell him how to come. He may come with a run, a jump, a skip, or a leap. He may come praying, shouting, singing, or even crying. It doesn't matter how he comes, so long as he comes."*

The same thing is true with salvation. It does not matter how we come to Christ; the important thing is that we do come to Him. Come now, just as you are. Someone has made an acrostic from the word come. C is for children, O is for old, M is for the middle-aged, E is for everybody. The fact is that God wants everyone to come to Him.

The last few verses in the Bible extend this invitation as a fitting climax to the Scriptures. Revelation 22:17 says: "And the Spirit and the bride say, Come. And let him that heareth say, Come. And let him that is athirst come. And whosoever will, let him take the water of life freely."

God the Father, God the Son, and God the Holy Spirit say, "Come." The church, the Bride of Christ, also says, "Come." The best possible response to God's favorite word is to come.

ON THE CROSS THE HANDS OF JESUS WERE
WIDE OPEN!

Monday—*God's long-suffering (Psalm 103:6-14)*
⁶The LORD performs righteous deeds,
  And judgments for all who are oppressed.
⁷He made known His ways to Moses,
  His acts to the sons of Israel.
⁸The LORD is compassionate and gracious,
  Slow to anger and abounding in lovingkindness.
⁹He will not always strive with us;

Nor will He keep His anger forever.
¹⁰He has not dealt with us according to our sins,
Nor rewarded us according to our iniquities.
¹¹For as high as the heavens are above the earth,
So great is His lovingkindness toward those who fear Him.
¹²As far as the east is from the west,
So far has He removed our transgressions from us.
¹³Just as a father has compassion on his children,
So the Lord has compassion on those who fear Him.
¹⁴For He Himself knows our frame;
He is mindful that we are but dust.

Tuesday—*God's mercy to Israel (Isaiah 65:1-5)*

¹"I permitted Myself to be sought by those who did not ask for
    Me;
I permitted Myself to be found by those who did not seek Me.
I said, 'Here am I, here am I,'
To a nation which did not call on My name.
²"I have spread out My hands all day long to a rebellious
    people,
Who walk in the way which is not good, following their own
    thoughts,
³A people who continually provoke Me to My face,
Offering sacrifices in gardens and burning incense on bricks;
⁴Who sit among graves, and spend the night in secret places;
Who eat swine's flesh,
And the broth of unclean meat is in their pots.
⁵"Who say, 'Keep to yourself, do not come near me,
For I am holier than you!'
These are smoke in My nostrils,
A fire that burns all the day."

Wednesday—*An invitation to rest (Hebrews 4:10-16)*

¹⁰For the one who has entered His rest has himself also rested
from his works, as God did from His. ¹¹Let us therefore be
diligent to enter that rest, lest anyone fall through following the
same example of disobedience. ¹²For the word of God is living
and active and sharper than any two-edged sword, and piercing
as far as the division of soul and spirit, of both joints and marrow, and able to judge the thoughts and intentions of the heart.
¹³And there is no creature hidden from His sight, but all things

are open and laid bare to the eyes of Him with whom we have to do. ¹⁴Since then we have a great high priest who has passed through the heavens, Jesus the Son of God, let us hold fast our confession. ¹⁵For we do not have a high priest who cannot sympathize with our weaknesses, but one who has been tempted in all things as we are, yet without sin. ¹⁶Let us therefore draw near with confidence to the throne of grace, that we may receive mercy and may find grace to help in time of need.

Thursday—*Jesus' invitation to the children (Mark 10:13-16)*
¹³And they began bringing children to Him, so that He might touch them; and the disciples rebuked them. ¹⁴But when Jesus saw this, He was indignant and said to them, "Permit the children to come to Me; do not hinder them; for the kingdom of God belongs to such as these. ¹⁵Truly I say to you, whoever does not receive the kingdom of God like a child shall not enter it at all." ¹⁶And He took them in His arms and began blessing them, laying His hands upon them.

Friday—*Jesus' call to the disciples (Mark 1:16-20)*
¹⁶And as He was going along by the Sea of Galilee, He saw Simon and Andrew, the brother of Simon, casting a net in the sea; for they were fishermen. ¹⁷And Jesus said to them, "Follow Me, and I will make you become fishers of men." ¹⁸And they immediately left the nets and followed Him. ¹⁹And going on a little farther, He saw James the son of Zebedee, and John his brother, who were also in the boat mending the nets. ²⁰And immediately He called them; and they left their father Zebedee in the boat with the hired servants, and went away to follow Him.

Saturday—*The final invitation (Revelation 22:16-21)*
¹⁶"I, Jesus, have sent My angel to testify to you these things for the churches. I am the root and the offspring of David, the bright morning star." ¹⁷And the Spirit and the bride say, "Come." And let the one who hears say, "Come." And let the one who is thirsty come; let the one who wishes take the water of life without cost. ¹⁸I testify to everyone who hears the words of prophecy of this book: if anyone adds to them, God shall add to him the plagues which are written in this book; ¹⁹and if anyone takes away from the words of the book of this prophecy,

God shall take away his part from the tree of life and from the holy city, which are written in this book. [20]He who testifies to these things says, "Yes, I am coming quickly." Amen. Come, Lord Jesus. [21]The grace of the Lord Jesus be with all. Amen.

2

Closed Doors

Sunday—*Prepared and unprepared wedding guests*
**   *(Matthew 25:1-13)***

[1]"Then the kingdom of heaven will be comparable to ten virgins, who took their lamps, and went out to meet the bridegroom. [2]And five of them were foolish, and five were prudent. [3]For when the foolish took their lamps, they took no oil with them, [4]but the prudent took oil in flasks along with their lamps. [5]Now while the bridegroom was delaying, they all got drowsy and began to sleep. [6]But at midnight there was a shout, 'Behold, the bridegroom! Come out to meet him.' [7]Then all those virgins arose, and trimmed their lamps. [8]And the foolish said to the prudent, 'Give us some of your oil, for our lamps are going out.' [9]But the prudent answered, saying, 'No, there will not be enough for us and you too; go instead to the dealers and buy some for yourselves.' [10]And while they were going away to make the purchase, the bridegroom came, and those who were ready went in with him to the wedding feast; and the door was shut. [11]And later the other virgins also came, saying, 'Lord, lord, open up for us.' [12]But he answered and said, 'Truly I say to you, I do not know you.' [13]Be on the alert then, for you do not know the day nor the hour.''

Matthew 25 relates a parable about ten virgins who were waiting for a bridegroom. Five of them were wise and prepared for his arrival, but five of them were foolish and waited until it was too late to prepare. They went out to buy oil for their lamps and missed the wedding. Matthew 25:10 simply states, "And while they went to buy, the bridegroom came; and they that were ready went in with him to the marriage: and the door was shut." Opportunities do not last forever.

A similar thought is expressed in the account of Noah and his family entering the ark. "And they that went in . . . and the LORD shut him in" (Genesis 7:16). God shut the door behind Noah, and no one else could get in. Open doors will ultimately close. The road marked Tomorrow leads to the town called Never.

We tend to think worse of sins of commission than we do of sins of omission. We have the idea that it is worse to do what we should not than to neglect doing what we should. But neglected opportunity results in lost opportunity. The sin of the priest and Levite in Luke 10 was that they did nothing. They passed by on the other side, numb to human need, and left the injured man to the good Samaritan.

The same neglect is seen in the story of the rich man and Lazarus in Luke 16:19-26. The rich man was not guilty of deliberate evil. His sin was failing to do good. His error was neglect. But he perished for his neglect.

Luke 19:20 tells of the man who hid his talent in a napkin. He committed no barbarous deeds, but he did nothing with his opportunity. He sinned. James 4:17 says, "To him that knoweth to do good, and doeth it not, to him it is sin."

Neglect is serious. Neglect of Christ's salvation is fatal. "How shall we escape, if we neglect so great salvation?" (Hebrews 2:3). Continued neglect results in closed doors.

Ivan Albright painted a picture now hanging in the Chicago Art Institute of an eight-foot door shaped like the lid of an old casket. The door is scarred and bruised, supposedly by the difficult experiences of life. A funeral wreath of wilted flowers hangs on the closed door. The colors are dull and somber. The painting is entitled, "That Which I Should Have Done I Did Not Do." What a sad thought!

The Scripture calls us to decide for or against Christ now, while it is today. In fact, God promises no tomorrow, only now. Now is the only sure moment. Now is the day of salvation and service. Jesus says, "Behold, I stand at the door, and knock: if any man hear my voice, and open the door, I will come in to him, and will sup with him, and he with me" (Revelation 3:20). He will not stand there knocking forever.

If you have never received Jesus Christ as your savior, receive Him now. If you have received Christ, bring glory to God now.

Undeveloped talents evaporate. Unused muscles atrophy. Undisturbed water pollutes. Unstirred air stagnates. Unwound clocks stop. Unentered doors close.

Neglect will ruin you.

THE ROAD MARKED "TOMORROW" LEADS TO
THE TOWN CALLED "NEVER."

Monday—*The ark boarded by ready passengers*
      (Genesis 7:7-16)

7Then Noah and his sons and his wife and his sons' wives with him entered the ark because of the water of the flood. 8Of clean animals and animals that are not clean and birds and everything that creeps on the ground, 9there went into the ark to Noah by twos, male and female, as God had commanded Noah. 10And it came about after the seven days, that the water of the flood came upon the earth. 11In the six hundredth year of Noah's life, in the second month, on the seventeenth day of the month, on the same day all the fountains of the great deep burst open, and the floodgates of the sky were

19

opened. ¹²And the rain fell upon the earth for forty days and forty nights. ¹³On the very same day Noah and Shem and Ham and Japheth, the sons of Noah, and Noah's wife and the three wives of his sons with them, entered the ark, ¹⁴they and every beast after its kind, and all the cattle after their kind, and every creeping thing that creeps on the earth after its kind, and every bird after its kind, all sorts of birds. ¹⁵So they went into the ark to Noah, by twos of all flesh in which was the breath of life. ¹⁶And those that entered, male and female of all flesh, entered as God had commanded him; and the LORD closed it behind him.

Tuesday—*An opportunity grasped by a Samaritan* (Luke 10:30-37)

³⁰Jesus replied and said, "A certain man was going down from Jerusalem to Jericho; and he fell among robbers, and they stripped him and beat him, and went off leaving him half dead. ³¹And by chance a certain priest was going down on that road, and when he saw him, he passed by on the other side. ³²And likewise a Levite also, when he came to the place and saw him, passed by on the other side. ³³But a certain Samaritan, who was on a journey, came upon him; and when he saw him, he felt compassion, ³⁴and came to him, and bandaged up his wounds, pouring oil and wine on them; and he put him on his own beast, and brought him to an inn, and took care of him. ³⁵And on the next day he took out two denarii and gave them to the innkeeper and said, 'Take care of him; and whatever more you spend, when I return, I will repay you.' ³⁶Which of these three do you think proved to be a neighbor to the man who fell into the robbers' hands?" ³⁷And he said, "The one who showed mercy toward him." And Jesus said to him, "Go and do the same."

Wednesday—*The cost of rich living in selfishness* (Luke 16:19-26)

¹⁹"Now there was a certain rich man, and he habitually dressed in purple and fine linen, gaily living in splendor every day. ²⁰And a certain poor man named Lazarus was laid at his gate, covered with sores, ²¹and longing to be fed with the crumbs which were falling from the rich man's table; besides,

even the dogs were coming and licking his sores. ²²Now it came about that the poor man died and he was carried away by the angels to Abraham's bosom; and the rich man also died and was buried. ²³And in Hades he lifted up his eyes, being in torment, and saw Abraham far away, and Lazarus in his bosom. ²⁴And he cried out and said, 'Father Abraham, have mercy on me, and send Lazarus, that he may dip the tip of his finger in water and cool off my tongue; for I am in agony in this flame.' ²⁵But Abraham said, 'Child, remember that during your life you received your good things, and likewise Lazarus bad things; but now he is being comforted here, and you are in agony. ²⁶And besides all this, between us and you there is a great chasm fixed, in order that those who wish to come over from here to you may not be able, and that none may cross over from there to us.' "

Thursday—*The parable of the wasted talent* *(Matthew 25:14-30)*

¹⁴"For it is just like a man about to go on a journey, who called his own slaves, and entrusted his possessions to them. ¹⁵And to one he gave five talents, to another, two, and to another, one, each according to his own ability; and he went on his journey. ¹⁶Immediately the one who had received the five talents went and traded with them, and gained five more talents. ¹⁷In the same manner the one who had received the two talents gained two more. ¹⁸But he who received the one talent went away and dug in the ground, and hid his master's money. ¹⁹Now after a long time the master of those slaves came and settled accounts with them. ²⁰And the one who had received the five talents came up and brought five more talents, saying, 'Master, you entrusted five talents to me; see, I have gained five more talents.' ²¹His master said to him, 'Well done, good and faithful slave; you were faithful with a few things, I will put you in charge of many things, enter into the joy of your master.' ²²The one also who had received the two talents came up and said, 'Master, you entrusted to me two talents; see, I have gained two more talents.' ²³His master said to him, 'Well done, good and faithful slave; you were faithful with a few things, I will put you in charge of many things; enter into the joy of your master.' ²⁴And the one also who had received the one talent came up and said, 'Master, I knew you to be a hard man, reap-

21

ing where you did not sow, and gathering where you scattered no seed. 25And I was afraid, and went away and hid your talent in the ground; see, you have what is yours.' 26But his master answered and said to him, 'You wicked, lazy slave, you knew that I reap where I did not sow, and gather where I scattered no seed. 27Then you ought to have put my money in the bank, and on my arrival I would have received my money back with interest. 28Therefore take away the talent from him, and give it to the one who has the ten talents.' 29For to everyone who has shall more be given, and he shall have an abundance; but from the one who does not have, even what he does have shall be taken away. 30And cast out the worthless slave into the outer darkness; in that place there shall be weeping and gnashing of teeth."

Friday—*Planning to do right included in right planning (James 4:13-17)*

13Come now, you who say, "Today or tomorrow, we shall go to such and such a city, and spend a year there and engage in business and make a profit." 14Yet you do not know what your life will be like tomorrow. You are just a vapor that appears for a little while and then vanishes away. 15Instead, you ought to say, "If the Lord wills, we shall live and also do this or that." 16But as it is, you boast in your arrogance; all such boasting is evil. 17Therefore, to one who knows the right thing to do, and does not do it, to him it is sin.

Saturday—*The time for work (John 9:1-7)*

1And as He passed by, He saw a man blind from birth. 2And His disciples asked Him, saying, "Rabbi, who sinned, this man or his parents, that he should be born blind?" 3Jesus answered, "It was neither that this man sinned, nor his parents; but it was in order that the works of God might be displayed in him. 4"We must work the works of Him who sent Me, as long as it is day; night is coming, when no man can work. 5"While I am in the world, I am the light of the world." 6When He had said this, He spat on the ground, and made clay of the spittle, and applied the clay to his eyes, 7and said to him, "Go, wash in the pool of Siloam" (which is translated, Sent). And so he went away and washed, and came back seeing.

3

Born Again

Sunday—*The need to be born twice (John 3:3-6)*

³Jesus answered and said to him, "Truly, truly, I say to you, unless one is born again, he cannot see the kingdom of God." ⁴Nicodemus said to Him, "How can a man be born when he is old? He cannot enter a second time into his mother's womb and be born, can he?" ⁵Jesus answered, "Truly, truly, I say to you, unless one is born of water and the Spirit, he cannot enter into the kingdom of God. ⁶That which is born of the flesh is flesh; and that which is born of the Spirit is spirit."

Recently I heard a secular news commentator use the phrase *born again* in speaking about a prominent man. The commentator doubted that any would understand the meaning of this quaint expression.

His comment prompted me to write him a kind letter suggesting that millions of voting-age Americans knew more about being born again than he could imagine.

Time magazine has suggested that there might be as many as forty million evangelical Christians in America. Of course, only God knows the validity of any profession of individual faith.

The phrase *born again* has been around since it was first used by Jesus. To a gifted leader, Jesus said, "Except a man be born again, he cannot see the kingdom of God" (John 3:3).

Martin Luther expressed his salvation experience this way: "When by the Spirit of God, I understood these words, 'The just shall live by faith,' I felt born again like a new man: I entered through the open doors into the very Paradise of God!"

Religion is very popular in our day. Many people say, "I believe in God. I believe in Christ, and I believe in the Bible." Sometimes the lives of such people do not correspond with their beliefs. Does that show a saving faith or a false faith?

The Bible reminds us that "faith without works is dead" (James 2:20), and "by their fruits ye shall know them" (Matthew 7:20). In other words, people whose beliefs do not affect their behavior are in the flesh and "shall of the flesh reap corruption" (Galatians 6:8).

Almost every criminal believes it is better to be honest, but that does not make him honest. Almost every drunkard believes it is better to be sober, but mere belief does nothing to change his condition.

Many see faith as a simple acquiescence to the truth of the Word of God. But this kind of faith is deadening and even damning. The Bible reminds us that "the devils also believe, and tremble" (James 2:19). The difference between heart belief and head belief is the difference between heaven and hell. Faith that does not result in a changed life is a false faith.

To be born again is to experience a spiritual birth (John 3:6). Although every human being is a creature of God through physical birth, we become the children of God only through a spiritual rebirth. "But as many as received him, to them gave he power to become the sons of God, even to them that believe on his name: *which were born,* not of blood, nor of the will of the flesh, nor of the will of man, but *of God*" (John 1:12-13, italics added).

To receive Christ is to have faith in Him, that He is the sinless Son of God and that He died voluntarily for our sins on the cross so that we might be free from spiritual death and judgment and have everlasting life. To receive Jesus Christ is to commit yourself completely to Him.

If we take the first three words and the last two words of John 1:13, we have the phrase, "Which were born . . . of God." That is a good biblical definition of what it means to be born again.

> THE DIFFERENCE BETWEEN HEART BELIEF
> AND HEAD BELIEF IS THE DIFFERENCE
> BETWEEN HEAVEN AND HELL.

Monday—*Born to hope (1 Peter 1:3-5)*

³Blessed be the God and Father of our Lord Jesus Christ, who according to His great mercy has caused us to be born again to a living hope through the resurrection of Jesus Christ from the dead, ⁴to obtain an inheritance which is imperishable and undefiled and will not fade away, reserved in heaven for you, ⁵who are protected by the power of God through faith for a salvation ready to be revealed in the last time.

Tuesday—*Christ's suffering for us (1 Peter 2:21-25)*

²¹For you have been called for this purpose, since Christ also suffered for you, leaving you an example for you to follow in His steps, ²²WHO COMMITTED NO SIN, NOR WAS ANY DECEIT

25

FOUND IN HIS MOUTH; ²³and while being reviled, He did not revile in return; while suffering, He uttered no threats, but kept entrusting Himself to Him who judges righteously; ²⁴and He Himself bore our sins in His body on the cross, that we might die to sin and live to righteousness; for by His wounds you were healed. ²⁵For you were continually straying like sheep, but now you have returned to the Shepherd and Guardian of your souls.

Wednesday—*Redemption in Christ (Romans 3:21-26)*

²¹But now apart from the Law the righteousness of God has been manifested, being witnessed by the Law and the Prophets; ²²even the righteousness of God through faith in Jesus Christ for all those who believe; for there is no distinction; ²³for all have sinned and fall short of the glory of God, ²⁴being justified as a gift by His grace through the redemption which is in Christ Jesus; ²⁵whom God displayed publicly as a propitiation in His blood through faith. This was to demonstrate His righteousness, because in the forbearance of God He passed over the sins previously committed; ²⁶for the demonstration, I say, of His righteousness at the present time, that He might be just and the justifier of the one who has faith in Jesus.

Thursday—*Not our works, but God's grace (Titus 3:4-9)*

⁴But when the kindness of God our Savior and His love for mankind appeared, ⁵He saved us, not on the basis of deeds which we have done in righteousness, but according to His mercy, by the washing of regeneration and renewing by the Holy Spirit, ⁶whom He poured out upon us richly through Jesus Christ our Savior, ⁷that being justified by His grace we might be made heirs according to the hope of eternal life. ⁸This is a trustworthy statement; and concerning these things I want you to speak confidently, so that those who have believed God may be careful to engage in good deeds. These things are good and profitable for men. ⁹But shun foolish controversies and genealogies and strife and disputes about the Law; for they are unprofitable and worthless.

Friday—*Being born of God proved by love (1 John 5:1-5)*

¹Whoever believes that Jesus is the Christ is born of God; and whoever loves the Father loves the child born of Him. ²By this

we know that we love the children of God, when we love God and observe His commandments. ³For this is the love of God, that we keep His commandments; and His commandments are not burdensome. ⁴For whatever is born of God overcomes the world; and this is the victory that has overcome the world—our faith. ⁵And who is the one who overcomes the world, but he who believes that Jesus is the Son of God?

Saturday—*A changed life (Galatians 6:6-12)*

⁶And let the one who is taught the word share all good things with him who teaches. ⁷Do not be deceived, God is not mocked; for whatever a man sows, this he will also reap. ⁸For the one who sows to his own flesh shall from the flesh reap corruption, but the one who sows to the Spirit shall from the Spirit reap eternal life. ⁹And let us not lose heart in doing good, for in due time we shall reap if we do not grow weary. ¹⁰So then, while we have opportunity, let us do good to all men, and especially to those who are of the household of the faith. ¹¹See with what large letters I am writing to you with my own hand. ¹²Those who desire to make a good showing in the flesh try to compel you to be circumcised, simply that they may not be persecuted for the cross of Christ.

4

The Good News

Sunday—*The resurrection of Christ (Matthew 28:1-8)*
¹Now after the Sabbath, as it began to dawn toward the first day of the week, Mary Magdalene and the other Mary came to look at the grave. ²And behold, a severe earthquake had occurred, for an angel of the lord descended from heaven and came and rolled away the stone and sat upon it. ³And his appearance was like lightning, and his garment as white as snow; ⁴and the guards shook for fear of him, and became like dead men. ⁵And the angel answered and said to the women, "Do not be afraid; for I know that you are looking for Jesus who has been crucified. ⁶He is not here, for He has risen, just as He said. Come, see the place where He was lying. ⁷And go quickly and tell His disciples that He has risen from the dead; and behold, He is going before you into Galilee, there you will see Him; behold, I have told you." ⁸And they departed quickly from the tomb with fear and great joy and ran to report it to His disciples.

Medicine is waging a worldwide war on sickness and death. In 1967, in Cape Town, South Africa, Dr. Christian Barnard performed the world's first heart transplant. The patient, a victim of advanced heart disease, lived only eighteen days. Since then, hundreds of heart transplants have been performed, some adding years to patients' lives.

Despite medical progress, however, death is still our greatest enemy. That is an inescapable fact of life.

But there is hope! The good news is that Jesus overcame death nearly two thousand years ago. The apostle Paul declares in 1 Corinthians 15:3-4, "Christ died for our sins according to the scriptures . . . was buried, and . . . rose again the third day."

Those are facts, not suppositions. Although Jesus Christ's resurrection took place nearly two thousand years ago, the details of it are among the best attested in all history. Matthew, Mark, Luke, John, the two followers who met Jesus on the Emmaus road, Thomas, and many others tell us Jesus died and rose again.

Jesus' enemies would have given their lives for a shred of evidence to disprove the resurrection. But they found none.

First, there is the fact that *Jesus really died*. That was the purpose of crucifixion, administered by Roman soldiers. After six hours of indescribable agony, the gospels tell us, He died. At the end of the day, when soldiers came to break the victims' legs, they found Him already dead.

Our Lord's body was then wrapped in spices—John says about one hundred pounds—and left in the grave. The tomb was closed with a huge stone and then sealed with the Roman seal. Any person moving it (impossible without several accomplices) would have been guilty of a crime against the Roman government. As if that were not enough, the tomb was guarded—not by one, but by several professional soldiers.

By Easter morning, however, the stone had been rolled

away. Only the empty body wrappings were left inside the tomb.

Second, *Jesus was seen alive by different people.* The list includes Mary Magdalene, the two Marys who came to the tomb together, Simon Peter, and two believers on the road to Emmaus. He also appeared to the disciples in the upper room when Thomas was absent and again when he was present. He met the disciples by the Sea of Tiberias. Could all of them have been deceived?

Third, *the believers who saw the risen Christ were changed;* they were convinced of Jesus' resurrection. Days earlier they were crushed, defeated, discouraged, and afraid. Then, a total change came over them. In the face of opposition and almost certain death, they went out with boldness to preach a living Christ everywhere. Why? Because they knew He was alive! Transformed lives testify to the truth of the resurrection.

Yes, Jesus Christ rose from the grave and lives today. But the good news is something more. It is the thrilling guarantee that every Christian who dies will one day be raised, even as Christ Himself was raised.

"Because I live," Jesus told His disciples in John 14:19, "ye shall live also." Anchor your faith to the good news of the resurrection.

> TRANSFORMED LIVES TESTIFY TO THE
> TRUTH OF THE RESURRECTION.

Monday—*Proof of the resurrection (1 Corinthians 15:1-8)*

¹Now I make known to you, brethren, the gospel which I preached to you, which also you received, in which also you stand, ²by which also you are saved, if you hold fast the word which I preached to you, unless you believed in vain. ³For I delivered to you as of first importance what I also received, that Christ died for our sins according to the Scriptures, ⁴and that He was buried, and that He was raised on the third day according to the Scriptures, ⁵and that He appeared to Cephas,

then to the twelve. [6]After that He appeared to more than five hundred brethren at one time, most of whom remain until now, but some have fallen asleep; [7]then He appeared to James, then to all the apostles; [8]and last of all, as it were to one untimely born, He appeared to me also.

Tuesday—*The importance of the resurrection* *(1 Corinthians 15:12-19)*

[12]Now if Christ is preached, that He has been raised from the dead, how do some among you say that there is no resurrection of the dead? [13]But if there is no resurrection of the dead, not even Christ has been raised; [14]and if Christ has not been raised, then our preaching is vain, your faith also is vain. [15]Moreover we are even found to be false witnesses of God, because we witnessed against God that He raised Christ, whom He did not raise, if in fact the dead are not raised. [16]For if the dead are not raised, not even Christ has been raised; [17]and if Christ has not been raised, your faith is worthless; you are still in your sins. [18]Then those also who have fallen asleep in Christ have perished. [19]If we have only hoped in Christ in this life, we are of all men most to be pitied.

Wednesday—*The principle of resurrection* *(1 Corinthians 15:35-44)*

[35]But some one will say, "How are the dead raised? And with what kind of body do they come?" [36]You fool! That which you sow does not come to life unless it dies; [37]and that which you sow, you do not sow the body which is to be, but a bare grain, perhaps of wheat or of something else. [38]But God gives it a body just as He wished, and to each of the seeds a body of its own. [39]All flesh is not the same flesh, but there is one flesh of men, and another flesh of beasts, and another flesh of birds, and another of fish. [40]There are also heavenly bodies and earthly bodies, but the glory of the heavenly is one, and the glory of the earthly is another. [41]There is one glory of the sun, and another glory of the moon, and another glory of the stars; for star differs from star in glory. [42]So also is the resurrection of the dead. It is sown a perishable body, it is raised an imperishable body; [43]it is sown in dishonor, it is raised in glory; it is sown in weakness, it is raised in power; [44]it is sown a natural body, it is raised a spiritual body. If there is a natural body, there is also a spiritual body.

Thursday—*The promise of resurrection*
(1 Corinthians 15:51-58)

[51]Behold, I tell you a mystery; we shall not all sleep, but we shall all be changed, [52]in a moment, in the twinkling of an eye, at the last trumpet; for the trumpet will sound, and the dead will be raised imperishable, and we shall be changed. [53]For this perishable must put on the imperishable, and this mortal must put on immortality. [54]But when this perishable will have put on the imperishable, and this mortal will have put on immortality, then will come about the saying that is written, "DEATH IS SWALLOWED UP IN VICTORY. [55]"O DEATH, WHERE IS YOUR VICTORY? O DEATH, WHERE IS YOUR STING?" [56]The sting of death is sin, and the power of sin is the law; [57]but thanks be to God, who gives us the victory through our Lord Jesus Christ. [58]Therefore, my beloved brethren, be steadfast, immovable, always abounding in the work of the Lord, knowing that your toil is not in vain in the Lord.

Friday—*The hope of redemption (Romans 8:18-23)*

[18]For I consider that the sufferings of this present time are not worthy to be compared with the glory that is to be revealed to us. [19]For the anxious longing of the creation waits eagerly for the revealing of the sons of God. [20]For the creation was subjected to futility, not of its own will, but because of Him who subjected it, in hope [21]that the creation itself also will be set free from its slavery to corruption into the freedom of the glory of the children of God. [22]For we know that the whole creation groans and suffers the pains of childbirth together until now. [23]And not only this, but also we ourselves, having the first fruits of the Spirit, even we ourselves groan within ourselves, waiting eagerly for our adoption as sons, the redemption of our body.

Saturday—*The final resurrections (Revelation 20:4-15)*

[4]And I saw thrones, and they sat upon them, and judgment was given to them. And I saw the souls of those who had been beheaded because of the testimony of Jesus and because of the word of God, and those who had not worshiped the beast or his image, and had not received the mark upon their forehead and upon their hand; and they came to life and reigned with Christ for a thousand years. [5]The rest of the dead did not come to life

until the thousand years were completed. This is the first resurrection. ⁶Blessed and holy is the one who has a part in the first resurrection; over these the second death has no power, but they will be priests of God and of Christ and will reign with Him for a thousand years. ⁷And when the thousand years are completed, Satan will be released from his prison, ⁸and will come out to deceive the nations which are in the four corners of the earth, Gog and Magog, to gather them together for the war; the number of them is like the sand of the seashore. ⁹And they came up on the broad plain of the earth and surrounded the camp of the saints and the beloved city, and fire came down from heaven and devoured them. ¹⁰And the devil who deceived them was thrown into the lake of fire and brimstone, where the beast and the false prophet are also; and they will be tormented day and night forever and ever. ¹¹And I saw a great white throne and Him who sat upon it, from whose presence earth and heaven fled away, and no place was found for them. ¹²And I saw the dead, the great and the small, standing before the throne, and books were opened; and another book was opened, which is the book of life; and the dead were judged from the things which were written in the books, according to their deeds. ¹³And the sea gave up the dead which were in it, and death and Hades gave up the dead which were in them; and they were judged, every one of them according to their deeds. ¹⁴And death and Hades were thrown into the lake of fire. This is the second death, the lake of fire. ¹⁵And if anyone's name was not found written in the book of life, he was thrown into the lake of fire.

5

What Is Your Favorite Game?

Sunday—*Jesus: life and light (John 1:1-14)*

¹In the beginning was the Word, and the Word was with God, and the Word was God. ²He was in the beginning with God. ³All things came into being through Him; and apart from Him nothing came into being that has come into being. ⁴In Him was life; and the life was the light of men. ⁵And the light shines in the darkness; and the darkness did not comprehend it. ⁶There came a man, sent from God, whose name was John. ⁷He came for a witness, that he might bear witness of the light, that all might believe through him. ⁸He was not the light, but came that he might bear witness of the light. ⁹There was the true light which, coming into the world, enlightens every man. ¹⁰He was in the world, and the world was made through Him, and the world did not know Him. ¹¹He came to His own, and those who were His own did not receive Him. ¹²But as many as received Him, to them He gave the right to become children of God, even to those who believe in His name: ¹³who were born not of blood, nor of the will of the flesh, nor of the will of man, but of God. ¹⁴And the Word became flesh, and dwelt among us, and we beheld His glory as of the only begotten from the Father, full of grace and truth.

Playing games is a common pastime, whether you realize it or not. Not checkers or dominoes or chess, but social games that we devise to make us feel closer to other people. I heard of a girl who turns on her radio every night just in time to hear the announcer say, "We bid you a very pleasant good night." All she wants is a human voice speaking to her.

An executive returns to his office after dinner, Sundays, and even holidays. He drives himself to fulfill his idea of success. But it has been years since he and his wife have spent any meaningful time together.

A grandmother goes shopping and buys another unneeded hat. She is disappointed because her husband has been called out of town again. So she is off to grab a new "thing" to try to cure her empty feeling.

A young divorcee goes back to her paint and canvas. As she structures her long new day with appointments to sell her sketches, she is offering a part of herself in the hope that someone will notice her.

One woman calls another to have lunch. They sip their coffee and talk all around themselves, but they never really make contact.

A bachelor plays house with an eager coed he has met. He wants someone in his apartment to talk with, to feel close to.

What is it that we hunt for in life? What do we really want? What moves us through day after day, month after month, year after year? What would make us sell out, or give up everything we have?

Our needs are many. Our desires are constant. We cry, "Gimme," by our attitudes, our glances, our conversations, our actions. We find many stopgap answers. But always there is the big hole, begging to be filled. The more we have been loved, it seems, the greater the hole yawns. We pour into it an astonishing collection of things: work projects, television, athletics, club memberships, travel, entertainment, volunteer service, study parties, barbiturates. But if we are honest, we have to admit that the human satisfaction we gain creates a longing for even greater fulfillment than anything we have yet experienced. The deepest want of all is to find what some people call "at-oneness." Some call it "peace of soul" or "peace with God."

The strange truth about our human involvements is that they both meet and do not meet our deepest needs. The more we have, the more we want—especially of love. So we improvise our own little games. We learn how to play them with increasing skill. They keep us occupied, and give to us a sense of temporary triumph and satisfaction.

All of life is spent in an effort to overcome the separation that is common to men and women everywhere. Even strangers passing in the night will wonder whether their coming together might create union, or further emphasize each one's aloneness. Loneliness is hell, and hell is irrevocable and final separateness.

The inner expectation of really belonging to someone drives us to a constant search for reunion. We know the blinding, superb moment of discovery as we find another being who seems poured from the same mold. But we also know the gradual dawning of realization that even this special person is not enough.

There is no substitute in man's experience for knowing God. He made us in His own image, and our reunion with Him is the foundation for everything else we seek. No game—not even marriage—is serious or permanent enough to satisfy our restless search for completeness.

The only way to realize satisfaction and fulfillment is to say yes to God, who is love, and in whose mold we are shaped. When we say no to His will, we are not only out of place with Him, but out of relationship with our fellowman.

People have been trying to bridge their separate existence since the world began. But God, being love, stepped over the gulf one day as a real human person. Christ Jesus is the one who invaded our world in a human form we can understand. He came as a servant to say yes to everything God asked of Him. He became obedient to the death of the cross so that we might be saved.

A true Christian believes that he was made by God, and that his highest usefulness is to love and serve Him. If that is true, we are wasting our time playing games to win satisfaction. Consider saying yes to Jesus Christ in everything, because that is what we were made for. And we will not ever be satisfied until we are at one with Jesus Christ.

> NO GAME, SERIOUS OR PERMANENT, NOT
> EVEN MARRIAGE, IS ENOUGH TO SATISFY
> OUR RESTLESS SEARCH FOR COMPLETENESS.

Monday—*Jesus: Revealer of God's love (John 3:13-21)*

[13]"And no one has ascended into heaven, but He who descended from heaven, even the Son of Man. [14]And as Moses lifted up the serpent in the wilderness, even so must the Son of Man be lifted up; [15]that whoever believes may in Him have eternal life. [16]For God so loved the world, that He gave His only begotten Son, that whoever believes in Him should not perish, but have eternal life. [17]For God did not send the Son into the world to judge the world; but that the world should be saved through Him. [18]He who believes in Him is not judged; he who does not believe has been judged already, because he has not believed in the name of the only begotten Son of God. [19]And this is the judgment, that the light is come into the world, and men loved the darkness rather than the light; for their deeds were evil. [20]For everyone who does evil hates the light, and does not come to the light, lest his deeds should be exposed. [21]But he who practices the truth comes to the light, that his deeds may be manifested as having been wrought in God."

Tuesday—*Jesus: the Bread of Life (John 6:28-40)*

[28]They said therefore to Him, "What shall we do, that we may work the works of God?" [29]Jesus answered and said to them, "This is the work of God, that you believe in Him whom He has

sent." 30They said therefore to Him, "What then do You do for a sign, that we may see, and believe You? What work do You perform? 31Our fathers ate the manna in the wilderness; as it is written, 'HE GAVE THEM BREAD OUT OF HEAVEN TO EAT.'" 32Jesus therefore said to them, "Truly, truly, I say to you, it is not Moses who has given you the bread out of heaven, but it is My Father who gives you the true bread out of heaven. 33For the bread of God is that which comes down out of heaven, and gives life to the world." 34They said therefore to Him, "Lord, evermore give us this bread. 35Jesus said to them, "I am the bread of life; he who comes to Me shall not hunger, and he who believes in Me shall never thirst. 36But I said to you, that you have seen Me, and yet do not believe. 37All that the Father gives Me shall come to Me; and the one who comes to Me I will certainly not cast out. 38For I have come down from heaven, not to do My own will, but the will of Him who sent Me. 39And this is the will of Him who sent Me, that of all that He has given Me I lose nothing, but raise it up on the last day. 40For this is the will of My Father, that every one who beholds the Son, and believes in Him, may have eternal life; and I Myself will raise him up on the last day."

Wednesday—*Jesus: Provider of living water (John 7:37-39)*

37Now on the last day, the great day of the feast, Jesus stood and cried out, saying, "If any man is thirsty, let him come to Me and drink. 38He who believes in Me, as the Scripture said, 'From his innermost being shall flow rivers of living water.'" 39But this He spoke of the Spirit, whom those who believed in Him were to receive; for the Spirit was not yet given, because Jesus was not yet glorified.

Thursday—*Jesus: Light of the world (John 9:1-7, 35-41)*

1And as He passed, He saw a man blind from birth. 2And His disciples asked Him, saying, "Rabbi, who sinned, this man, or his parents, that he should be born blind?" 3Jesus answered, "It was neither that this man sinned, nor his parents; but it was in order that the works of God might be displayed in him. 4We must work the works of Him who sent Me, as long as it is day; night is coming, when no man can work. 5While I am in the world, I am the light of the world." 6When He had said this, He spat on the ground, and made clay of the spittle, and applied the clay to his eyes, [7]and said to him, "Go, wash in the pool of Siloam" (which is translated, Sent). And so he went away and washed, and came back seeing. . . . [35]Jesus heard that they had put him out; and finding him, He said, "Do you believe in the Son of Man?" [36]He answered and said, "And who is He, Lord, that I may believe in Him?" [37]Jesus said to him, "You have both seen Him, and He is the one who is talking with you." [38]And he said, "Lord, I believe." And he worshiped Him. [39]And Jesus said, "For judgment I came into this world, that those who do not see may see; and that those who see may become blind." [40]Those of the Pharisees who were with Him heard these things, and said to Him, "We are not blind too, are we?" [41]Jesus said to them, "If you were blind, you would have no sin; but now you say, 'We see'; your sin remains."

Friday—*Jesus: the Good Shepherd (John 10:7-15)*

[7]Jesus therefore said to them again, "Truly, truly, I say to you, I am the door of the sheep. [8]All who came before Me are thieves and robbers; but the sheep did not hear them. [9]I am the door; if anyone enters through Me, he shall be saved, and shall go in and out, and find pasture. [10]The thief comes only to steal, and kill, and destroy; I came that they might have life, and might have it abundantly. [11]I am the good shepherd; the good shepherd lays down His life for the sheep. [12]He who is a hireling, and not a shepherd, who is not the owner of the sheep, beholds the wolf coming, and leaves the sheep, and flees, and the wolf snatches them, and scatters them. [13]He flees because he is a hireling, and is not concerned about the sheep. [14]I am the good shepherd; and I know My own, and My own know Me, [15]even as the Father knows Me and I know the Father; and I lay down My life for the sheep."

Saturday—*Jesus: Recipient of worship and faith (John 20:24-31)*

[24]But Thomas, one of the twelve, called Didymus, was not with them when Jesus came. [25]The other disciples therefore were saying to him, "We have seen the Lord!" But he said to them, "Unless I shall see in His hands the imprint of the nails, and put my finger into the place of the nails, and put my hand into His side, I will not believe." [26]And after eight days again His disciples were inside, and Thomas with them. Jesus came,

the doors having been shut, and stood in their midst, and said, "Peace be with you." ²⁷Then He said to Thomas, "Reach here your finger, and see My hands; and reach here your hand, and put it into My side; and be not unbelieving, but believing." ²⁸Thomas answered and said to Him, "My Lord and my God!" ²⁹Jesus said to him, "Because you have seen Me, have you believed? Blessed are they who did not see, and yet believed." ³⁰Many other signs therefore Jesus also performed in the presence of the disciples, which are not written in this book; ³¹but these have been written that you may believe that Jesus is the Christ, the Son of God; and that believing you may have life in His name.

GROWTH

6

Our Blueprint

Sunday—*Asking sincerely for wisdom (James 1:5-8)*

⁵But if any of you lacks wisdom, let him ask of God, who gives to all men generously and without reproach, and it will be given to him. ⁶But let him ask in faith without any doubting, for the one who doubts is like the surf of the sea driven and tossed by the wind. ⁷For let not that man expect that he will receive anything from the Lord, ⁸being a double-minded man, unstable in all his ways.

The Bible is God speaking to us. It is God's instrument in salvation and God's means for growing Christians. It is our blueprint for living. How can we use it profitably?

The first step in understanding the Bible is salvation. The uncoverted person can read the Bible and might receive some inspiration, but the twice-born person receives infinitely more than mere inspiration. Here are some suggestions on how to read the Bible:

Read the Bible prayerfully. Prayer is the key to opening ourselves to the Bible. All of us in reading some current book have wished the author were present to answer and explain some things, but that is rarely possible. Amazing as it seems, we can speak directly to the Author of the Bible. James said, "If any of you lack wisdom let him ask of God" (James 1:5). God delights to give us wisdom and understanding, especially with regard to His Word.

The Holy Spirit, who inspired the writers of Scripture, longs to lead us to understand its truth. Without the guidance of the Holy Spirit, we read the Scriptures in vain.

Read the Bible carefully. Of the Berean Christians it could be said, "These were more noble than those in Thessalonica, in that they received the word with all readiness of mind" (Acts 17:11).

The Bereans also "searched the scriptures daily." That required work, for the great truths of God are not gathered by the careless reader. Diamonds are not found on the sidewalk. We must linger on the Bible's chapters, verses, phrases, and words, eagerly seeking to understand its message.

Martin Luther studied the Bible as one would gather apples: "First I shake the whole tree, that the ripest might fall. Then I climb the tree and shake each limb, and then each branch and then each twig, and then I look under each leaf."

Read the Bible systematically. Set aside a definite time for Bible reading, preferably at the beginning of the day when your mind is alert. At a prescribed time, in a quiet place, systematically read the Word of God. Nothing should interfere, because nothing is more important. Many well-meaning Christians who sincerely love the Lord are up and down in their Christian experience because they have no definite time with God. Beware of the barrenness of an overactive life.

Begin at the beginning. In reading any other book we start with chapter one. To start a novel or biography in the middle results in confusion. The same thing holds true for the Bible. We cannot adequately understand Exodus apart from Genesis, or Hebrews apart from Leviticus. Too often we become so attached to certain favorite portions that we neglect the remainder of the Bible. Begin where God began, Genesis 1:1, and go through to Revelation 22:21.

Secure a notebook and jot down some questions such as Who is speaking? To whom was it written? What were the backgrounds of the writer and the receiver? What are the main ideas? What seems to be the key verse? What message is there for my heart today? As you read, fill in the answers. Learn the facts, then apply them.

Read the Bible believingly. "Without faith it is impossible to please him" (Hebrews 11:6). Growth as well as salvation depend upon faith. Faith is necessary in understanding the Bible. That is exactly where Israel failed. "The word preached did not profit them, not being mixed with faith in them that heard it" (Hebrews 4:2). We must believe God's Word.

The Bible is alive! If the Lord came personally to you, would you ignore Him? He has spoken personally to us in the Bible! We dare not neglect His Word. Think of it—the Bible is not man's word but God's Word! Say with Samuel, "Speak, LORD; for thy servant heareth" (1 Samuel 3:9).

THE HOLY SPIRIT, WHO INSPIRED THE
WRITERS OF SCRIPTURE, LONGS TO LEAD US
TO UNDERSTAND ITS TRUTHS.

Monday—*The Spirit revealing the things of God*
(1 Corinthians 2:6-10)

⁶Yet we do speak wisdom among those who are mature; a wisdom, however, not of this age, nor of the rulers of this age, who are passing away; ⁷but we speak God's wisdom in a mystery, the hidden wisdom, which God predestined before the ages to our glory; ⁸the wisdom which none of the rulers of this age has understood; for if they had understood it, they would not have crucified the Lord of glory; ⁹but just as it is written, "THINGS WHICH EYE HAS NOT SEEN AND EAR HAS NOT HEARD, AND which HAVE NOT ENTERED THE HEART OF MAN, ALL THAT GOD HAS PREPARED FOR THOSE WHO LOVE HIM." ¹⁰For to us God revealed them through the Spirit; for the Spirit searches all things, even the depths of God.

Tuesday—*The Spirit instructing us in the things of God*
(1 Corinthians 2:11-16)

¹¹For who among men knows the thoughts of a man except the spirit of the man, which is in him? Even so the thoughts of God no one knows except the Spirit of God. ¹²Now we have received, not the spirit of the world, but the Spirit who is from God, that we might know the things freely given to us by God. ¹³which things we also speak, not in words taught by human wisdom, but in those taught by the Spirit, combining spiritual thoughts with spiritual words. ¹⁴But a natural man does not accept the things of the Spirit of God; for they are foolishness to him, and he cannot understand them, because they are spiritually appraised. ¹⁵But he who is spiritual appraises all things, yet he himself is appraised by no man. ¹⁶For WHO HAS KNOWN THE MIND OF THE LORD, THAT HE SHOULD INSTRUCT HIM? But we have the mind of Christ.

Wednesday—*Preaching tested by the Scriptures*
(Acts 17:10-12)

¹⁰And the brethren immediately sent Paul and Silas away by night to Berea; and when they arrived, they went into the synagogue of the Jews. ¹¹Now these were more noble-minded than those in Thessalonica, for they received the word with great eagerness, examining the Scriptures daily, to see whether these things were so. ¹²Many of them therefore believed, along with a number of prominent Greek women and men.

Thursday—*Samuel's eagerness to hear God speak*
**   *(1 Samuel 3:1-10)***

¹Now the boy Samuel was ministering to the LORD before Eli. And word from the LORD was rare in those days, visions were infrequent. ²And it happened at that time as Eli was lying down in his place (now his eyesight had begun to grow dim and he could not see well), ³and the lamp of God had not yet gone out, and Samuel was lying down in the temple of the LORD where the ark of God was, ⁴that the LORD called Samuel; and he said, "Here I am." ⁵Then he ran to Eli and said, "Here I am, for you called me." But he said, "I did not call, lie down again." So he went and lay down. ⁶And the LORD called yet again, "Samuel!" So Samuel arose and went to Eli, and said, "Here I am, for you called me." But he answered, "I did not call, my son, lie down again." ⁷Now Samuel did not yet know the LORD, nor had the word of the LORD yet been revealed to him. ⁸So the LORD called Samuel again for the third time. And he arose and went to Eli, and said, "Here I am, for you called me." Then Eli discerned that the LORD was calling the boy. ⁹And Eli said to Samuel, "Go lie down, and it shall be if He calls you, that you shall say, 'Speak, LORD, for Thy servant is listening.'" So Samuel went and lay down in his place. ¹⁰Then the LORD came and stood and called as at other times, "Samuel! Samuel!" And Samuel said, "Speak, for Thy servant is listening."

Friday—*Faith as a source of understanding (Hebrews 11:1-6)*

¹Now faith is the assurance of things hoped for, the conviction of things not seen. ²For by it the men of old gained approval. ³By faith we understand that the worlds were prepared by the word of God, so that what is seen was not made out of things which are visible. ⁴By faith Abel offered to God a better sacrifice than Cain, through which he obtained the testimony that he was righteous, God testifying about his gifts, and through faith, though he is dead, he still speaks. ⁵By faith Enoch was taken up so that he should not see death; and he was not found because God took him up; for he obtained the witness that before his being taken up he was pleasing to God. ⁶And without faith it is impossible to please Him, for he who comes to God must believe that He is, and that He is a rewarder of those who seek Him.

Saturday—*Making the Word a part of your life*
             (Psalm 119:9-16)

[9]How can a young man keep his way pure?
  By keeping it according to Thy word.
[10]With all my heart I have sought Thee;
  Do not let me wander from Thy commandments.
[11]Thy word I have treasured in my heart,
  That I may not sin against Thee.
[12]Blessed art Thou, O LORD;
  Teach me Thy statutes.
[13]With my lips I have told of
  All the ordinances of Thy mouth.
[14]I have rejoiced in the way of Thy testimonies,
  As much as in all riches.
[15]I will mediate on Thy precepts,
  And regard Thy ways.
[16]I shall delight in Thy statutes;
  I shall not forget Thy word.

7

I Will Build My Church

Sunday—*The church founded on Christ (Matthew 16:16-18)*

16And Simon Peter answered and said, "Thou art the Christ, the Son of the living God." 17And Jesus answered and said to him, "Blessed are you, Simon Barjona, because flesh and blood did not reveal this to you, but My Father who is in heaven. 18And I also say to you that you are Peter, and upon this rock I will build My church; and the gates of Hades shall not overpower it."

To attack the church appears to be a popular thing to do in our time. One accuser labeled the church as "outdated, ineffective, irrelevant, and not worth a bullet to shoot it." Another has described the church as "a devouring monster to be supported rather than a place of service to mankind."

Some have rather brazenly asked the question, Has the church had it? In every generation, some churches have obviously had it. Even Jesus felt that the Laodicean church had had it. "So then because thou art lukewarm, and neither cold nor hot, I will spew thee out of my mouth. Because thou sayest, I am rich, and increased with goods, and have need of nothing; and knowest not that thou art wretched, and miserable, and poor, and blind, and naked" (Revelation 3:16-17).

In appraising the present situation, it is important to remember that the church as an institution is both human and divine. As a human institution, the church reflects all the characteristics of humanity. All of us experience moments of fervor as well as moments of fainting, periods of saintliness, and times of stupidity. The church is not a hothouse for the exhibition of eminent saints, but rather a nursery for the newborn. The church is a school for our spiritual education and an armory for training. There is no reason to expect it to be without problems.

In a very real sense the church is a reflection of each member. Perhaps the present-day criticism of the church from within is a form of confession. But what is needed in the church is not criticism but personal confession and cleansing. Each church member should strive to be an asset and not a liability to the church.

The church is also a divine institution, and that truth affords great strength. Jesus said, "I will build my church; and the gates of hell shall not prevail against it" (Matthew 16:18).

It is sobering to remember the church's origin. The church belongs to Jesus, and He calls it "my church." In fact, Jesus guarantees the success of the church. He is the Owner and Builder, and He promises ultimate victory. There is nothing in heaven or on earth that God has given to us that is more meaningful than the church. To attack it is to attack the work of God.

The church has been in the plan of God since the day of Pentecost. The book of Acts relates vividly how believers gladly received His word. They had agreed with the Bible's indictment of guilt and sin and had an experience of salvation. They openly confessed their allegiance to Christ and were added to the church. Their being added to the church was a natural result of their conversions; every believer became a church member.

The first church, as related in Acts 2, was conceived in a "rushing mighty wind," and then it moved like a hurricane. In seventy years those first Christians went over mountain peaks and tossing seas to rock the imperial city of Rome with the gospel of Jesus Christ. The postapostolic church was equally aggressive. In the face of bitter persecution, the church marched forward to evangelize her generation.

Christians down through the centuries have found that it is vital to fellowship together in local assemblies. The writer of Hebrews reminds us that it is dangerous to forsake the assembling of ourselves together (Hebrews 10:25). Martin Luther said, "To gather with God's people in united adoration of the Father is as necessary to the Christian life as prayer."

Some time ago, I suggested to a Christian friend of many years' standing that he become a member of a local church where his family attended. "Oh," he said, "you don't have to be a church member to be a Christian."

I suggested that one could cross the ocean without the use of a plane or boat, but I would not recommend it. The church is certainly God's vehicle for carrying us through the rough seas of our journey on this earth. It is a colossal mistake to ignore the church.

> THE CHURCH IS NOT A HOTHOUSE FOR THE
> EXHIBITION OF EMINENT SAINTS BUT
> RATHER A NURSERY FOR THE NEWBORN.

Monday—*Coming together for encouragement (Hebrews 10:23-25)*

[23]Let us hold fast the confession of our hope without wavering, for He who promised is faithful; [24]and let us consider how to stimulate one another to love and good deeds, [25]not forsaking our own assembling together, as is the habit of some, but encouraging one another; and all the more, as you see the day drawing near.

Tuesday—*Characteristics of the early church (Acts 2:41-47)*

[41]So then, those who had received his word were baptized; and there were added that day about three thousand souls. [42]And they were continually devoting themselves to the apostles' teaching and to fellowship, to the breaking of bread and to prayer. [43]And everyone kept feeling a sense of awe; and many wonders and signs were taking place through the apostles. [44]And all those who had believed were together, and had all things in common; [45]and they began selling their property and possessions, and were sharing them with all, as anyone might have need. [46]And day by day continuing with one mind in the temple, and breaking bread from house to house, they were taking their meals together with gladness and sincerity of heart, [47]praising God, and having favor with all the people. And the Lord was adding to their number day by day those who were being saved.

Wednesday—*Christ as the head of the church (Ephesians 5:23-27)*

[23]For the husband is the head of the wife, as Christ also is the head of the church, He Himself being the Savior of the body. [24]But as the church is subject to Christ, so also the wives ought to be to their husbands in everything. [25]Husbands, love your wives, just as Christ also loved the church and gave Himself up for her; [26]that He might sanctify her, having cleansed her by the washing of water with the word, [27]that He might present to

Himself the church in all her glory, having no spot or wrinkle or any such thing; but that she should be holy and blameless.

Thursday—*Many members, one body*
(1 Corinthians 12:12-16)

[12]For even as the body is one and yet has many members, and all the members of the body, though they are many, are one body, so also is Christ. [13]For by one Spirit we were all baptized into one body, whether Jews or Greeks, whether slaves or free, and we were all made to drink of one Spirit. [14]For the body is not one member, but many. [15]If the foot should say, "Because I am not a hand, I am not a part of the body," it is not for this reason any the less a part of the body. [16]And if the ear should say, "Because I am not an eye, I am not a part of the body," it is not for this reason any the less a part of the body.

Friday—*The need of each member for the others*
(1 Corinthians 12:17-21)

[17]If the whole body were an eye, where would the hearing be? If the whole were hearing, where would the sense of smell be? [18]But now God has placed the members, each one of them, in the body, just as He desired. [19]And if they were all one member, where would the body be? [20]But now there are many members, but one body. [21]And the eye cannot say to the hand, "I have no need of you"; or again the head to the feet, "I have no need of you."

Saturday—*Joy and sorrow shared by all*
(1 Corinthians 12:22-26)

[22]On the contrary, it is much truer that the members of the body which seem to be weaker are necessary; [23]and those members of the body, which we deem less honorable, on these we bestow more abundant honor, and our unseemly members come to have more abundant seemliness, [24]whereas our seemly members have no need of it. But God has so composed the body, giving more abundant honor to that member which lacked, [25]that there should be no division in the body, but that the members should have the same care for one another. [26]And if one member suffers, all the members suffer with it; if one member is honored, all the members rejoice with it.

52

8

Be Kind

Sunday—*Dorcas living a life of kindness (Acts 9:36-41)*

[36]Now in Joppa there was a certain disciple named Tabitha (which translated in Greek is called Dorcas); this woman was abounding with deeds of kindness and charity, which she continually did. [37]And it came about at that time that she fell sick and died; and when they had washed her body, they laid it in an upper room. [38]And since Lydda was near Joppa, the disciples, having heard that Peter was there, sent two men to him, entreating him, "Do not delay to come to us." [39]And Peter arose and went with them. And when he had come, they brought him into the upper room; and all the widows stood beside him weeping, and showing all the tunics and garments that Dorcas used to make while she was with them. [40]But Peter sent them all out and knelt down and prayed, and turning to the body, he said, "Tabitha, arise." And she opened her eyes, and when she saw Peter, she sat up. [41]And he gave her his hand and raised her up; and calling the saints and widows, he presented her alive.

Our world is starving for kindness. The word *kind* comes from *kin* or *kindred* and carries in its meaning the idea of love for those who are our own flesh and blood. Goethe claimed that "kindness is the golden chain by which society is bound together." Everyone you meet is carrying a burden, so be kind.

Kindness characterizes God and should mark each believer. Kindness and love are inseparable. In spite of our personal shortcomings and our unloveliness, God keeps loving us and *is kind* to us. Those of us who are His children ought to reflect God's kindness to others.

Each follower of Jesus Christ should be kind, as He was, even when misunderstood and falsely accused. Our human tendency is to be hasty, hotheaded, and unkind. But divine love is different. Paul reminds us, "[Love] suffereth long, and is kind" (1 Corinthians 13:4).

Some years ago, I was misunderstood and criticized by a friend whom I expected would know better. I desperately wanted to retaliate, or at least present my version of the story. With bulldog determination, I clenched my fist, bit my lip, and managed to keep my mouth closed. But surely I was not kind, nor did I display much graciousness. I was wrong. Love *is kind.*

A large part of being kind is the patient willingness to put up with abuse or misunderstanding. Usually that patience is exhausted just when it is needed most. Often our tolerance wears thin at the wrong time and our kindness melts away. Real love is kind and never gives up. G. K. Chesterton has an interesting comment: "There is no such thing as being a gentleman at important moments; it is at unimportant moments that a man is a gentleman. . . . If once his mind is possessed in any strong degree with the knowledge that he is a gentleman, he will soon cease to be one."

Jesus Christ spent His life ministering to others. For thirty-three years He went about doing kind deeds, ministering to the sick, feeding the hungry, comforting the bereaved, always helping others. Although He was often misunderstood, Jesus was kind.

Our Saviour was long-suffering with His weak-willed disciples who disappointed Him so often. He was merciful to the despised and the mentally disturbed. He was long-suffering with Pilate, with the Roman centurion, and with the crucified thief. Jesus suffered long and was kind even in His dying hours. After the nails had done their ugly work, He called out, "Father, forgive them; for they know not what they do" (Luke 23:34). That was kindness such as no mere man could display.

The kindness that Jesus demonstrated goes beyond human understanding; yet that is the very attitude of love in which God would live through us.

When Stephen, one of the early church deacons, was being stoned, he prayed, "Lord, lay not this sin to their charge" (Acts 7:60). What spirit does that show? The spirit of Christ. It is divine kindness amid ignorance, bigotry, and violence. That kind of love is possible only through Jesus Christ. He gives us the capacity to love and to be kind.

Remember the admonition of Paul, "And be ye kind one to another, tenderhearted, forgiving one another, even as God for Christ's sake hath forgiven you" (Ephesians 4:32). God showed His kindness by forgiving us. Don't we have an obligation to cultivate that same kindness in our lives?

EVERYONE YOU MEET IS CARRYING A
BURDEN . . . . SO BE KIND.

Monday—*David's kindness to Saul's grandson* *(2 Samuel 9:1-13)*

¹Then David said, "Is there yet anyone left of the house of Saul, that I may show him kindness for Jonathan's sake?" ²Now there was a servant of the house of Saul whose name was Ziba,

55

and they called him to David; and the king said to him, "Are you Ziba?" And he said, "I am your servant." ³And the king said, "Is there not yet anyone of the house of Saul to whom I may show the kindness of God?" And Ziba said to the king, "There is still a son of Jonathan who is crippled in both feet." ⁴So the king said to him, "Where is he?" And Ziba said to the king, "Behold, he is in the house of Machir the son of Ammiel in Lo-debar." ⁵Then King David sent and brought him from the house of Machir the son of Ammiel, from Lo-debar. ⁶And Mephibosheth, the son of Jonathan the son of Saul, came to David and fell on his face and prostrated himself. And David said, "Mephibosheth." And he said, "Here is your servant!" ⁷And David said to him, "Do not fear, for I will surely show kindness to you for the sake of your father Jonathan, and will restore to you all the land of your grandfather Saul; and you shall eat at my table regularly." ⁸Again he prostrated himself and said, "What is your servant, that you should regard a dead dog like me?" ⁹Then the king called Saul's servant Ziba, and said to him, "All that belonged to Saul and to all his house I have given to your master's grandson. ¹⁰And you and your sons and your servants shall cultivate the land for him, and you shall bring in the produce so that your master's grandson may have food; nevertheless Mephibosheth your master's grandson shall eat at my table regularly." Now Ziba had fifteen sons and twenty servants. ¹¹Then Ziba said to the king, "According to all that my lord the king commands his servant so your servant will do." So Mephibosheth ate at David's table as one of the king's sons. ¹²And Mephibosheth had a young son whose name was Mica. And all who lived in the house of Ziba were servants to Mephibosheth. ¹³So Mephibosheth lived in Jerusalem, for he ate at the king's table regularly. Now he was lame in both feet.

Tuesday—*Kind acts done to the Lord (Matthew 25:34-40)*

³⁴"Then the King will say to those on His right, 'Come, you who are blessed of My Father, inherit the kingdom prepared for you from the foundation of the world. ³⁵For I was hungry, and you gave Me something to eat; I was thirsty, and you gave Me drink; I was a stranger, and you invited Me in; ³⁶naked, and you clothed Me; I was sick, and you visited Me; I was in prison, and you came to Me.' ³⁷Then the righteous will answer Him, saying, 'Lord, when did we see You hungry, and feed You, or thirsty,

and give You drink? ³⁸And when did we see You a stranger, and invite You in, or naked, and clothe You? ³⁹And when did we see You sick, or in prison, and come to You?' ⁴⁰And the King will answer and say to them, 'Truly I say to you, to the extent that you did it to one of these brothers of Mine, even the least of them, you did it to Me.' "

Wednesday—*Abraham's kindness toward Lot*
 (Genesis 13:8-12)

⁸Then Abram said to Lot, "Please let there be no strife between you and me, nor between my herdsmen and your herdsmen, for we are brothers. ⁹Is not the whole land before you? Please separate from me: if to the left, then I will go to the right; or if to the right, then I will go to the left." ¹⁰And Lot lifted up his eyes and saw all the valley of the Jordan, that it was well watered everywhere—this was before the LORD destroyed Sodom and Gomorrah—like the garden of the LORD, like the land of Egypt as you go to Zoar. ¹¹So Lot chose for himself all the valley of the Jordan; and Lot journeyed eastward. Thus they separated from each other. ¹²Abram settled in the land of Canaan, while Lot settled in the cities of the valley, and moved his tents as far as Sodom.

Thursday—*Jesus' kindness to a kind man (Luke 7:1-10)*

¹When He had completed all His discourse in the hearing of the people, He went to Capernaum. ²And a certain centurion's slave, who was highly regarded by him, was sick and about to die. ³And when he heard about Jesus, he sent some Jewish elders asking Him to come and save the life of his slave. ⁴And when they had come to Jesus, they earnestly entreated Him, saying, "He is worthy for You to grant this to him; ⁵for he loves our nation, and it was he who built us our synagogue." ⁶Now Jesus started on His way with them; and when He was already not far from the house, the centurion sent friends, saying to Him, "Lord, do not trouble Yourself further, for I am not fit for You to come under my roof; ⁷for this reason I did not even consider myself worthy to come to You, but just say the word, and my servant will be healed. ⁸"For indeed, I am a man under authority, with soldiers under me; and I say to this one, 'Go!' and he goes; and to another 'Come!' and he comes; and to my slave, 'Do this!' and he does it." ⁹And when Jesus heard this, He

marveled at him, and turned and said to the multitude that was following Him, "I say to you, not even in Israel have I found such great faith." [10]And when those who had been sent returned to the house, they found the slave in good health.

Friday—*Living for others (Romans 15:1-7)*

[1]Now we who are strong ought to bear the weaknesses of those without strength and not just please ourselves. [2]Let each of us please his neighbor for his good, to his edification. [3]For even Christ did not please Himself; but as it is written, "THE REPROACHES OF THOSE WHO REPROACHED THEE FELL UPON ME." [4]For whatever was written in earlier times was written for our instruction, that through perseverance and the encouragement of the Scriptures we might have hope. [5]Now may the God who gives perseverance and encouragement grant you to be of the same mind with one another according to Christ Jesus; [6]that with one accord you may with one voice glorify the God and Father of our Lord Jesus Christ. [7]Wherefore, accept one another, just as Christ also accepted us to the glory of God.

Saturday—*A place prepared for Elisha (2 Kings 4:8-11)*

[8]Now there came a day when Elisha passed over to Shunem, where there was a prominent woman, and she persuaded him to eat food. And so it was as often as he passed by, he turned in there to eat food. [9]And she said to her husband, "Behold now, I perceive that this is a holy man of God passing by us continually. [10]Please, let us make a little walled upper chamber and let us set a bed for him there, and a table and a chair and a lampstand; and it shall be, when he come to us, that he can turn in there." [11]One day he came there and turned in to the upper chamber and rested.

9

Follow After Love

[7]Beloved, I am not writing a new commandment to you, but an old commandment which you have had from the beginning; the old commandment is the word which you have heard. [8]On the other hand, I am writing a new commandment to you, which is true in Him and in you, because the darkness is passing away, and the true light is already shining. [9]The one who says he is in the light and yet hates his brother is in the darkness until now. [10]The one who loves his brother abides in the light and there is no cause for stumbling in him. [11]But the one who hates his brother is in the darkness and walks in the darkness, and does not know where he is going because the darkness has blinded his eyes.

Life is too short to read all the books, see all the sights, hear all the people, and participate in all the exciting activities. The biggest problem facing us is that of *selection*. Constantly we must choose the best way and the greatest good.

Paul, in writing to the believers at Corinth, listed many spiritual gifts, but he concluded that the way of divine love is "a more excellent way" (1 Corinthians 12:31). He announced plainly that love is better and greater than any other conceivable gift.

Peter came to the same conclusion. He taught the early church many principles for living, but he too rated God's love as the supreme pursuit of life. "And *above all things* have fervent [love] among yourselves; for [love] shall cover the multitude of sins" (1 Peter 4:8, italics added).

During the first century after Christ, Tertullian, an early Christian theologian, wrote: "It is our care for the helpless, our practice of lovingkindness, that brands us in the eyes of many of our opponents. 'Look,' they say, 'how they love one another. Look how they are prepared to die for one another.' "

Tradition tells us about the aged apostle John bidding farewell to his congregation. Once again he encouraged them to love one another. They nodded carelessly and said, "We want something new—give us a new commandment." He quoted, "A new commandment-I give unto you, that ye love one another" (John 13:34).

John had nothing else to say. Everything was wrapped up in one big bundle of love for Christ, for one another, for a needy world. Three major New Testament writers—Peter, Paul, and John—identified the pursuit of God's love as the greatest goal of life.

Many readily admit their need and even their desire to know more of God's love. The big question is, How can I experience that love? Paul challenges all believers to follow after love (1 Corinthians 14:1). The word "follow" is not a passive word but an active word. It involves dedication, determination, and discipline. The pursuit of God's love is a full-time, lifelong vocation.

A variety of signals alerted me to the supreme calling of love. Perhaps the earliest occurred when I was a student at Moody Bible Institute. A serious illness led to major surgery. My bed in the Swedish Covenant Hospital became my altar as I dedicated myself anew to the will of God. I vowed to "follow after love."

Some time later I was speaking in a little church in Michigan where I was leading a seven-day series of meetings. After the service one morning I was acutely aware that I was failing. There seemed to be no explanation for it, but nothing had gone right. After the people had left the church, I stayed behind and knelt at the front pew. As I prayed, the Lord made me painfully aware of my dishonest self and of my own personal, selfish ambitions. I told the Lord that I needed His help—right away.

That morning, as I poured out my soul in confession, I made up my mind to pray daily for the gift of love. I vowed not to let any obstacle hinder the development of this gift. I asked that my life would become a straightforward following after love, and I decided to make that pursuit the mainstream of my life, as Paul urged. The difference in my own life has been revolutionary since I decided to "follow after love."

> THE PURSUIT OF GOD'S LOVE IS A
> FULL-TIME, LIFELONG VOCATION.

Monday—*Love as proof of who knows God (1 John 4:7-12)*

[7]Beloved, let us love one another, for love is from God; and every one who loves is born of God and knows God. [8]The one who does not love does not know God, for God is love. [9]By this the love of God was manifested in us, that God has sent His only begotten Son into the world so that we might live through Him. [10]In this is love, not that we loved God, but that He loved us and sent His Son to be the propitiation for our sins. [11]Beloved, if God so loved us, we also ought to love one another.

[12]No one has beheld God at any time; if we love one another, God abides in us, and His love is perfected in us.

Tuesday—*Love helping others (1 Peter 4:7-11)*

[7]The end of all things is at hand; therefore, be of sound judgment and sober spirit for the purpose of prayer. [8]Above all, keep fervent in your love for one another, because love covers a multitude of sins. [9]Be hospitable to one another without complaint. [10]As each one has received a special gift, employ it in serving one another, as good stewards of the manifold grace of God. [11]Whoever speaks, let him speak, as it were, the utterances of God; whoever serves, let him do so as by the strength which God supplies; so that in all things God may be glorified through Jesus Christ, to whom belongs the glory and dominion forever and ever. Amen.

Wednesday—*Jesus' example of love for others (John 13:3-15)*

[3]Jesus, knowing that the Father had given all things into His hands, and that He had come forth from God, and was going back to God, [4]rose from supper, and laid aside His garments; and taking a towel, girded Himself about. [5]Then He poured water into the basin, and began to wash the disciples' feet, and to wipe them with the towel with which He was girded. [6]And so He came to Simon Peter. He said to Him, "Lord, do You wash my feet?" [7]Jesus answered and said to him, "What I do you do not realize now; but you shall understand hereafter." [8]Peter said to Him, "Never shall You wash my feet!" Jesus answered him, "If I do not wash you, you have no part with Me." [9]Simon Peter said to Him, "Lord, not my feet only, but also my hands and my head." [10]Jesus said to him, "He who has bathed needs only to wash his feet, but is completely clean; and you are clean, but not all of you." [11]For He knew the one who was betraying Him; for this reason He said, "Not all of you are clean." [12]And so when He had washed their feet, and taken His garments, and reclined at table again, He said to them, "Do you know what I have done to you? [13]You call me Teacher and Lord; and you are right; for so I am. [14]If I then, the Lord and the Teacher, washed your feet, you also ought to wash one another's feet. [15]For I gave you an example that you also should do as I did to you."

Thursday—*Honest love shown in activity (Romans 12:9-13)*

⁹Let love be without hypocrisy. Abhor what is evil; cling to what is good. ¹⁰Be devoted to one another in brotherly love; give preference to one another in honor; ¹¹not lagging behind in diligence, fervent in spirit, serving the Lord; ¹²rejoicing in hope, persevering in tribulation, devoted to prayer, ¹³contributing to the needs of the saints, practicing hospitality.

Friday—*Love as service to others (Galatians 5:13-18)*

¹³For you were called to freedom, brethren; only do not turn your freedom into an opportunity for the flesh, but through love serve one another. ¹⁴For the whole Law is fulfilled in one word, in the statement, "YOU SHALL LOVE YOUR NEIGHBOR AS YOURSELF." ¹⁵But if you bite and devour one another, take care lest you be consumed by one another. ¹⁶But I say, walk by the Spirit, and you will not carry out the desire of the flesh. ¹⁷For the flesh sets its desire against the Spirit, and the Spirit against the flesh; for these are in opposition to one another, so that you may not do the things that you please. ¹⁸But if you are led by the Spirit, you are not under the Law.

Saturday—*Love being gentle (1 Thessalonians 2:7-12)*

⁷But we proved to be gentle among you, as a nursing mother tenderly cares for her own children. ⁸Having thus a fond affection for you, we were well pleased to impart to you not only the gospel but also our own lives, because you had become very dear to us. ⁹For you recall, brethren, our labor and hardship, how working night and day so as not to be a burden to any of you, we proclaimed to you the gospel of God. ¹⁰You are witnesses, and so is God, how devoutly and uprightly and blamelessly we behaved toward you believers; ¹¹just as you know how we were exhorting and encouraging and imploring each one of you as a father would his own children, ¹²so that you may walk in a manner worthy of the God who calls you into His own kingdom and glory.

10

Pressure Produces

Sunday—*Pressure leading to completion (James 1:2-5)*

²Consider it all joy, my brethren, when you encounter various trials; ³knowing that the testing of your faith produces endurance. ⁴And let endurance have its perfect result, that you may be perfect and complete, lacking in nothing. ⁵But if any of you lacks wisdom, let him ask of God, who gives to all men generously and without reproach, and it will be given to him.

A familiar saying is that a Christian is like a tea bag: he is not worth much until he has been through some hot water.

Times of pressure can be eternally profitable. God tests us, not to destroy us but to demonstrate us. It is the pressed flower that releases the enchanting aroma. The crushed fruit gives the tasty juice. The fiery furnace yields the best steel. Soil is rock that has been crushed, pounded, and pulverized. The pressure and heat of the earth's elements create a costly diamond. As A. B. Simpson wrote,

> Out of the presses of pain,
> Cometh the souls' best wine.
> The eyes that have shed no rain,
> Can shed but little shine.

Pressure produces!

Remember three things about pressures. First, they are the common experience of all, a part of living. No one is immune. Second, they may appear to be eternal, but they are temporary. Third, they are grand opportunities to learn and therefore should not be wasted.

Our Lord never promised us an easy journey, but He did promise a safe and triumphant landing.

What does pressure produce? The apostle James tells us that "the trying of [our] faith worketh patience" (James 1:3). Pressure plus faith produces patience. The pressures God permits are to develop character and dependability in us.

Pressure also produces completeness. C. B. Williams translates James 1:4, "Let your endurance come to its perfect product, so that you may be fully developed and perfectly equipped, without any defects." James is saying, "Don't try to wiggle out of your troubles, because God isn't finished with you yet." Pressure produces a full-grown soul.

What are we to do about the pressures of life? We are to accept them joyfully (James 1:2); accept them confidently (James 1:3); and accept them trustingly (James 1:5). The first thing we must do with pressure is to seek the Lord and ask for divine wisdom (James 1:5).

In Eden's garden, Eve went for wisdom to the tree of the knowledge of good and evil. Today many are running here and there in a futile search for wisdom. Only the Scriptures give an adequate answer. We are to "ask of God" (James 1:5) and we are to "ask in faith" (James 1:6). We are to "look up" and "hook up."

I challenge you to meet life's pressures, not with dull resignation but with a positive, enthusiastic spirit of trust and cooperation with the plan of God.

This Bible formula helps: Pressure plus faith equals patience and completeness.

> GOD TESTS US, NOT TO DESTROY US BUT TO
> DEMONSTRATE US.

Monday—*Pressure leading to character and hope*
(Romans 5:1-5)

[1]Therefore having been justified by faith, we have peace with God through our Lord Jesus Christ, [2]through whom also we have obtained our introduction by faith into this grace in which we stand; and we exult in hope of the glory of God. [3]And not only this, but we also exult in our tribulations; knowing that tribulation brings about perseverance; [4]and perseverance, proven character; and proven character, hope; [5]and hope does not disappoint; because the love of God has been poured out within our hearts through the Holy Spirit who was given to us.

Tuesday—*Pressure leading to favor with God*
(1 Peter 2:18-25)

[18]Servants, be submissive to your masters with all respect, not only to those who are good and gentle, but also to those who are unreasonable. [19]For this finds favor, if for the sake of conscience toward God a man bears up under sorrows when suffering unjustly. [20]For what credit is there if, when you sin and are harshly treated, you endure it with patience? But if when you do what is right and suffer for it you patiently endure

it, this finds favor with God. ²¹For you have been called for this purpose, since Christ also suffered for you, leaving you an example for you to follow in His steps, ²²WHO COMMITTED NO SIN, NOR WAS ANY DECEIT FOUND IN HIS MOUTH; ²³and while being reviled, He did not revile in return; while suffering, He uttered no threats, but kept entrusting Himself to Him who judges righteously; ²⁴and He Himself bore our sins in His body on the cross, that we might die to sin and live to righteousness; for by His wounds you were healed. ²⁵For you were continually straying like sheep, but now you have returned to the Shepherd and Guardian of your souls.

Wednesday—*Pressure leading to fruitful service* *(2 Peter 1:5-11)*

⁵Now for this very reason also, applying all diligence, in your faith supply moral excellence, and in your moral excellence, knowledge; ⁶and in your knowledge, self-control, and in your self-control, perseverance, and in your perseverance, godliness; ⁷and in your godliness, brotherly kindness, and in your brotherly kindness, Christian love. ⁸For if these qualities are yours and are increasing, they render you neither useless nor unfruitful in the true knowledge of our Lord Jesus Christ. ⁹For he who lacks these qualities is blind or short-sighted, having forgotten his purification from his former sins. ¹⁰Therefore, brethren, be all the more diligent to make certain about His calling and choosing you; for as long as you practice these things, you will never stumble; ¹¹for in this way the entrance into the eternal kingdom of our Lord and Savior Jesus Christ will be abundantly supplied to you.

Thursday—*Qualities God wants built into you* *(Colossians 3:12-17)*

¹²And so, as those who have been chosen of God, holy and beloved, put on a heart of compassion, kindness, humility, gentleness and patience; ¹³bearing with one another, and forgiving each other, whoever has a complaint against any one; just as the Lord forgave you, so also should you. ¹⁴And beyond all these things put on love, which is the perfect bond of unity. ¹⁵And let the peace of Christ rule in your hearts, to which indeed you were called in one body; and be thankful. ¹⁶Let the word of Christ richly dwell within you; with all wisdom

teaching and admonishing one another with psalms and hymns and spiritual songs, singing with thankfulness in your hearts to God. [17]And whatever you do in word or deed, do all in the name of the Lord Jesus, giving thanks through Him to God the Father.

Friday—*The active Christian life—what to pursue (1 Timothy 6:11-16)*

[11]But flee from these things, you man of God; and pursue righteousness, godliness, faith, love, perseverance and gentleness. [12]Fight the good fight of faith; take hold of the eternal life to which you were called, and you made the good confession in the presence of many witnesses. [13]I charge you in the presence of God, who gives life to all things, and of Christ Jesus, who testified the good confession before Pontius Pilate; [14]that you keep the commandment without stain or reproach, until the appearing of our Lord Jesus Christ, [15]which He will bring about at the proper time—He who is the blessed and only Sovereign, the King of kings and Lord of lords; [16]who alone possesses immortality and dwells in unapproachable light; whom no man has seen or can see. To Him be honor and eternal dominion! Amen.

Saturday—*A worthy walk (Ephesians 4:1-3)*

[1]I, therefore, the prisoner of the Lord, entreat you to walk in a manner worthy of the calling with which you have been called, [2]with all humility and gentleness, with patience, showing forbearance to one another in love, [3]being diligent to preserve the unity of the Spirit in the bond of peace.

11

Singleness of Purpose

Sunday—*Paul's single purpose (Philippians 3:9-14)*

⁹and may be found in Him, not having a righteousness of my own derived from the Law, but that which is through faith in Christ, the righteousness which comes from God on the basis of faith, ¹⁰that I may know Him, and the power of His resurrection and the fellowship of His sufferings, being conformed to His death; ¹¹in order that I may attain to the resurrection from the dead. ¹²Not that I have already obtained it, or have already become perfect, but I press on in order that I may lay hold of that for which also I was laid hold of by Christ Jesus. ¹³Brethren, I do not regard myself as having laid hold of it yet; but one thing I do: forgetting what lies behind and reaching forward to what lies ahead. ¹⁴I press on toward the goal for the prize of the upward call of God in Christ Jesus.

If there is anything I admire it is the person who is good at his or her work, whether that person is a teacher, truck driver, secretary, housewife, or window washer. I am excited by the person who does things well.

The apostle Paul possessed an all-consuming, dynamic purpose. Whether he was starting a new church or writing a letter to a congregation, or mending tents to earn his keep, his all-embracing purpose was clearly before him. What was that purpose? He expressed it in that beautiful phrase: "That I may know him" (Philippians 3:10). Paul possessed a passionate enthusiasm and total commitment to that purpose. He actually hungered for all that God had for him—not just to know *about* God, but to know Him deeply and intimately.

One of Britain's great prime ministers, Benjamin Disraeli, said, "The secret of success is constancy of purpose." That is what Paul had in mind when he wrote, "This one thing I do" (Philippians 3:13). Single-mindedness is the most indispensable quality of all. Owen Meredith wrote,

He who seeks all things wherever he goes
Only reaps from the hopes which around him he sows
A harvest of barren regrets.

D. L. Moody used to say, "Give me a man who says, 'this one thing I do,' and not, 'these fifty things I dabble in.'" Never sacrifice depth for area.

As a boy, I owned a versatile, inexpensive jackknife. It had three blades, a can opener, gimlet, corkscrew, nail file, and miniature pair of scissors. The whole thing cost a dollar but was not worth a dime. The knife was so versatile that it was useless. Too much versatility can render us ineffective. Beware of spreading yourself too thin.

Single-mindedness does not appear to come naturally with talent. It is not a natural commodity. Rather, it is something we have to pray for, work at, encourage, and maintain.

Jesus said, "If . . . thine eye be single, thy whole body shall be full of light" (Matthew 6:22). Our Lord was really saying, "Be narrow in your purpose." James reminds us that "a double minded man is unstable in all his ways" (James 1:8).

Few of us come anywhere near realizing 100 percent of our potential. We are told that most of us only use 20 percent of our capacity. God did not create us to live and minister at 20 percent of our potential. Living at 20 percent of one's potential throws everything else out of balance.

D. L. Moody heard Henry Varley say, "The world has yet to see what God will do with a man fully surrendered to Him." Moody said, "By the grace of God, I'll be that man." D. L. Moody had singleness of purpose.

The apostle Paul was determined that nothing in life should sway him from his purpose. He laid aside every hindrance and as a disciplined runner pressed forward for the prize. At the close of his life he was able to say, "I have fought a good fight, I have finished my course, I have kept the faith" (2 Timothy 4:7).

I urge you to strive for singleness of purpose.

NEVER SACRIFICE DEPTH FOR AREA.

Monday—*Running the race, with the joy set before us (Hebrews 12:1-6)*

¹Therefore, since we have so great a cloud of witnesses surrounding us, let us also lay aside every encumbrance, and the sin which so easily entangles us, and let us run with endurance the race that is set before us, ²fixing our eyes on Jesus, the author and perfecter of faith, who for the joy set before Him endured the cross, despising the shame, and has sat down at the right hand of the throne of God. ³For consider Him who has endured such hostility by sinners against Himself, so that you may not grow weary and lose heart. ⁴You have not yet resisted to the point of shedding blood, in your striving against sin; ⁵and you have forgotten the exhortation which is addressed to you as sons,

"MY SON, DO NOT REGARD LIGHTLY THE DISCIPLINE OF THE
    LORD,
NOR FAINT WHEN YOU ARE REPROVED BY HIM;
⁶FOR THOSE WHOM THE LORD LOVES HE DISCIPLINES,
AND HE SCOURGES EVERY SON WHOM HE RECEIVES."

Tuesday—*God directing our purpose (Proverbs 3:3-8)*

³Do not let kindness and truth leave you;
  Bind them around your neck,
  Write them on the tablet of your heart.
⁴So you will find favor and good repute
  In the sight of God and man.
⁵Trust in the LORD with all your heart,
  And do not lean on your own understanding.
⁶In all your ways acknowledge Him,
  And He will make your paths straight.
⁷Do not be wise in your own eyes;
  Fear the LORD and turn away from evil.
⁸It will be healing to your body,
  And refreshment to your bones.

Wednesday—*Daniel's purpose not to defile himself (Daniel 1:8-20)*

⁸But Daniel made up his mind that he would not defile himself with the king's choice food or with the wine which he drank; so he sought permission from the commander of the officials that he might not defile himself. ⁹Now God granted Daniel favor and compassion in the sight of the commander of the officials, ¹⁰and the commander of the officials said to Daniel, "I am afraid of my lord the king, who has appointed your food and your drink; for why should he see your faces looking more haggard than the youths who are your own age? Then you would make me forfeit my head to the king." ¹¹But Daniel said to the overseer whom the commander of the officials had appointed over Daniel, Hananiah, Mishael and Azariah, ¹²"Please test your servants for ten days, and let us be given some vegetables to eat and water to drink. ¹³Then let our appearance be observed in your presence, and the appearance of the youths who are eating the king's choice food; and deal with your servants according to what you see. ¹⁴So he listened to them in this matter and tested them for ten days. ¹⁵And at the

end of ten days their appearance seemed better and they were fatter than all the youths who had been eating the king's choice food. 16So the overseer continued to withhold their choice food and the wine they were to drink, and kept giving them vegetables. 17And as for these four youths, God gave them knowledge and intelligence in every branch of literature and wisdom; Daniel even understood all kinds of visions and dreams. 18Then at the end of the days which the king had specified for presenting them, the commander of the officials presented them before Nebuchadnezzar. 19And the king talked with them, and out of them all not one was found like Daniel, Hananiah, Mishael and Azariah; so they entered the king's personal service. 20And as for every matter of wisdom and understanding about which the king consulted them, he found them ten times better than all the magicians and conjurers who were in all his realm.

Thursday—*The result of Bartimaeus's persistence (Mark 10:46-52)*

46And they came to Jericho. And as He was going out from Jericho with His disciples and a great multitude, a blind beggar named Bartimaeus, the son of Timaeus, was sitting by the road. 47And when he heard that it was Jesus the Nazarene, he began to cry out and say, "Jesus, Son of David, have mercy on me!" 48And many were sternly telling him to be quiet, but he began crying out all the more, "Son of David, have mercy on me!" 49And Jesus stopped and said, "Call him here." And they called the blind man, saying to him, "Take courage, arise! He is calling for you." 50And casting aside his cloak, he jumped up, and came to Jesus. 51And answering him, Jesus said, "What do you want Me to do for you?" And the blind man said to Him, "Rabboni, I want to regain my sight!" 52And Jesus said to him, "Go your way; your faith has made you well." And immediately he received his sight and began following Him on the road.

Friday—*The one thing Mary wanted (Luke 10:38-42)*

38Now as they were traveling along, He entered a certain village; and a woman named Martha welcomed Him into her home. 39And she had a sister called Mary, who moreover was listening to the Lord's word, seated at His feet. 40But Martha was distracted with all her preparations; and she came up to

Him, and said, "Lord, do You not care that my sister has left me to do all the serving alone? Then tell her to help me." ⁴¹But the Lord answered and said to her, "Martha, Martha, you are worried and bothered about so many things; ⁴²but only a few things are necessary, really only one: for Mary has chosen the good part, which shall not be taken away from her."

Saturday—*Intent on one purpose (Philippians 2:1-4)*

¹If therefore there is any encouragement in Christ, if there is any consolation of love, if there is any fellowship of the Spirit, if any affection and compassion, ²make my joy complete by being of the same mind, maintaining the same love, united in spirit, intent on one purpose. ³Do nothing from selfishness or empty conceit, but with humility of mind let each of you regard one another as more important than himself; ⁴do not merely look out for your own personal interests, but also for the interests of others.

12

Are We for Real?

7You are looking at things as they are outwardly. If any one is confident in himself that he is Christ's, let him consider this again within himself, that just as he is Christ's, so also are we. 8For even if I should boast somewhat further about our authority, which the Lord gave for building you up and not for destroying you, I shall not be put to shame, 9for I do not wish to seem as if I would terrify you by my letters. 10For they say, "His letters are weighty and strong, but his personal presence is unimpressive, and his speech contemptible." 11Let such a person consider this, that what we are in word by letters when absent, such persons we are also in deed when present. 12For we are not bold to class or compare ourselves with some of those who commend themselves; but when they measure themselves by themselves, and compare themselves with themselves, they are without understanding. 13But we will not boast beyond our measure, but within the measure of the sphere which God apportioned to us as a measure, to reach even as far as you. 14For we are not overextending ourselves, as if we did not reach to you, for we were the first to come even as far as you in the gospel of Christ; 15not boasting beyond our measure, that is, in other men's labors, but with the hope that as your faith grows, we shall be, within our sphere, enlarged even more by you, 16so as to preach the gospel even to the regions beyond you, and not to boast in what has been accomplished in the sphere of another. 17But HE WHO BOASTS, LET HIM BOAST IN THE LORD. 18For not he who commends himself is approved, but whom the Lord commends.

You cannot read the gospels without being impressed with the reality of Jesus. His life and His words said the same things.

He taught His disciples to deny themselves, take up their crosses, and follow Him. Of Jesus we read, "Christ pleased not himself" (Romans 15:3).

He taught that whoever would be great must become a servant, and He said, "I am among you as he that serveth" (Luke 22:27).

He taught His disciples to keep the commandments, and He said, "I have kept my Father's commandments" (John 15:10).

He urged His disciples to pray in secret, and He sent the crowds away as He departed into a mountain alone to pray (Matthew 14:23).

He told His disciples to tarry in Jerusalem until they were empowered by the Holy Spirit to evangelize. Jesus Himself did not enter His ministry until after His baptism, when the Holy Spirit in the shape of a dove descended upon Him; then Jesus, full of the Holy Ghost, returned from the Jordan to minister (Luke 4:14).

Jesus practiced what He preached. He was "for real." Are we? Let us look at three areas of our lives where we especially need reality.

First, we should practice reality in our *speech*. There are so many evidences of unreality in our speech: deceit, injurious words, exaggeration, cutting criticism, and hypocrisy. Even our silence on certain subjects accuses us of unreality. Are we genuine in our speech? Do the things we profess to believe really hold us? Are we totally persuaded?

We say that Jesus Christ is Lord. But is He really Lord? Does He control our time, talents, and money? We urge people to start the day with God. Do we ourselves spend time systematically in Bible study and prayer? We urge others to witness for Christ. Do we? Are we following in the steps of the Lord Jesus, the master soul-winner?

Second, we must practice reality in our *thoughts*. The

real Christian is the person through whom Christ is thinking. The mind of Christ has no time for selfish thoughts, proud thoughts, impure thoughts, or dishonorable thoughts. We are told to think about things that are true, honest, just, pure, lovely, and of good report (Philippians 4:8).

Third, we must be "real" in our *spiritual development*. Are we more like Christ than a year ago? Is God's truth having its way with us? Are we experiencing greater achievements in our prayer life? Are we stronger to live righteously and to serve mankind? Are we involved in God's program of world evangelization?

It takes time to develop reality. Let us study all that Jesus said about hypocrisy until it moves us to act. Then let us cultivate the deeper life by an earnest personal approach to Bible study. Let us yield continuously to the Holy Spirit, who will guard our words and thoughts as we seek reality.

JESUS PRACTICED WHAT HE PREACHED. HE
WAS FOR REAL.

Monday—*Importance of what you say (James 3:2-12)*

²For we stumble in many ways. If any one does not stumble in what he says, he is a perfect man, able to bridle the whole body as well. ³Now if we put the bits into the horses' mouths so that they may obey us, we direct their entire body as well. ⁴Behold, the ships also, though they are so great and are driven by strong winds, are still directed by a very small rudder, wherever the inclination of the pilot desires. ⁵So also the tongue is a small part of the body, and yet it boasts of great things. Behold, how great a forest is set aflame by such a small fire! ⁶And the tongue is a fire, the very world of iniquity; the tongue is set among our members as that which defiles the entire body, and sets on fire the course of our life, and is set on fire by hell. ⁷For every species of beasts and birds, of reptiles and creatures of the sea, is tamed, and has been tamed by the human race. ⁸But no one can tame the tongue; it is a restless evil and full of deadly

poison. ⁹With it we bless our Lord and Father; and with it we curse men, who have been made in the likeness of God; ¹⁰from the same mouth come both blessing and cursing. My brethren, these things ought not to be this way. ¹¹Does a fountain send out from the same opening both fresh and bitter water? ¹²Can a fig tree, my brethren, produce olives, or a vine produce figs? Neither can salt water produce fresh.

Tuesday—*Truth in speech and behavior (Ephesians 4:20-32)*

²⁰But you did not learn Christ in this way, ²¹if indeed you have heard Him and have been taught in Him, just as truth is in Jesus, ²²that, in reference to your former manner of life, you lay aside the old self, which is being corrupted in accordance with the lusts of deceit, ²³and that you be renewed in the spirit of your mind, ²⁴and put on the new self, which in the likeness of God has been created in righteousness and holiness of the truth. ²⁵Therefore, laying aside falsehood, SPEAK TRUTH, EACH ONE of you, WITH HIS NEIGHBOR, for we are members of one another. ²⁶BE ANGRY, AND yet DO NOT SIN; do not let the sun go down on your anger, ²⁷and do not give the devil an opportunity. ²⁸Let him who steals steal no longer; but rather let him labor, performing with his own hands what is good, in order that he may have something to share with him who has need. ²⁹Let no unwholesome word proceed from your mouth, but only such a word as is good for edification according to the need of the moment, that it may give grace to those who hear. ³⁰And do not grieve the Holy Spirit of God, by whom you were sealed for the day of redemption. ³¹Let all bitterness and wrath and anger and clamor and slander be put away from you, along with all malice. ³²And be kind to one another, tender-hearted, forgiving each other, just as God in Christ also has forgiven you.

Wednesday—*Right speech (Proverbs 12:17-23)*

¹⁷He who speaks truth tells what is right,
  But a false witness, deceit.
¹⁸There is one who speaks rashly like the thrusts of a sword,
  But the tongue of the wise brings healing.
¹⁹Truthful lips will be established forever,
  But a lying tongue is only for a moment.
²⁰Deceit is in the heart of those who devise evil,

But counselors of peace have joy.
²¹No harm befalls the righteous,
But the wicked are filled with trouble.
²²Lying lips are an abomination to the LORD,
But those who deal faithfully are His delight.
²³A prudent man conceals knowledge,
But the heart of fools proclaims folly.

Thursday—*Serving God in truth (1 Samuel 12:20-25)*

²⁰And Samuel said to the people, "Do not fear. You have committed all this evil, yet do not turn aside from following the LORD, but serve the LORD with all your heart. ²¹And you must not turn aside, for then you would go after futile things which can not profit or deliver, because they are futile. ²²For the LORD will not abandon His people on account of His great name, because the LORD has been pleased to make you a people for Himself. ²³Moreover, as for me, far be it from me that I should sin against the LORD by ceasing to pray for you; but I will instruct you in the good and right way. ²⁴Only fear the LORD and serve Him in truth with all your heart; for consider what great things He has done for you. ²⁵But if you still do wickedly, both you and your king shall be swept away."

Friday—*How to think (Philippians 4:6-8)*

⁶Be anxious for nothing, but in everything by prayer and supplication with thanksgiving let your requests be made known to God. ⁷And the peace of God, which surpasses all comprehension, shall guard your hearts and your minds in Christ Jesus. ⁸Finally, brethren, whatever is true, whatever is honorable, whatever is right, whatever is pure, whatever is lovely, whatever is of good repute, if there is any excellence and if anything worthy of praise, let your mind dwell on these things.

Saturday—*The mind of Christ (1 Corinthians 2:1-16)*

¹And when I came to you, brethren, I did not come with superiority of speech or of wisdom, proclaiming to you the testimony of God. ²For I determined to know nothing among you except Jesus Christ, and Him crucified. ³And I was with you in weakness and in fear and in much trembling. ⁴And my message and my preaching were not in persuasive words of

wisdom, but in demonstration of the Spirit and of power, ⁵that your faith should not rest on the wisdom of men, but on the power of God. ⁶Yet we do speak wisdom among those who are mature; a wisdom, however, not of this age, nor of the rulers of this age, who are passing away; ⁷but we speak God's wisdom in a mystery, the hidden wisdom, which God predestined before the ages to our glory; ⁸the wisdom which none of the rulers of this age has understood; for if they had understood it, they would not have crucified the Lord of glory; ⁹but just as it is written,

"THINGS WHICH EYE HAS NOT SEEN AND EAR HAS NOT HEARD,
AND which HAVE NOT ENTERED THE HEART OF MAN,
ALL THAT GOD HAS PREPARED FOR THOSE WHO LOVE HIM."

¹⁰For to us God revealed them through the Spirit; for the Spirit searches all things, even the depths of God. ¹¹For who among men knows the thoughts of a man except the spirit of the man, which is in him? Even so the thoughts of God no one knows except the Spirit of God. ¹²Now we have received, not the spirit of the world, but the Spirit who is from God, that we might know the things freely given to us by God, ¹³which things we also speak, not in words taught by human wisdom, but in those taught by the Spirit, combining spiritual thoughts with spiritual words. ¹⁴But a natural man does not accept the things of the Spirit of God; for they are foolishness to him, and he cannot understand them, because they are spiritually ap-praised. ¹⁵But he who is spiritual appraises all things, yet he himself is appraised by no man. ¹⁶For WHO HAS KNOWN THE MIND OF THE LORD, THAT HE SHOULD INSTRUCT HIM? But we have the mind of Christ.

13

Law of Abundance

Sunday—*The first deacons (Acts 6:1-6)*

[1]Now at this time while the disciples were increasing in number, a complaint arose on the part of the Hellenistic Jews against the native Hebrews, because their widows were being overlooked in the daily serving of food. [2]And the twelve summoned the congregation of the disciples and said, "It is not desirable for us to neglect the word of God in order to serve tables. [3]But select from among you, brethren, seven men of good reputation, full of the Spirit and of wisdom, whom we may put in charge of this task. [4]But we will devote ourselves to prayer, and to the ministry of the word." [5]And the statement found approval with the whole congregation; and they chose Stephen, a man full of faith and of the Holy Spirit, and Philip, Prochorus, Nicanor, Timon, Parmenas and Nicolas, a proselyte from Antioch. [6]And these they brought before the apostles; and after praying, they laid their hands on them.

The word *abundance* finds its origin in the Latin word *undore*. The word pictures the waves of the sea overflowing and splashing in every direction. The word *abundance* carries that exciting and dynamic meaning.

Jesus announced that the purpose of His coming into the world was to provide life more abundantly (John 10:10). It is really God's intention that all of us live our lives at floodtide.

God's abundance is seen throughout the Bible. David described his life as a full cup that "runneth over" (Psalm 23:5). When Solomon asked the Lord for an understanding heart, God generously added riches and honor.

Luke's gospel pictures God as giving "good measure, pressed down, and shaken together, and running over" (Luke 6:38). James encourages all who need wisdom and guidance to "ask of God, that giveth to all men *liberally*" (James 1:5, italics added).

When I think of the cross, I even like to think of it as a giant plus sign, suggesting something of the abundant, overflowing, limitless mercy of God.

The book of Acts tells of a layman who was a living example of God's abundance. Of Stephen we read that he was full of *wisdom, faith, power,* and the *Holy Spirit* (Acts 6). He knew God's abundance by personal experience.

Stephen was full of wisdom. He was obviously sensitive to the Scriptures. According to Acts 7, he was quite familiar with his Bible. Perhaps some good questions for us to ask are, Am I a growing person? Am I full of Bible wisdom?

Stephen was full of faith. He realized that apart from faith it was impossible to please God (Hebrews 11:6). We begin our spiritual pilgrimage by faith, and we must continue by faith all the way.

Stephen also was full of grace. The word *grace* originally suggested balance, symmetry, and charm. Paul took that word and poured into it the fullness of God's love and redemption for lost sinners. Even Stephen's facial expression reminded the ungodly council of an angel (Acts 6:15). God's grace showed through and caused his face to shine.

Stephen was full of power. He lived powerfully, prayed powerfully, preached powerfully, and died powerfully. God's abundance gave him the hidden strength to take it. His life would have been nothing without the power of God.

But above and beyond everything else, Stephen was full of the Holy Spirit. His wisdom, faith, grace, and power all came through the Holy Spirit, and that was the secret of his abundant life. He was fully yielded to the Spirit. Are we?

As we begin a brand-new week, let us ask ourselves the searching question, Am I controlled by the Holy Spirit? Abundant life is not just for Stephen, Solomon, and David, but for you and me as well. For every need, there is a corresponding abundance in Jesus Christ.

FOR EVERY NEED THERE IS A
CORRESPONDING ABUNDANCE IN
JESUS CHRIST.

Monday—*Stephen full of faith (Acts 6:7-15)*

7And the word of God kept on spreading; and the number of the disciples continued to increase greatly in Jerusalem, and a great many of the priests were becoming obedient to the faith. 8And Stephen, full of grace and power, was performing great wonders and signs among the people. 9But some men from what was called the Synagogue of the Freedmen, including both Cyrenians and Alexandrians, and some from Cilicia and Asia, rose up and argued with Stephen. 10And yet they were unable to cope with the wisdom and the Spirit with which he was speaking. 11Then they secretly induced men to say, "We have heard him speak blasphemous words against Moses and against God." 12And they stirred up the people, the elders and the scribes, and they came upon him and dragged him away, and brought him before the Council. 13And they put forward false witnesses who said, "This man incessantly speaks against this holy place, and the Law; ¹⁴for we have heard him say that this Nazarene, Jesus, will destroy this place and alter the customs which Moses handed down to us." ¹⁵And fixing their gaze on him, all who were sitting in the Council saw his face like the face of an angel.

Tuesday—*Stephen's persecution (Acts 7:54-60)*

⁵⁴Now when they heard this, they were cut to the quick, and they began gnashing their teeth at him. ⁵⁵But being full of the Holy Spirit, he gazed intently into heaven and saw the glory of God, and Jesus standing at the right hand of God; ⁵⁶and he said, "Behold, I see the heavens opened up and the Son of Man standing at the right hand of God." ⁵⁷But they cried out with a loud voice, and covered their ears, and they rushed upon him with one impulse. ⁵⁸And when they had driven him out of the city, they began stoning him, and the witnesses laid aside their robes at the feet of a young man named Saul. ⁵⁹And they went on stoning Stephen as he called upon the Lord and said, "Lord Jesus, receive my spirit!" ⁶⁰And falling on his knees, he cried out with a loud voice, "Lord, do not hold this sin against them!" And having said this, he fell asleep.

Wednesday—*God's liberal giving (Luke 6:35-38)*

³⁵"But love your enemies, and do good, and lend, expecting nothing in return; and your reward will be great, and you will be sons of the Most High; for He Himself is kind to ungrateful and evil men. ³⁶Be merciful, just as your Father is merciful. ³⁷And do not pass judgment and you will not be judged; and do not condemn, and you shall not be condemned; pardon, and you will be pardoned. ³⁸Give, and it will be given to you; good measure, pressed down, shaken together, running over, they will pour into your lap. For whatever measure you deal out to others, it will be dealt to you in return."

Thursday—*Solomon's gift of wisdom (2 Chronicles 1:7-12)*

⁷In that night God appeared to Solomon and said to him, "Ask what I shall give you." ⁸And Solomon said to God, "Thou hast dealt with my father David with great lovingkindness, and hast made me king in his place. ⁹Now, O LORD God, Thy promise to my father David is fulfilled; for Thou hast made me king

over a people as numerous as the dust of the earth. [10]Give me now wisdom and knowledge, that I may go out and come in before this people; for who can rule this great people of Thine?" [11]And God said to Solomon, "Because you had this in mind, and did not ask for riches, wealth, or honor, or the life of those who hate you, nor have you even asked for long life, but you have asked for yourself wisdom and knowledge, that you may rule My people, over whom I have made you king, [12]wisdom and knowledge have been granted to you. And I will give you riches and wealth and honor, such as none of the kings who were before you has possessed, nor those who will come after you."

Friday—*Jesus full of grace and truth (John 1:14-18)*

[14]And the Word became flesh, and dwelt among us, and we beheld His glory, glory as of the only begotten from the Father, full of grace and truth. [15]John bore witness of Him, and cried out, saying, "This was He of whom I said, 'He who comes after me has a higher rank than I, for He existed before me.'" [16]For of His fulness we have all received, and grace upon grace. [17]For the law was given through Moses; grace and truth were realized through Jesus Christ. [18]No man has seen God at any time; the only begotten God, who is in the bosom of the Father, He has explained Him.

Saturday—*Fullness of Christ (Ephesians 3:14-19)*

[14]For this reason, I bow my knees before the Father, [15]from whom every family in heaven and on earth derives its name, [16]that He would grant you, according to the riches of His glory, to be strengthened with power through His Spirit in the inner man; [17]so that Christ may dwell in your hearts through faith; and that you, being rooted and grounded in love, [18]may be able to comprehend with all the saints what is the breadth and length and height and depth, [19]and to know the love of Christ which surpasses knowledge, that you may be filled up to all the fulness of God.

14

The Quiet Time

Sunday—*The importance of God's Word (Matthew 4:1-6)*
¹Then Jesus was led up by the Spirit into the wilderness to be tempted by the devil. ²And after He had fasted forty days and forty nights, He then became hungry. ³And the tempter came and said to Him, "If You are the Son of God, command that these stones become bread." ⁴But He answered and said, "It is written, 'MAN SHALL NOT LIVE ON BREAD ALONE, BUT ON EVERY WORD THAT PROCEEDS OUT OF THE MOUTH OF GOD.'" ⁵Then the devil took Him into the holy city; and he stood Him on the pinnacle of the temple, ⁶and said to Him, "If You are the son of God throw Yourself down; for it is written,

'HE WILL GIVE HIS ANGELS CHARGE CONCERNING YOU;
AND ON THEIR HANDS THEY WILL BEAR YOU UP,
LEST YOU STRIKE YOUR FOOT AGAINST A STONE.'"

We are living in a hectic world.

The pace at which most of us operate is frightening. More than ever before we need to budget our time to accomplish those things that need to be done. Each of us must decide what our priorities will be. Someone has said, "Beware of the barrenness of an overbusy life."

Unfortunately, for many Christians a daily time of devotion or "quiet time" does not rank high enough on the list. That activity, which should be most important, is pushed aside and neglected, resulting in spiritual lives that are feeble and undernourished.

What is the quiet time and why is it so important? A Christian's quiet time is the definite time set aside each day for prayer, meditation, and the study of God's Word. The quiet time is like a spiritual bath. It cleanses, it refreshes, and it restores. It helps to protect us from the moral corruption that surrounds us, and it prepares us, as Christian soldiers, for the spiritual warfare we are in.

Christians today are bombarded by distractions. Noise pollution takes its toll on every one of us. Radios and television sets blare all day long. Telephones ring incessantly. Automobiles and airplanes make us insensitive to the beauty of solitude. Our mechanized society with all its labor-saving devices has actually become more hectic than ever. When we finally do set aside a few moments for devotion, we find that our minds are still occupied with the many activities of the day. So on and on we go, never seeming to find time to spend with God.

The quiet time is more than just a commendable idea. No matter who you are—new Christian, old Christian, pastor, or layman—you have little hope of living victoriously unless you spend time regularly with your heavenly Father.

How can we maintain a successful quiet time? How can we be still and know God in the midst of this high-pressure society? Here are some suggestions I have found to be extremely helpful in my own experience:

First, be convinced of the importance of a quiet time. It

is a fact of life that we are never truly successful at what we do unless we are committed to achieve success.

Because we believe food is vital to our physical well-being, we eat three times a day. We must feed spiritually for the same reason. Jesus said, "Man shall not live by bread alone, but by every word that proceedeth out of the mouth of God" (Matthew 4:4).

Martin Luther said that "to be a Christian without prayer is no more possible than to be alive without breathing." Communication with our heavenly Father through prayer and through His Word is the spiritual lifeline of every believer.

Second, cultivate a taste for fellowship with God. Jeremiah declared, "Thy words were found, and I did eat them; and thy word was unto me the joy and rejoicing of mine heart" (Jeremiah 15:16). We must meditate upon the Word of God, digest it, and let it become a part of our lives.

We should also desire to talk with God, to be with Him in prayer. Because I love my wife, I want to be with her. I enjoy talking to her. When I am traveling away from home, I look forward to calling her on the phone. If we truly love God we should have a desire to be in constant contact with Him.

Third, work hard to maintain a quiet time. Avoid all interruptions. Do not let the telephone rob you of your time with God. Arrange your schedule so that you can be alone—totally alone and undisturbed—for a specific length of time each day.

I have found that people have time for just about anything that is really important to them. If we want to look attractive, we spend the necessary time in front of the mirror. If we enjoy watching television or reading, we are likely to give several hours a day to those activities. Civic work, even church work, takes up our time because we are convinced of its importance.

But what about communion with God? If we do not maintain that time each day, it is not because we are too busy; it is because we do not feel it is important enough—that it is worth sacrificing for.

Fourth, be consistent. Try to meet God in the same place and at the same time each day. A definite time and place will help a great deal in insuring regularity.

Consistency is the important thing, but I have personally found the morning to be the best time for my quiet time with God. The psalmist declared, "My voice shalt thou hear in the morning, O LORD; in the morning will I direct my prayer unto thee, and will look up" (Psalm 5:3).

If you are like most people, you are probably more alert in the morning than you are just before bedtime. But in order to meet God regularly in the morning, you must get to bed at a reasonable time at night. You may have to put that book or magazine down a little earlier. You may have to switch off the television. Consistency requires faithfulness. The apostle Paul wrote, "Moreover it is required in stewards, that a man be found faithful" (1 Corinthians 4:2). Each one of us is a steward. We have twenty-four hours to spend every day. How are you using your time?

Fifth, expect God to do something for you each day. Pray expecting Him to meet a specific need in your life.

Do not hurry through your personal devotions. Be still before the Lord. Ask God for one word of instruction that you can take with you for the day.

Do you lack power in your life? Does it feel as if there is something missing in your Christian experience? Why not purpose in your heart right now that you will spend time with God? Begin today to read His Word and pray, and He will bless your life in a way you have never known before.

BEWARE OF THE BARRENNESS OF AN
OVERBUSY LIFE.

Monday—*Jesus' use of the Word (Matthew 4:7-11)*

7Jesus said to him, "On the other hand, it is written, 'YOU

89

SHALL NOT TEMPT THE LORD YOUR GOD.'" [8]Again, the devil took Him to a very high mountain, and showed Him all the kingdoms of the world, and their glory; [9]and he said to Him, "All these things will I give You, if You fall down and worship me." [10]Then Jesus said to him, "Begone, Satan! For it is written, 'YOU SHALL WORSHIP THE LORD YOUR GOD, AND SERVE HIM ONLY.'" [11]Then the devil left Him; and behold, angels came and began to minister to Him.

Tuesday—*The Word of God in the midst of trouble (Jeremiah 15:15-16)*

[15]Thou who knowest, O LORD;
  Remember me, take notice of me,
  And take vengeance for me on my persecutors.
  Do not, in view of Thy patience, take me away;
  Know that for Thy sake I endure reproach.
[16]Thy words were found and I ate them,
  And Thy words became for me a joy and the delight of my
      heart;
  For I have been called by Thy name,
  O LORD God of hosts.

Wednesday—*Morning prayers and regular worship (Psalm 5:1-7)*

[1]Give ear to my words, O LORD,
  Consider my groaning.
[2]Heed the sound of my cry for help, my King and my God,
  For to Thee do I pray.
[3]In the morning, O LORD, Thou wilt hear my voice;
  In the morning I will order my prayer to Thee and eagerly
      watch.
[4]For Thou art not a God who takes pleasure in wickedness;
  No evil dwells with thee.
[5]The boastful shall not stand before Thine eyes;
  Thou dost hate all who do iniquity.
[6]Thou dost destroy those who speak falsehood;
  The LORD abhors the man of bloodshed and deceit.
[7]But as for me, by Thine abundant lovingkindness I will enter
      Thy house,
  At Thy holy temple I will bow in reverence for Thee.

Thursday—*Faithfulness in small and big things (Luke 16:10-13)*

[10]"He who is faithful in a very little thing is faithful also in much; and he who is unrighteous in a very little thing is unrighteous also in much. [11]If therefore you have not been faithful in the use of unrighteous mammon, who will entrust the true riches to you? [12]And if you have not been faithful in the use of that which is another's, who will give you that which is your own? [13]No servant can serve two masters; for either he will hate the one, and love the other, or else he will hold to one, and despise the other. You cannot serve God and mammon."

Friday—*Seeking God's fellowship (Psalm 27:4-8)*

[4]One thing I have asked from the LORD, that I shall seek;
  That I may dwell in the house of the LORD all the days of my
    life,
  To behold the beauty of the LORD,
  And to meditate in His temple.
[5]For in the day of trouble He will conceal me in His tabernacle;
  In the secret place of His tent He will hide me;
  He will lift me up on a rock.
[6]And now my head will be lifted up above my enemies around
    me;
  And I will offer in His tent sacrifices with shouts of joy;
  I will sing, yes, I will sing praises to the LORD.
[7]Hear, O LORD, when I cry with my voice,
  And be gracious to me and answer me.
[8]When Thou didst say, "Seek My face," my heart said to Thee,
  "Thy face, O LORD, I shall seek."

Saturday—*God's teaching and leading (Psalm 27:8-11)*

[8]When Thou didst say, "Seek My face," my heart said to Thee,
  "Thy face, O LORD, I shall seek."
[9]Do not hide Thy face from me,
  Do not turn Thy servant away in anger;
  Thou hast been my help;
  Do not abandon me nor forsake me,
  O God of my salvation!
[10]For my father and my mother have forsaken me,
  But the LORD will take me up.

[11]Teach me Thy way, O Lord,
And lead me in a level path,
Because of my foes.

15

Grow Up

Sunday—*Beginning life (John 3:1-8)*

¹Now there was a man of the Pharisees, named Nicodemus, a ruler of the Jews; ²this man came to Him by night, and said to Him, "Rabbi, we know that You have come from God as a teacher; for no one can do these signs that You do unless God is with him." ³Jesus answered and said to him, "Truly, truly, I say to you, unless one is born again, he cannot see the kingdom of God." ⁴Nicodemus said to Him, "How can a man be born when he is old? He cannot enter a second time into his mother's womb and be born, can he?" ⁵Jesus answered, "Truly, truly, I say to you, unless one is born of water and the Spirit, he cannot enter into the kingdom of God. ⁶That which is born of the flesh is flesh; and that which is born of the Spirit is spirit. ⁷Do not marvel that I said to you, 'You must be born again.' ⁸The wind blows where it wishes and you hear the sound of it, but do not know where it comes from and where it is going; so is every one who is born of the Spirit."

Recently I read a book entitled *Grow Up or Blow Up*. The book asserted that civilization must mature or it will destroy itself. Our atomic capability is hundreds of times greater than in World War II, and world destruction is very possible.

Robert Browning wrote, "Man was made to grow." The apostles continually underscored the need for growth in the spiritual realm. Peter challenged all Christians to "grow in grace."

The first essential to growth is *life*. When a child is born, the first cry indicates life. If there is life, a world of possibilities beckons to this new baby. Where there is no *life*, all is hopeless. A fence post placed in the ground will not grow, but a little seed will. Drop a stone into the richest soil and it will be exactly the same size years later. Place a seed into the ground and it will spring up and produce a stalk and flowers. The difference is plain: one has *life* while the other does not. Dead things may accumulate, but they cannot grow. Life is the first prerequisite for growth.

Unless men and women have life from above, religious practices and environment mean nothing. In fact, they cause a person to rest in a false hope.

Divine life may be imitated, but the imitation is worthless; it is false, unnatural, and mechanical. False righteousness is self-righteousness, and self-righteousness is not righteousness at all.

How can spiritual growth be attained? First, it is important to see that Christian growth is not the dream of a starry-eyed idealist, but the very purpose and plan of God. Jesus said, "Be ye therefore perfect [mature], even as your Father which is in heaven is perfect (Matthew 5:48).

The word *grow* denotes continuous action. If we stop growing physically, it is a bad sign, a mark of sickness. A mother would be alarmed if day after day and week after week her baby showed no signs of growth. A farmer would be dismayed if his crops never yielded their harvest. Erratic growth results in death. A cankered tree does not send forth new shoots. When the human body stops growing, it begins to deteriorate. Death ultimately results. The first law of life is expansion. Grow or decay! Advance or regress! Live or die! There is no time or place to stop growing. Growth is according to the law of nature and according to God's plan.

Jesus said, "Every branch in me that beareth not fruit he taketh away; and every branch that beareth fruit, he purgeth it, that it may bring forth more fruit" (John 15:2).

Our twentieth century finds masses of people living and literally dying for material possessions. An unparalleled desire for wealth sickens the populace while spiritual values are ignored. We have forgotten that the true measure of success in life cannot be counted in dollars and cents or in physical or mental accomplishments. We have stopped growing and begun to decay.

Let me make five suggestions concerning how one grows.

1. *Naturally*

Jesus said, "Consider the lilies of the field, how they grow; they toil not, neither do they spin; and yet I say unto you, That even Solomon in all his glory was not arrayed like one of these" (Matthew 6:28-29).

Notice the phrase "how they grow." Well, how do the lilies grow? What is their secret of growth? The lily, according to God's plan, simply unfolds the life within. We do not tell a lily to grow; it grows naturally, spontaneously. It does not fuss or fret, toil or turn, strain or stretch; it just grows. Growth is natural and inevitable when there is life, and more so when there is divine life.

2. *By eating*

We also grow by eating. All living things eat, and what we eat affects our growth. The Bible says, "Eat ... that which is good" (Isaiah 55:2). No book will help you grow like the Bible.

D. L. Moody used to hoe potatoes when a boy, and he said that he hoed them so poorly that he always had to mark where he stopped. I wonder, is that how we read the Bible?

3. *By breathing*

What breathing is to the physical man, prayer is to the spiritual man. Our Savior was a man of prayer. The common atmosphere was stifling to Him, and He frequently sought communion with God in places apart from the crowd. If Jesus, the sinless Son of God, found prayer important, we sinful creatures dare not live without it.

4. *By resting*

This is what Jesus was talking about when He asked, "Which of you by taking thought can add one cubit unto his stature?" (Matthew 6:27). Anxiety will not add to your spiritual size; worry will not add one fraction to your stature.

The Christian life is not a nervous hanging on to God, but a resting in the hollow of His hand. I will not grow by toiling and turning, stretching and straining, but rather by yielding completely to Christ's control.

5. *By exercising*

The Bible places great stress on work. Show me a person who does not work, and I will show you a person who is weak. If you faithfully work, you will eat and sleep right. People often complain that they are not spiritually fed, but probably they are not spiritually hungry, and they are not hungry because they are not working. Broken-down tissues call for nourishment. So those broken down in toil in the Lord's harvest field call out for the Bread of Life. If a believer will sincerely work in the vineyard of God, he will grow in grace.

Friend, are you glorifying God more this week than last week? Are you nearer the Savior now than at your hour of decision? Is your delight in the law of the Lord, and are you meditating upon it day and night?

I would encourage you to grow, grow, grow until that wonderful day when we shall see Him and be like Him!

> NO OTHER BOOK WILL HELP YOU GROW AS THE BIBLE WILL.

Monday—*Growth as a vine (John 15:1-8)*

[1]"I am the true vine, and My Father is the vinedresser. [2]Every branch in Me that does not bear fruit, He takes away; and every branch that bears fruit, He prunes it, that it may bear more fruit. [3]You are already clean because of the word which I have spoken to you. [4]Abide in Me, and I in you. As the branch cannot bear fruit of itself, unless it abides in the vine, so neither can you, unless you abide in Me. [5]I am the vine, you are the branches; he who abides in Me, and I in him, he bears much fruit; for apart from Me you can do nothing. [6]If anyone does not abide in Me, he is thrown away as a branch, and dries up; and they gather them, and cast them into the fire, and they are burned. [7]If you abide in Me, and My words abide in you, ask whatever you wish, and it shall be done for you. [8]By this is My Father glorified, that you bear much fruit, and so prove to be My disciples."

Tuesday—*Growing up into Christ (Ephesians 4:11-16)*

[11]And He gave some as apostles, and some as prophets, and some as evangelists, and some as pastors and teachers, [12]for the equipping of the saints for the work of service, to the building up of the body of Christ; [13]until we all attain to the unity of the faith, and of the knowledge of the Son of God, to a mature man, to the measure of the stature which belongs to the fulness of Christ. [14]As a result, we are no longer to be children, tossed here and there by waves, and carried about by every wind of doctrine, by the trickery of men, by craftiness in deceitful scheming; [15]but speaking the truth in love, we are to grow up in all aspects into Him, who is the head, even Christ, [16]from whom the whole body, being fitted and held together by that which every joint supplies, according to the proper working of each individual part, causes the growth of the body for the building up of itself in love.

97

Wednesday—*Growth by the Word (Psalm 1)*
¹How blessed is the man who does not walk in the counsel of
    the wicked,
Nor stand in the path of sinners,
Nor sit in the seat of scoffers!
²But his delight is in the law of the LORD,
And in His law he meditates day and night.
³And he will be like a tree firmly planted by streams of water,
Which yields its fruit in its season,
And its leaf does not wither;
And in whatever he does, he prospers.
⁴The wicked are not so,
But they are like chaff which the wind drives away.
⁵Therefore the wicked will not stand in the judgment,
Nor sinners in the assembly of the righteous.
⁶For the LORD knows the way of the righteous,
But the way of the wicked will perish.

Thursday—*Growing like a new baby (1 Peter 2:1-3)*
¹Therefore, putting aside all malice and all guile and hypocrisy and envy and all slander, ²like newborn babes, long for the
pure milk of the word, that by it you may grow in respect to
salvation, ³if you have tasted the kindness of the Lord.

Friday—*The sower planting seed (Mark 4:3-20)*
³"Listen to this! Behold, the sower went out to sow; ⁴and it
came about that as he was sowing, some seed fell beside the
road, and the birds came and ate it up. ⁵And other seed fell on
the rocky ground where it did not have much soil; and immediately it sprang up because it had no depth of soil. ⁶And
after the sun had risen, it was scorched; and because it had no
root, it withered away. ⁷And other seed fell among the thorns,
and the thorns grew up and choked it, and it yielded no crop.
⁸And other seeds fell into the good soil and as they grew up and
increased, they were yielding a crop and were producing thirty,
sixty, and a hundredfold." ⁹And He was saying, "He who has
ears to hear, let him hear." ¹⁰And as soon as He was alone, His
followers, along with the twelve, began asking Him about the
parables. ¹¹And He was saying to them, "To you has been given
the mystery of the kingdom of God; but those who are outside

get everything in parables; [12]in order that WHILE SEEING, THEY MAY SEE AND NOT PERCEIVE; AND WHILE HEARING, THEY MAY HEAR AND NOT UNDERSTAND LEST THEY RETURN AGAIN AND BE FORGIVEN." [13]And He said to them, "Do you not understand this parable? And how will you understand all the parables? [14]The sower sows the word. [15]And these are the ones who are beside the road where the word is sown; and when they hear, immediately Satan comes and takes away the word which has been sown in them. [16]And in a similar way these are the ones on whom seed was sown on the rocky places, who, when they hear the word, immediately receive it with joy; [17]and they have no firm root in themselves, but are only temporary; then, when affliction or persecution arises because of the word, immediately they fall away. [18]And others are the ones on whom seed was sown among the thorns; these are the ones who have heard the word, [19]and the worries of the world, and the deceitfulness of riches, and the desires for other things enter in and choke the word, and it becomes unfruitful. [20]And those are the ones on whom seed was sown on the good ground; and they hear the word and accept it, and bear fruit, thirty, sixty, and a hundredfold."

Saturday—*Growth patterns to imitate*
(Luke 2:51-52; 1 Samuel 2:21-26)

[51]And He went down with them, and came to Nazareth; and He continued in subjection to them; and His mother treasured all these things in her heart. [52]And Jesus kept increasing in wisdom and stature, and in favor with God and men. . . . [21]And the LORD visited Hannah; and she conceived and gave birth to three sons and two daughters. And the boy Samuel grew before the LORD. [22]Now Eli was very old; and he heard all that his sons were doing to all Israel, and how they lay with the women who served at the doorway of the tent of meeting. [23]And he said to them, "Why do you do such things, the evil things that I hear from all these people? [24]"No, my sons; for the report is not good which I hear the LORD's people circulating. [25]"If one man sins against another, God will mediate for him; but if a man sins against the LORD, who can intercede for him?" But they would not listen to the voice of their father, for the LORD desired to put them to death. [26]Now the boy Samuel was growing in stature and in favor both with the LORD and with men.

16

The Secret of Self-Control

Sunday—*David's self-control (1 Samuel 24:1-15)*

¹Now it came about when Saul returned from pursuing the Philistines, he was told, saying, "Behold, David is in the wilderness of Engedi." ²Then Saul took three thousand chosen men from all Israel, and went to seek David and his men in front of the Rocks of the Wild Goats. ·³And he came to the sheepfolds on the way, where there was a cave; and Saul went in to relieve himself. Now David and his men were sitting in the inner recesses of the cave. ⁴And the men of David said to him, "Behold, this is the day of which the LORD said to you, 'Behold; I am about to give your enemy into your hand, and you shall do to him as it seems good to you.' " Then David arose and cut off the edge of Saul's robe secretly. ⁵And it came about afterward that David's conscience bothered him because he had cut off the edge of Saul's robe. ⁶So he said to his men, "Far be it from me because of the LORD that I should do this thing to my lord, the LORD's anointed, to stretch out my hand against him, since he is the LORD's anointed." ⁷And David persuaded his men with these words and did not allow them to rise up against Saul. And Saul arose, left the cave, and went on his way. ⁸Now afterward David arose and went out of the cave and called after Saul, saying, "My lord the king!" And when Saul looked behind him, David bowed with his face to the ground and prostrated himself. ⁹And David said to Saul, "Why do you listen to the words of men, saying, 'Behold, David seeks to harm you'? ¹⁰Behold, this day your eyes have seen that the LORD had given you today into my hand in the cave, and some said to kill you, but my eye had pity on you; and I said, 'I will not stretch out my

hand against my lord, for he is the LORD's anointed.' [11]Now, my father, see! Indeed, see the edge of your robe in my hand! For in that I cut off the edge of your robe and did not kill you, know and perceive that there is no evil or rebellion in my hands, and I have not sinned against you, though you are lying in wait for my life to take it. [12]May the LORD judge between you and me, and may the LORD avenge me on you; but my hand shall not be against you. [13]As the proverb of the ancients says, 'Out of the wicked comes forth wickedness'; but my hand shall not be against you. [14]After whom has the king of Israel come out? After whom are you pursuing? After a dead dog, after a single flea? [15]The LORD therefore be judge and decide between you and me; and may He see and plead my cause, and deliver me from your hand."

No more worlds to conquer! That was the cry of Alexander the Great after his Grecian armies swept across the then known world. Bold and impulsive Alexander was one of the few men in history who deserved to be called "great."

Anger was not generally a part of Alexander's nature. Several times in his life, however, he was tragically defeated by temper. On one of those occasions, Cletus, a dear friend of Alexander's and a general in his army, became intoxicated and began to ridicule the emperor in front of his men. Blinded by anger, Alexander snatched a spear from a soldier and hurled it at Cletus. Although he had only intended to scare the drunken general, his spear took the life of his childhood friend.

Deep remorse followed his anger. Overcome with guilt, Alexander attempted to take his own life with the same spear, but his men stopped him. For days he lay sick, calling for Cletus, chiding himself as a murderer. Alexander the Great conquered many cities, but he had failed to conquer his own spirit.

Throughout history many have destroyed their lives by passion and pride. James offers a tried and proven remedy, "Let every man be swift to hear, slow to speak, slow to wrath" (James 1:19).

Be swift to hear. Psychotherapists tell us that listening is probably the most simple and effective technique for helping troubled people. Poor listening causes a tremendous waste in education and industry. Thousands of marriages are ended each year because the husband and wife stopped listening to each other.

James says, "Be swift to hear." Swift to hear what? Swift to hear the Word of God. The first step in conversion is hearing. The Bible tells us that "faith cometh by hearing, and hearing by the word of God" (Romans 10:17). It is sad when men and women fail to listen to one another, but it is eternally fatal when they fail to listen to God.

Be slow to speak. Everybody seems to have something

102

to say. Never before in history have so many said so much and done so little! Zeno, the ancient philosopher, once said, "We have two ears and one mouth; therefore we should listen twice as much as we speak." That is good advice! Unfortunately, some people shift their minds into neutral and stomp the gas pedal of wild talk. Solomon wrote, "Whoso keepeth his mouth and his tongue keepeth his soul from troubles" (Proverbs 21:23).

Be slow to wrath. Why should we be slow to wrath or anger? James continues, "For the wrath of man worketh not the righteousness of God" (James 1:20). Man's anger hinders God's work. When you lose your temper, you really lose the ability to think sanely and to make balanced decisions. Anger borders on insanity. When we are angry, we say irrational things. May we practice the Word of God.

THE SECRET OF SELF-CONTROL IS CHRIST-CONTROL.

Monday—*Fruits of maturity (2 Peter 1:5-9)*

[5]Now for this very reason also, applying all diligence, in your faith supply moral excellence, and in your moral excellence, knowledge; [6]and in your knowledge, self-control, and in your self-control, perseverance, and in your perseverance, godliness; [7]and in your godliness, brotherly kindness, and in your brotherly kindness, Christian love. [8]For if these qualities are yours and are increasing, they render you neither useless nor unfruitful in the true knowledge of our Lord Jesus Christ. [9]For he who lacks these qualities is blind or short-sighted, having forgotten his purification from his former sins.

Tuesday—*Christ's example (Romans 15:1-7)*

[1]Now we who are strong ought to bear the weaknesses of those without strength and not just please ourselves. [2]Let each of us please his neighbor for his good, to his edification. [3]For even Christ did not please Himself; but as it is written, "THE REPROACHES OF THOSE WHO REPROACHED THEE FELL UPON ME."

⁴For whatever was written in earlier times was written for our instruction, that through perseverance and the encouragement of the Scriptures we might have hope. ⁵Now may the God who gives perseverance and encouragement grant you to be of the same mind with one another according to Christ Jesus; ⁶that with one accord you may with one voice glorify the God and Father of our Lord Jesus Christ. ⁷Wherefore, accept one another, just as Christ also accepted us to the glory of God.

Wednesday—*Following in His steps (1 Peter 2:21-25)*

²¹For you have been called for this purpose, since Christ also suffered for you, leaving you an example for you to follow in His steps, ²²WHO COMMITTED NO SIN, NOR WAS ANY DECEIT FOUND IN HIS MOUTH; ²³and while being reviled, He did not revile in return; while suffering, He uttered no threats, but kept entrusting Himself to Him who judges righteously; ²⁴and He Himself bore our sins in His body on the cross, that we might die to sin and live to righteousness; for by His wounds you were healed. ²⁵For you were continually straying like sheep, but now you have returned to the Shepherd and Guardian of your souls.

Thursday—*Overcoming the world (1 John 4:4-11)*

⁴You are from God, little children, and have overcome them; because greater is He who is in you than he who is in the world. ⁵They are from the world; therefore they speak as from the world, and the world listens to them. ⁶We are from God; he who knows God listens to us; he who is not from God does not listen to us. By this we know the spirit of truth and the spirit of error. ⁷Beloved, let us love one another, for love is from God; and every one who loves is born of God and knows God. ⁸The one who does not love does not know God, for God is love. ⁹By this the love of God was manifested in us, that God has sent His only begotten Son into the world so that we might live through Him. ¹⁰In this is love, not that we loved God, but that He loved us and sent His Son to be the propitiation for our sins. ¹¹Beloved, if God so loved us, we also ought to love one another.

Friday—*The law of sacrifice (John 12:24-26)*

²⁴Truly, truly, I say to you, unless a grain of wheat falls into the earth and dies, it remains by itself alone; but if it dies, it bears much fruit. ²⁵He who loves his life loses it; and he who

hates his life in this world shall keep it to life eternal. ²⁶If any one serves Me, let him follow Me; and where I am, there shall My servant also be; if any one serves Me, the Father will honor him."

Saturday—*The Beatitudes (Matthew 5:3-11)*

³"Blessed are the poor in spirit, for theirs is the kingdom of heaven. ⁴Blessed are those who mourn, for they shall be comforted. ⁵Blessed are the gentle, for they shall inherit the earth. ⁶Blessed are those who hunger and thirst for righteousness, for they shall be satisfied. ⁷Blessed are the merciful, for they shall receive mercy. ⁸Blessed are the pure in heart, for they shall see God. ⁹Blessed are the peacemakers, for they shall be called sons of God. ¹⁰Blessed are those who have been persecuted for the sake of righteousness, for theirs is the kingdom of heaven. ¹¹Blessed are you when men revile you, and persecute you, and say all kinds of evil against you falsely, on account of Me."

17

How to Whip Worry

Sunday—*God's provision in nature (Matthew 6:25-30)*

²⁵"For this reason I say to you, do not be anxious for your life, as to what you shall eat, or what you shall drink; nor for your body, as to what you shall put on. Is not life more than food, and the body than clothing? ²⁶Look at the birds of the air, that they do not sow, neither do they reap, nor gather into barns; and yet your heavenly Father feeds them. Are you not worth much more than they? ²⁷And which of you by being anxious can add a single cubit to his life's span? ²⁸And why are you anxious about clothing? Observe how the lilies of the field grow; they do not toil nor do they spin, ²⁹yet I say to you that even Solomon in all his glory did not clothe himself like one of these. ³⁰But if God so arrays the grass of the field, which is alive today and tomorrow is thrown into the furnace, will He not much more do so for you, O men of little faith?"

Worry is one of the world's leading ailments. Unfortunately, it is also contagious—easily caught and fearfully experienced.

The Greek word for worry, *merimnao,* is a combination of two words—*merizo* ("to divide") and *nous* ("mind"). Worry actually means "a divided mind."

Worry weakens our ability to act single-mindedly. It diminishes our power to will. Worry sometimes leaves people unable to make even the smallest decisions.

But despite the worry epidemic, there is a scriptural, step-by-step cure for the willing patient. First, *pray.* In Luke 18:1 we read, "Men ought always to pray, and not to faint." Prayer is one of God's cures for a caved-in life. Do what the great hymn suggests, "Take it to the Lord *in prayer."*

Paul encourages us along the same lines: "Be careful for nothing; but in every thing by prayer and supplication with thanksgiving let your requests be made known unto God. And the peace of God, which passeth all understanding, shall keep your hearts and minds through Christ Jesus" (Philippians 4:6-7).

Second, *rejoice.* Philippians 4:4 also suggests, "Rejoice in the Lord alway: and again I say, Rejoice." You may say, "But I'm not in a rejoicing mood. I just don't feel like rejoicing." Although most people let circumstances control them, the verb in Philippians 4:4 makes rejoicing mandatory, regardless of our situation. Paul does not say, "If you are so inclined, please let me suggest that you rejoice." Instead, he says, "Keep on rejoicing in the Lord." Praise to God is another of His cures for worry.

Third, Psalm 37 tells us to *trust.* "Trust in the LORD, and do good" (Psalm 37:3). Fretting is the opposite of trusting. It creates useless friction by heating the axle without generating any motion or speed.

In a way, fretting or worrying is a form of atheism. It denies God's concern and Christ's intercessory work. No amount of worry will resolve your problem, but trust in your heavenly Father will.

Fourth, Psalm 37:3 also suggests that we *work* as a worry remedy. "Trust in the LORD, and do good." Work is one of the best cures for worry. "It is not work that kills men," wrote Henry Ward Beecher, "it is worry. Work is healthy . . . worry is rust upon the blade." Matthew affirms: "But seek ye first the kingdom of God, and his righteousness; and all these things shall be added unto you" (Matthew 6:33). If we put the Lord and His work first, He will provide us with all that is necessary in life.

Fifth, *count your blessings*. Thank God for loved ones, a husband or wife, parents, children, your job, your country, your health, your possessions. Thank Him for your church fellowship, the Word of God, and your personal faith in Christ.

Do you want to rid yourself of anxiety? Do you want to win out over worry? Then stop seeking the trivial; do not major in the minor things of life. Instead, view life from God's perspective—through the lens of eternity. Concern yourself with the Kingdom of God. J. B. Phillips paraphrased Matthew 6:33 this way: "Set your heart on his kingdom and his goodness, and all these things will come to you as a matter of course."

Commit yourself completely to Jesus Christ, and He will free you from a divided mind.

PRAISE TO GOD IS ANOTHER OF HIS CURES
FOR WORRY.

Monday—*Taking no thought (Matthew 6:31-34)*

[31]"Do not be anxious then, saying, 'What shall we eat?' or, 'What shall we drink?' or, 'With what shall we clothe ourselves?' [32]For all these things the Gentiles eagerly seek; for your heavenly Father knows that you need all these things. [33]But seek first His kingdom, and His righteousness; and all these things shall be added to you. [34]Therefore do not be anxious for tomorrow; for tomorrow will care for itself. Each day has enough trouble of its own."

108

Tuesday—*God's provision for Elijah (1 Kings 17:2-9)*

²And the word of the LORD came to him, saying, ³"Go away from here and turn eastward, and hide yourself by the brook Cherith, which is east of the Jordan. ⁴And it shall be that you shall drink of the brook, and I have commanded the ravens to provide for you there." ⁵So he went and did according to the word of the LORD, for he went and lived by the brook Cherith, which is east of the Jordan. ⁶And the ravens brought him bread and meat in the morning and bread and meat in the evening, and he would drink from the brook. ⁷And it happened after a while, that the brook dried up, because there was no rain in the land. ⁸Then the word of the LORD came to him, saying, ⁹"Arise, go to Zarephath, which belongs to Sidon, and stay there; behold, I have commanded a widow there to provide for you."

Wednesday—*Water from the rock (Exodus 17:5-7)*

⁵Then the LORD said to Moses, "Pass before the people and take with you some of the elders of Israel; and take in your hand your staff with which you struck the Nile, and go. ⁶Behold, I will stand before you there on the rock at Horeb; and you shall strike the rock, and water will come out of it, that the people may drink." And Moses did so in the sight of the elders of Israel. ⁷And he named the place Massah and Meribah because of the quarrel of the sons of Israel, and because they tested the LORD, saying, "Is the LORD among us, or not?"

Thursday—*Foolish thinking (Psalm 63:1-6)*

¹O God, Thou are my God; I shall seek Thee earnestly;
My soul thirsts for Thee, my flesh yearns for Thee,
In a dry and weary land where there is no water.
²Thus I have beheld Thee in the sanctuary,
To see Thy power and Thy glory.
³Because Thy lovingkindness is better than life,
My lips will praise Thee.
⁴So I will bless Thee as long as I live;
I will lift up my hands in Thy name.
⁵My soul is satisfied as with marrow and fatness.
And my mouth offers praises with joyful lips;
⁶When I remember Thee on my bed.
I meditate on Thee in the night watches.

Friday—*David's fearlessness (Psalm 27:1-6)*

¹The LORD is my light and my salvation;
 Whom shall I fear?
 The LORD is the defense of my life;
 Whom shall I dread?
²When evildoers came upon me to devour my flesh,
 My adversaries and my enemies, they stumbled and fell.
³Though a host encamp against me,
 My heart will not fear;
 Though war arise against me,
 In spite of this I shall be confident.
⁴One thing I have asked from the LORD, that I shall seek:
 That I may dwell in the house of the LORD all the days of my
  life,
 To behold the beauty of the LORD,
 And to meditate in His temple.
⁵For in the day of trouble He will conceal me in His tabernacle;
 In the secret place of His tent He will hide me;
 He will lift me up on a rock.
⁶And now my head will be lifted up above my enemies around
  me;
 And I will offer in His tent sacrifices with shouts of joy;
 I will sing, yes, I will sing praises to the LORD.

Saturday—*Being unafraid (Matthew 10:28-34)*

²⁸"And do not fear those who kill the body, but are unable to kill the soul; but rather fear Him who is able to destroy both soul and body in hell. ²⁹Are not two sparrows sold for a cent? And yet not one of them will fall to the ground apart from your Father. ³⁰But the very hairs of your head are all numbered. ³¹Therefore do not fear; you are of more value than many sparrows. ³²Every one therefore who shall confess Me before men, I will also confess him before My Father who is in heaven. ³³But whoever shall deny Me before men, I will also deny him before My Father who is in heaven. ³⁴Do not think that I came to bring peace on the earth; I did not come to bring peace, but a sword."

110

18

Blessed Are the Balanced

Sunday—*Balanced living (Proverbs 30:7-9)*
   [7]Two things I asked of Thee,
   Do not refuse me before I die:
   [8]Keep deception and lies far from me,
   Give me neither poverty nor riches,
   Feed me with the food that is my portion,
   [9]Lest I be full and deny Thee and say, "Who is the LORD?"
   Or lest I be in want and steal,
   And profane the name of my God.

In some ways, it is natural to be negative. Since the curse of God in the Garden of Eden, all creation groans under the process of decay (Romans 8:22).

There is a negative ring throughout creation, like some solemn tune in a minor key. Roses have thorns and day turns to night. The voice of nature cries out continually—the howling wind, the bleating of sheep, the rolling thunder—reminding us of God's judgment on man's sin.

We too participate in this groaning. Paul writes, "We ourselves groan within ourselves, waiting for the adoption . . . the redemption of our body" (Romans 8:23).

Some time ago my wife and I were climbing a very steep hill. I was panting and complaining about how difficult it was when she teasingly suggested that I stop groaning.

"Why should I?" I asked. "It's scriptural."

However, another truth needs to be kept in mind—"Christ in you, the hope of glory" (Colossians 1:27). There is a real possibility that each believer can "reign in life by one, Jesus Christ" (Romans 5:17). Victory is possible in and through Jesus Christ right now!

Someone has suggested that a good beatitude would be, "Blessed are the balanced." There is a tendency to be either too optimistic or too pessimistic.

The person who is always optimistic often fails to come to grips with reality. He can have a blind eye. Vance Havner once said, "An optimist is a person with misty optics." It is not good to be unreasonably optimistic, to refuse to see things realistically.

Pessimism, on the other hand, inspires no enthusiasm for anything, not even for its pessimism. A person who is constantly pessimistic may have forgotten that Christ is the Victor and God is working all things for ultimate good. Remember that Jesus, who passed through Gethsemane, Calvary, and the tomb, is now cheering you on to victory.

Balance requires the harmonious intermingling of both optimism and pessimism. It is not a Jekyll and Hyde combination, but a Moody and Sankey, traveling in beautiful harmony, each inspiring and checking one another.

Imbalance is harmful to Christian living. Imbalance in doctrine can lead to theological heresy. Even extreme emphasis on the dedication of one's life can inspire unhealthy introspection, while the neglect of self-examination can result in callousness. Balance is important to a full spiritual experience.

Perfect balance is expressed in the words of the apostle Paul in Philippians 4:12-13, "I know how to be *abased*, and I know how to *abound*: every where and in all things I am instructed both to be *full* and to be *hungry*, both to *abound* and to suffer *need*. I can do all things through Christ which strengtheneth me" (italics added). At times God loads our arms with *blessings* and our backs with *burdens*, just to keep us *balanced*.

VICTORY IS POSSIBLE IN AND THROUGH JESUS CHRIST RIGHT NOW.

Monday—*Paul's balance (Philippians 4:11-13)*

[11]Not that I speak from want; for I have learned to be content in whatever circumstances I am. [12]I know how to get along with humble means, and I also know how to live in prosperity; in any and every circumstance I have learned the secret of being filled and going hungry, both of having abundance and suffering need. [13]I can do all things through Him who strengthens me.

Tuesday—*Wisdom in our walk (Ephesians 5:11-18)*

[11]And do not participate in the unfruitful deeds of darkness, but instead even expose them; [12]for it is disgraceful even to speak of the things which are done by them in secret. [13]But all things become visible when they are exposed by the light, for everything that becomes visible is light. [14]For this reason it says,

> "AWAKE, SLEEPER,
> AND ARISE FROM THE DEAD,
> AND CHRIST WILL SHINE ON YOU."

¹⁵Therefore be careful how you walk, not as unwise men, but as wise, ¹⁶making the most of your time, because the days are evil. ¹⁷So then do not be foolish, but understand what the will of the Lord is. ¹⁸And do not get drunk with wine, for that is dissipation, but be filled with the Spirit.

Wednesday—*Overcoming evil with good (Romans 12:17-21)*

¹⁷Never pay back evil for evil to anyone. Respect what is right in the sight of all men. ¹⁸If possible, so far as it depends on you, be at peace with all men. ¹⁹Never take your own revenge, beloved, but leave room for the wrath of God, for it is written, "VENGEANCE IS MINE, I WILL REPAY, SAYS THE LORD." ²⁰"BUT IF YOUR ENEMY IS HUNGRY, FEED HIM, AND IF HE IS THIRSTY, GIVE HIM A DRINK; FOR IN SO DOING YOU WILL HEAP BURNING COALS UPON HIS HEAD." ²¹Do not be overcome by evil, but overcome evil with good.

Thursday—*The promise of triumph (2 Corinthians 2:14-17)*

¹⁴But thanks be to God, who always leads us in His triumph in Christ, and manifests through us the sweet aroma of the knowledge of Him in every place. ¹⁵For we are a fragrance of Christ to God among those who are being saved and among those who are perishing; ¹⁶to the one an aroma from death to death, to the other an aroma from life to life. And who is adequate for these things? ¹⁷For we are not like many, peddling the word of God, but as from sincerity, but as from God, we speak in Christ in the sight of God.

Friday—*Balancing truth with love (2 John 1-6)*

¹The elder to the chosen lady and her children, whom I love in truth; and not only I, but also all who know the truth, ²for the sake of the truth which abides in us and will be with us forever: ³Grace, mercy and peace will be with us, from God the Father and from Jesus Christ, the Son of the Father, in truth and love. ⁴I was very glad to find some of your children walking in truth, just as we have received commandment to do from the Father. ⁵And now I ask you, lady, not as writing to you a new commandment, but the one which we have had from the beginning, that we love one another. ⁶And this is love, that we walk according to His commandments. This is the commandment, just as you have heard from the beginning, that you should walk in it.

Saturday—*Balancing love with truth (2 John 7-13)*

[7]For many deceivers have gone out into the world, those who do not acknowledge Jesus Christ as coming in the flesh. This is the deceiver and the antichrist. [8]Watch yourselves, that you might not lose what we have accomplished, but that you may receive a full reward. [9]Any one who goes too far and does not abide in the teaching of Christ, does not have God; the one who abides in the teaching, he has both the Father and the Son. [10]If any one comes to you and does not bring this teaching, do not receive him into your house, and do not give him a greeting; [11]for the one who gives him a greeting participates in his evil deeds. [12]Having many things to write to you, I do not want to do so with paper and ink; but I hope to come to you and speak face to face, that your joy may be made full. [13]The children of your chosen sister greet you.

19

Discovering True Happiness

Sunday—*A new self (2 Corinthians 5:14-19)*

[14]For the love of Christ controls us, having concluded this, that one died for all, therefore all died; [15]and He died for all, that they who live should no longer live for themselves, but for Him who died and rose again on their behalf. [16]Therefore from now on we recognize no man according to the flesh; even though we have known Christ according to the flesh, yet now we know Him thus no longer. [17]Therefore if any man is in Christ, he is a new creature; the old things passed away; behold, new things have come. [18]Now all these things are from God, who reconciled us to Himself through Christ, and gave us the ministry of reconciliation, [19]namely, that God was in Christ reconciling the world to Himself, not counting their trespasses against them, and He has committed to us the word of reconciliation.

We all want happiness. Most people live a moment at a time. When the taste of life is good, they respond with happiness. When it is bitter or flat, their days become a burden.

Is there really any way to be happy? I can say yes with assurance. Happiness is possible through a little-known way of life.

Some years ago I heard a popular lecturer point out that everyone needs at least three things for a happy life: a self fit to live with, a faith fit to live by, and a work fit to live for.

Do you have *a self fit to live with*? Or are you living with a self that makes each day a struggle? If you need a self fit to live with, the only answer is found in Jesus Christ. He majors in changing men and women for now and all eternity.

After receiving Jesus Christ as Savior, you should be building *a faith fit to live by*.

Many start out in the Christian life but fall by the wayside. Keep going on. Read the Bible and obey it. Pray. Tell others about Jesus Christ. Find a Bible-loving church and make it yours. Then you will have a growing, vital faith.

But I want to emphasize the third requirement. Assuming that you have the other two, you need *a work that is fit to live for*.

Everyone needs a valid reason for living. It is not enough to eat and sleep and make the payments on a house. It is not even enough to like our work, although that is important.

Several times the Lord Jesus challenged individuals with two explosive words: "Follow me." To follow Jesus means to make Him first in your life and thinking. It means putting aside your personal program to get involved in His program.

That is what the disciples did. Andrew, Peter, James, and John were fishermen. But when Jesus called, they left fishing. Matthew had probably worked for years to get his post as a tax collector. But when Jesus came along, he left his table and his title for more important things.

The point is not that they changed their occupations, but that they switched from serving themselves to serving Jesus Christ.

Have you done that? If the year ahead seems hardly worth the trouble, it may be that you have never found your larger job. Perhaps you have never fully followed Jesus. How can you follow Him?

First, you will have to volunteer. Jesus said, "If any man will come after me, let him deny himself" (Luke 9:23). Jesus was not only speaking to the disciples, but to the larger group of less committed people. Wherever you are in your spiritual experience, you can say yes or no to this call.

Second, you will have to pay a price. "If any man will come after me, let him deny himself, and take up his cross daily" (Luke 9:23). A cross was used for execution.

Years ago I discovered that I cannot serve myself and still serve Jesus Christ. Only as I forget about myself and get wrapped up in serving Jesus, does anything happen that counts for Him.

Third, you will have to follow in His footsteps. Jesus' deepest purpose in life was to carry out the will of His Father. He said, "I have meat to eat that ye know not of" (John 4:32). And then He explained, "My meat is to do the will of him that sent me, and to finish his work" (4:34).

Is it the purpose of our lives to do God's will and finish His work? Following Jesus is costly but rewarding. I could have no better wish for you than that you may know the joy and happiness of truly following Jesus Christ.

EVERYONE NEEDS A VALID REASON FOR LIVING.

Monday—*Happiness from wisdom (Proverbs 3:13-18)*

[13]How blessed is the man who finds wisdom,
  And the man who gains understanding.
[14]For its profit is better than the profit of silver,
  And its gain than fine gold.
[15]She is more precious than jewels;
  And nothing you desire compares with her.
[16]Long life is in her right hand;
  In her left hand are riches and honor.
[17]Her ways are pleasant ways,
  And all her paths are peace.
[18]She is a tree of life to those who take hold of her,
  And happy are all who hold her fast.

Tuesday—*Work leading to fruit bearing (John 15:2-8)*

[2]"Every branch in Me that does not bear fruit, He takes away; and every branch that bears fruit, He prunes it, that it may bear more fruit. [3]You are already clean because of the word which I have spoken to you. [4]Abide in Me, and I in you. As the branch cannot bear fruit of itself, unless it abides in the vine, so neither can you, unless you abide in Me. [5]I am the vine, you are the branches; he who abides in Me, and I in him, he bears much fruit; for apart from Me you can do nothing. [6]If anyone does not abide in Me, he is thrown away as a branch, and dries up; and they gather them, and cast them into the fire, and they are burned. [7]If you abide in Me, and My words abide in you, ask whatever you wish, and it shall be done for you. [8]By this is My Father glorified, that you bear much fruit, and so prove to be My disciples."

Wednesday—*Listening to the Word (James 1:22-25)*

[22]But prove yourselves doers of the word, and not merely hearers who delude themselves. [23]For if any one is a hearer of the word and not a doer, he is like a man who looks at his natural face in a mirror; [24]for once he has looked at himself and gone away, he has immediately forgotten what kind of person he was. [25]But one who looks intently at the perfect law, the law of liberty and abides by it, not having become a forgetful hearer but an effectual doer, this man shall be blessed in what he does.

119

Thursday—*Costly discipleship (Luke 9:23-27)*

23And He was saying to them all, "If anyone wishes to come after Me, let him deny himself, and take up his cross daily, and follow Me. 24For whoever wishes to save his life shall lose it, but whoever loses his life for My sake, he is the one who will save it. 25For what is a man profited if he gains the whole world, and loses or forfeits himself? 26For whoever is ashamed of Me and My words, of him will the Son of Man be ashamed when He comes in His glory, and the glory of the Father and of the holy angels. 27But I tell you truly, there are some of those standing here who shall not taste death until they see the kingdom of God."

Friday—*Good works to do (1 Timothy 5:7-10)*

7Prescribe these things as well, so that they may be above reproach. 8But if any one does not provide for his own, and especially for those of his household, he has denied the faith, and is worse than an unbeliever. 9Let a widow be put on the list only if she is not less than sixty years old, having been the wife of one man, 10having a reputation for good works; and if she has brought up children, if she has shown hospitality to strangers, if she has washed the saints' feet, if she has assisted those in distress, and if she had devoted herself to every good work.

Saturday—*Jesus' call for a change in work (Matthew 5:18-22)*

18"For truly I say to you, until heaven and earth pass away, not the smallest letter or stroke shall pass away from the Law, until all is accomplished. 19Whoever then annuls one of the least of these commandments, and so teaches others, shall be called least in the kingdom of heaven; but whoever keeps and teaches them, he shall be called great in the kingdom of heaven. 20For I say to you, that unless your righteousness surpasses that of the scribes and Pharisees, you shall not enter the kingdom of heaven. 21"You have heard that the ancients were told, 'YOU SHALL NOT COMMIT MURDER' and 'WHOEVER COMMITS MURDER SHALL BE LIABLE TO THE COURT.' 22But I say to you that every one who is angry with his brother shall be guilty before the court; and whoever shall say to his brother, 'Raca,' shall be guilty before the supreme court; and whoever shall say, 'You fool,' shall be guilty enough to go into the hell of fire."

COMMITMENT

20

God's Will and Your Happiness

Sunday—*Steps to God's will (Romans 12:1-2)*

¹I urge you therefore, brethren, by the mercies of God, to present your bodies a living and holy sacrifice, acceptable to God, which is your spiritual service of worship. ²And do not be conformed to this world, but be transformed by the renewing of your mind, and that you may prove what the will of God is, that which is good and acceptable and perfect.

Are you afraid of God's will? One of the greatest mis-understandings any person can have is that God's will is unpleasant. No one should ever be afraid of God's will.

Many people are living defeated, miserable lives be-cause they are afraid to accept God's plan and purpose for them. According to the Word of God, such fear is totally unfounded.

Consider these three important truths:

First, God wants us to be happy in His will. God is no Scrooge. He is not some celestial dictator who is always trying to crack the whip over our heads. God wants His very best for us. He is a God of love and kindness, not a cranky, vengeful overseer.

In fact, God is much more concerned that we enjoy ourselves than we are. Some people act as if God is out to take all their pleasures away, but what He really wants is to direct us into true pleasure that brings lasting satisfac-tion.

When we seek God's will we find that He helps us make the right decisions. He opens and closes doors and shapes our interests and desires so that we will not stumble and fall into pitfalls along life's way.

God's will is that you and I be happy. There is abso-lutely no reason to be afraid of His direction in our lives. In his letter to the church at Rome, Paul speaks of "that good, and acceptable, and [even more, that] perfect, will of God" (Romans 12:2).

At times we all make the mistake of thinking that our choice is between doing what we want to do and being happy, and doing what God wants us to do and being miserable. Nothing could be further from the truth.

Second, God's will does not have to be contrary to ours. Some people become alarmed whenever they have a strong desire to do anything, because they are convinced that it cannot possibly be God's will for them.

I remember counseling some time ago with a young man who was depressed because the greatest desire he had in life was to become a doctor. Despite the fact that his interests, aptitude, and educational background all indicated that he was ideally suited for that profession, he was sure it must not be God's will because he wanted it so much. Why do we so often demonstrate this kind of distrust?

David said, "Delight thyself . . . in the LORD; and he shall give thee the desires of thine heart" (Psalm 37:4). God wants us to have our hearts' desires met, and He wants to meet them. He does not want to dictate His will to us or force us to obey. We are not to be robots but mature believers with the wisdom to make the right decisions.

If a person is spending time in Bible study and prayer, and if he is growing in his walk with the Lord, he is going to have the maturity he needs to make the right choices. God will give him the wisdom and attitude so that his will will coincide with God's will. A. W. Tozer said, "The man or woman who is wholly, joyously surrendered to Christ can't make a wrong choice—any choice will be the right one."

Third, living in God's will is the only way to be successful and happy in the Christian life. We cannot expect to ignore the revealed will and Word of God deliberately and be happy.

Paul commands us to understand "what the will of the Lord is" (Ephesians 5:17). That is imperative! A complete peace and calm can be found only in the center of God's will. Let us understand the will of the Lord, and then obey it.

> NO ONE SHOULD EVER BE AFRAID OF GOD'S WILL.

Monday—*The choice God offered Solomon*
(2 Chronicles 1:7-12)
⁷In that night God appeared to Solomon and said to him, "Ask what I shall give you." ⁸And Solomon said to God,

124

"Thou hast dealt with my father David with great lovingkindness, and hast made me king in his place. 9Now, O LORD God, Thy promise to my father David is fulfilled; for Thou hast made me king over a people as numerous as the dust of the earth. 10Give me now wisdom and knowledge, that I may go out and come in before this people; for who can rule this great people of Thine?" 11And God said to Solomon, "Because you had this in mind, and did not ask for riches, wealth, or honor, or the life of those who hate you, nor have you even asked for long life, but you have asked for yourself wisdom and knowledge, that you may rule My people, over whom I have made you king, 12wisdom and knowledge have been granted to you. And I will give you riches and wealth and honor, such as none of the kings who were before you has possessed, nor those who will come after you."

Tuesday—*God's guidance and your delight (Psalm 37:3-6)*
3Trust in the LORD, and do good;
Dwell in the land and cultivate faithfulness.
4Delight yourself in the LORD;
And He will give you the desires of your heart.
5Commit your way to the LORD,
Trust also in Him, and He will do it.
6And He will bring forth your righteousness as the light,
And your judgment as the noonday.

Wednesday—*Family happiness from doing God's will (Psalm 128)*
1How blessed is everyone who fears the LORD,
Who walks in His ways.
2When you shall eat of the fruit of your hands,
You will be happy and it will be well with you.
3Your wife shall be like a fruitful vine,
Within your house,
Your children like olive plants
Around your table.
4Behold, for thus shall the man be blessed
Who fears the LORD.
5The LORD bless you from Zion,
And may you see the prosperity of Jerusalem all the days of
your life.

125

⁶Indeed, may you see your children's children.
  Peace be upon Israel!

Thursday—*Delight in doing God's will (Psalm 40:4-8)*

⁴How blessed is the man who has made the LORD his trust,
  And has not turned to the proud, nor to those who lapse into
    falsehood.
⁵Many, O LORD my God, are the wonders which Thou hast
    done,
  And Thy thoughts toward us;
  There is none to compare with Thee;
  If I would declare and speak of them,
  They would be too numerous to count.
⁶Sacrifice and meal offering Thou hast not desired;
  My ears Thou hast opened;
  Burnt offering and sin offering Thou hast not required.
⁷Then I said, "Behold, I come;
  In the scroll of the book it is written of me;
⁸I delight to do Thy will, O my God;
  Thy Law is within my heart."

Friday—*Loving God's commandments (Psalm 119:41-48)*

⁴¹May Thy lovingkindnesses also come to me, O LORD,
  Thy salvation according to Thy word;
⁴²So I shall have an answer for him who reproaches me,
  For I trust in Thy word.
⁴³And do not take the word of truth utterly out of my mouth,
  For I wait for Thine ordinances.
⁴⁴So I will keep Thy law continually,
  Forever and ever,
⁴⁵And I will walk at liberty,
  For I seek Thy precepts.
⁴⁶I will also speak of Thy testimonies before kings,
  And shall not be ashamed.
⁴⁷And I shall delight in Thy commandments,
  Which I love.
⁴⁸And I shall lift up my hands to Thy commandments, which I
    love;
  And I will meditate on Thy statutes.

Saturday—*Happiness from doing what you know to do*
(*John 13:13-17*)

[13]"You call me Teacher, and Lord; and you are right; for so I am. [14]If I then, the Lord and the Teacher, washed your feet, you also ought to wash one another's feet. [15]For I gave you an example that you also should do as I did to you. [16]Truly, truly, I say to you, a slave is not greater than his master; neither one who is sent greater than the one who sent him. [17]If you know these things, you are blessed if you do them."

21

Knowing God's Will

Sunday—*God's guiding word (Psalm 119:105-112)*

[105]Thy word is a lamp to my feet,
  And a light to my path.
[106]I have sworn, and I will confirm it,
  That I will keep Thy righteous ordinances.
[107]I am exceedingly afflicted;
  Revive me, O LORD, according to Thy word.
[108]O accept the freewill offerings of my mouth, O LORD,
  And teach me Thine ordinances.
[109]My life is continually in my hand,
  Yet I do not forget Thy law.
[110]The wicked have laid a snare for me,
  Yet I have not gone astray from Thy precepts.
[111]I have inherited Thy testimonies forever,
  For they are the joy of my heart.
[112]I have inclined my heart to perform Thy statutes
  Forever, even to the end.

Christians frequently ask, "How can I be sure of God's will in my life?" People sometimes think of God's will as a magical blueprint that drops from heaven into our lap. They are looking for a neat, little, prepackaged formula that will outline, day by day, each step for the rest of their lives. But God does not usually work that way. He does not want to make us robots. But how can we know His will? Unfortunately, for many people that is a difficult question. It should not be. God does not hide His will from us.

Always remember that the will of God is never contrary to the Word of God and that the overwhelming majority of God's will is found in God's Word.

It is also very important to remember the place of prayer in discovering the will of God. Too often we hurry from one meeting to the next, desperately seeking some catchy outline or formula while neglecting the God-appointed means of daily prayer in seeking His will.

Although there are no magic steps for determining God's will, let me suggest some guidelines.

Salvation is where it all begins. A person must know Jesus Christ as his or her personal Savior before he or she can ever hope to know the fullness of God's will. Salvation is the first step.

The Bible points out that it is impossible to see further into God's will until we surrender to what we already know. If we reject or disobey what God has made clear to us, we can expect no further revelation of His will. He leads us a step at a time. A surrendered heart is the basis of an understanding mind. That is the teaching of Romans 12:1-2.

We must be separated from evil and evil associations. God's will can be fully discovered only by those with clean hearts and hands. Paul wrote, "For this is the will of God, even your sanctification. . . . For God hath not called us unto uncleanness, but unto holiness" (1 Thessalonians 4:3-7). It is the will of God that we be clean and set apart for His glory. Known or unconfessed sin blocks an understanding of God's will.

Third, we must be sincere. If we are to know the will of God, there must be far more than mere intellectual agreement. There must be a yearning, burning, sincere desire *to do* God's will. I like to paraphrase John 7:17 like this, "If anyone wants to be doing His will, then he shall know about the teaching."

If you are right in these three areas, do anything you want to do! Why? Because if you are truly right in those areas, your only desire will be to bring glory to God. Psalm 37:4 verifies this. "Delight thyself also in the LORD; and he shall give thee the desires of thine heart."

KNOWN OR UNCONFESSED SIN BLOCKS AN
UNDERSTANDING OF GOD'S WILL.

Monday—*Not enough to hear (James 1:22-27)*

22But prove yourselves doers of the word, and not merely hearers who delude themselves. 23For if any one is a hearer of the word and not a doer, he is like a man who looks at his natural face in a mirror; 24for once he has looked at himself and gone away, he has immediately forgotten what kind of person he was. 25But one who looks intently at the perfect law, the law of liberty and abides by it, not having become a forgetful hearer but an effectual doer, this man shall be blessed in what he does. 26If any one thinks himself to be religious, and yet does not bridle his tongue but deceives his own heart, this man's religion is worthless. 27This is pure and undefiled religion in the sight of our God and Father, to visit orphans and widows in their distress, and to keep oneself unstained by the world.

Tuesday—*Discernment from being willing to obey God (John 7:14-18)*

14But when it was now the midst of the feast Jesus went up into the temple, and began to teach. 15The Jews therefore were marveling, saying, "How has this man become learned, having never been educated?" 16Jesus therefore answered them, and said, "My teaching is not Mine, but His who sent Me. 17If any man is willing to do His will, he shall know of the teaching, whether it is of God, or whether I speak from Myself. [18]He who speaks from himself seeks his own glory; but He who is seeking the glory of the one who sent Him, He is true, and there is no unrighteousness in Him.''

Wednesday—*Desiring God's will on earth (Matthew 6:9-13)*

[9]"Pray, then, in this way:
   'Our Father who art in heaven,
     Hallowed be Thy name.
   [10]Thy kingdom come.
     Thy will be done,
     On earth as it is in heaven.
   [11]Give us this day our daily bread.
   [12]And forgive us our debts, as we also have forgiven
     our debtors.
   [13]And do not lead us into temptation, but deliver us
     from evil. [For Thine is the kingdom, and the
     power, and the glory, forever. Amen].' ''

Thursday—*God's will for everlasting life for believers (2 Peter 3:8-13)*

[8]But do not let this one fact escape your notice, beloved, that with the Lord one day is as a thousand years, and a thousand years as one day. [9]The Lord is not slow about His promise, as some count slowness, but is patient toward you, not wishing for any to perish but for all to come to repentance. [10]But the day of the Lord will come like a thief, in which the heavens will pass away with a roar and the elements will be destroyed with intense heat, and the earth and its works will be burned up. [11]Since all these things are to be destroyed in this way, what sort of people ought you to be in holy conduct and godliness, [12]looking for and hastening the coming of the day of God, on account of which the heavens will be destroyed by burning, and the elements will melt with intense heat! [13]But according to His promise we are looking for new heavens and a new earth, in which righteousness dwells.

Friday—*God's will of purity (1 Thessalonians 4:3-8)*

[3]For this is the will of God, your sanctification; that is that you abstain from sexual immorality; [4]that each of you know

how to possess his own vessel in sanctification and honor, ⁵not in lustful passion, like the Gentiles who do not know God; ⁶and that no man transgress and defraud his brother in the matter because the Lord is the avenger in all these things, just as we also told you before and solemnly warned you. ⁷For God has not called us for the purpose of impurity, but in sanctification. ⁸Consequently, he who rejects this is not rejecting man but the God who gives His Holy Spirit to you.

Saturday—*Trusting God's guidance (Proverbs 3:5-7)*
⁵Trust in the LORD with all your heart,
  And do not lean on your own understanding.
⁶In all your ways acknowledge Him,
  And He will make your paths straight.
⁷Do not be wise in your own eyes;
  Fear the LORD and turn away from evil.

22

Being Filled with the Spirit

Sunday—*The coming and work of the Holy Spirit*
(John 14:16-26)

16"And I will ask the Father, and He will give you another Helper, that He may be with you forever; 17that is the Spirit of truth, whom the world cannot receive, because it does not behold Him or know Him, but you know Him because He abides with you, and will be in you. 18I will not leave you as orphans; I will come to you. 19After a little while the world will behold Me no more; but you will behold Me; because I live, you shall live also. 20In that day you shall know that I am in My Father, and you in Me, and I in you. 21He who has My commandments, and keeps them, he it is who loves Me; and he who loves Me shall be loved by My Father, and I will love him, and will disclose Myself to him." 22Judas (not Iscariot) said to Him, "Lord, what then has happened that You are going to disclose Yourself to us, and not to the world?" 23Jesus answered and said to him, "If anyone loves Me, he will keep My word; and My Father will love him, and We will come to him, and make Our abode with him. 24He who does not love Me does not keep My words; and the word which you hear is not Mine, but the Father's who sent Me. 25These things I have spoken to you, while abiding with you. 26But the Helper, the Holy Spirit, whom the Father will send in My name, He will teach you all things, and bring to your remembrance all that I said to you."

The Bible teaches that each believer in Jesus Christ is the dwelling place of God the Holy Spirit. That is a staggering and life-changing fact. Think of it. God in us, all the time.

The day of Pentecost marked a tremendous change in the way the Holy Spirit ministered to men. In Old Testament times the Spirit of God was active in human affairs, but in a limited way. The Old Testament contains more than eighty references to the Holy Spirit. He was present in creation, for we read, "And the Spirit of God moved upon the face of the waters" (Genesis 1:2). Of Samson we read, "The Spirit of the LORD came mightily upon him" (Judges 14:6). Old Testament passages reveal that the Holy Spirit would come for a specific task and then leave when His work was done. The Holy Spirit indwelt a relatively few for a specific ministry, but His indwelling was not universal or permanent.

Then Jesus promised the disciples in John 14:16-17 that the Holy Spirit would be with them and in them *forever*. Acts 2:2-4 gives the thrilling story of the coming of the Holy Spirit: "And suddenly there came a sound from heaven as of a rushing mighty wind, and it filled all the house where they were sitting. . . . And they were all filled with the Holy Ghost." From that momentous day on, the Holy Spirit has indwelt every believer *continuously*.

Whether a person is seven years old or seventy, when he trusts Jesus Christ, the Holy Spirit indwells him all the time. To the carnal Corinthian church, which was plagued by problems, Paul wrote, "What! know ye not that your body is the temple of the Holy Ghost which is in you, which ye have of God" (1 Corinthians 6:19). Each one of us is the temple of God, individually indwelt.

The Holy Spirit in us can convict us, guide us, teach us, and empower us. It is only through His ministry that we are enabled to live the Christian life. When we disobey the Holy Spirit, we grieve Him (Ephesians 4:30). The Holy Spirit may be grieved, but He is never absent.

134

Isn't that a great motivation to be obedient to the Holy Spirit? We know that He is with us forever, ministering to us and teaching us. We also know that the love of God flows through Him to us. We can show our love to Him by our obedience. Let us yield to the Holy Spirit and allow Him to fill us.

THE HOLY SPIRIT MAY BE GRIEVED, BUT HE IS NEVER ABSENT.

Monday—*The Spirit at Pentecost (Acts 2:1-10)*

¹And when the day of Pentecost had come, they were all together in one place. ²And suddenly there came from heaven a noise like a violent, rushing wind, and it filled the whole house where they were sitting. ³And there appeared to them tongues as of fire distributing themselves, and they rested on each one of them. ⁴And they were all filled with the Holy Spirit and began to speak with other tongues, as the Spirit was giving them utterance. ⁵Now there were Jews living in Jerusalem, devout men, from every nation under heaven. ⁶And when this sound occurred, the multitude came together, and were bewildered, because they were each one hearing them speak in his own language. ⁷And they were amazed and marveled, saying, "Why, are not all these who are speaking Galileans? ⁸And how is it that we each hear them in our own language to which we were born? ⁹Parthians and Medes and Elamites, and residents of Mesopotamia, Judea and Cappadocia, Pontus and Asia, ¹⁰Phrygia and Pamphylia, Egypt and the districts of Libya around Cyrene, and visitors from Rome, both Jews and proselytes."

Tuesday—*Peter's explanation about the Spirit's coming (Acts 2:12-21)*

¹²And they continued in amazement and great perplexity, saying to one another, "What does this mean?" ¹³But others were mocking and saying, "They are full of sweet wine." ¹⁴But Peter, taking his stand with the eleven, raised his voice and declared to them: "Men of Judea, and all you who live in Jerusalem, let this be known to you, and give heed to my words.

¹⁵For these men are not drunk, as you suppose, for it is only the third hour of the day; ¹⁶but this is what was spoken of through the prophet Joel:

¹⁷'AND IT SHALL BE IN THE LAST DAYS, GOD SAYS,
THAT I WILL POUR FORTH OF MY SPIRIT UPON ALL MANKIND;
AND YOUR SONS AND YOUR DAUGHTERS SHALL PROPHESY,
AND YOUR YOUNG MEN SHALL SEE VISIONS,
AND YOUR OLD MEN SHALL DREAM DREAMS;
¹⁸EVEN UPON MY BONDSLAVES, BOTH MEN AND WOMEN,
I WILL IN THOSE DAYS POUR FORTH OF MY SPIRIT
And they shall prophesy.
¹⁹AND I WILL GRANT WONDERS IN THE SKY ABOVE,
AND SIGNS ON THE EARTH BENEATH,
BLOOD, AND FIRE, AND VAPOR OF SMOKE.
²⁰THE SUN SHALL BE TURNED INTO DARKNESS,
AND THE MOON INTO BLOOD,
BEFORE THE GREAT AND GLORIOUS DAY OF THE LORD SHALL
    COME.
²¹AND IT SHALL BE, THAT EVERY ONE WHO CALLS ON THE NAME
    OF
THE LORD SHALL BE SAVED.'"

Wednesday—*Results of the filling of the Spirit*
(Ephesians 5:15-21)

¹⁵Therefore be careful how you walk, not as unwise men, but as wise, ¹⁶making the most of your time, because the days are evil. ¹⁷So then do not be foolish, but understand what the will of the Lord is. ¹⁸And do not get drunk with wine, for that is dissipation, but be filled with the Spirit, ¹⁹speaking to one another in psalms and hymns and spiritual songs, singing and making melody with your heart to the Lord; ²⁰always giving thanks for all things in the name of our Lord Jesus Christ to God, even the Father; ²¹and be subject to one another in the fear of Christ.

Thursday—*The temple of the Holy Spirit*
(1 Corinthians 6:14-20)

¹⁴Now God has not only raised the Lord, but will also raise us up through His power. ¹⁵Do you not know that your bodies are members of Christ? Shall I then take away the members of Christ and make them members of a harlot? May it never be!

¹⁶Or do you not know that the one who joins himself to a harlot is one body with her? For He says, "THE TWO WILL BECOME ONE FLESH." ¹⁷But the one who joins himself to the Lord is one spirit with Him. ¹⁸Flee immorality. Every other sin that a man commits is outside the body, but the immoral man sins against his own body. ¹⁹Or do you not know that your body is a temple of the Holy Spirit who is in you, whom you have from God, and that you are not your own? ²⁰For you have been bought with a price: therefore glorify God in your body.

Friday—*Things that grieve the Holy Spirit (Ephesians 4:25-32)*

²⁵Therefore, laying aside falsehood, SPEAK TRUTH, EACH ONE of you, WITH HIS NEIGHBOR, for we are members of one another. ²⁶Be ANGRY, AND yet DO NOT SIN; do not let the sun go down on your anger, ²⁷and do not give the devil an opportunity. ²⁸Let him who steals steal no longer; but rather let him labor, performing with his own hands what is good, in order that he may have something to share with him who has need. ²⁹Let no unwholesome word proceed from your mouth, but only such a word as is good for edification according to the need of the moment, that it may give grace to those who hear. ³⁰And do not grieve the Holy Spirit of God, by whom you were sealed for the day of redemption. ³¹Let all bitterness and wrath and anger and clamor and slander be put away from you, along with all malice. ³²And be kind to one another, tender-hearted, forgiving each other, just as God in Christ also has forgiven you.

Saturday—*The Holy Spirit in creation (Genesis 1:1-5)*

¹In the beginning God created the heavens and the earth. ²And the earth was formless and void, and darkness was over the surface of the deep; and the Spirit of God was moving over the surface of the waters. ³Then God said, "Let there be light"; and there was light. ⁴And God saw that the light was good; and God separated the light from the darkness. ⁵And God called the light day, and the darkness He called night. And there was evening and there was morning, one day.

23

A Call to Greatness

Sunday—*John's birth foretold (Luke 1:13-17)*

13But the angel said to him, "Do not be afraid, Zacharias, for your petition has been heard, and your wife Elizabeth will bear you a son, and you will give him the name John. 14And you will have joy and gladness, and many will rejoice at his birth. 15For he will be great in the sight of the Lord, and he will drink no wine or liquor; and he will be filled with the Holy Spirit, while yet in his mother's womb. 16And he will turn back many of the sons of Israel to the Lord their God. 17And it is he who will go as a forerunner before Him in the spirit and power of Elijah, TO TURN THE HEARTS OF THE FATHERS BACK TO THE CHILDREN, and the disobedient to the attitude of the righteous; so as to make ready a people prepared for the Lord."

Historian Arthur Schlesinger has written, "Ours is an age without heroes . . . today no one bestrides our narrow world like a colossus." Is that true? Is this the age of the common man? Is there a famine of great men and women in our world today?

Of all the characters in the Bible, who would you say was the greatest? Jesus answered that question. "Among them that are born of women," He said, "there hath not risen a greater than John the Baptist" (Matthew 11:11). Luke's gospel records what the angel of the Lord said about John: "He shall be great in the sight of the Lord" (Luke 1:15).

The predominant characteristic of John's life was his humility. The philosophy of our age is "Sell yourself. Toot your own horn. Look out for number one." Our arrogant world cannot equate greatness with humility. Yet Jesus underscored humility as basic to greatness. To His followers He said, "He that is least among you all, the same shall be great" (Luke 9:48).

Ultimate greatness will never be found in muscle or money but in the heart of the person who walks humbly with God.

A father and son walked through a wheat field inspecting the harvest. The boy called attention to the stems that stood erect and said, "Those that let their heads hang could not be of much value." The father said, "Son, you're wrong. The stalks that stand so straight are lightheaded and almost good for nothing, while those that hang their heads are full of beautiful grain."

When a committee from Jerusalem tried to discover John's identity, he simply replied, "I am the voice of one crying in the wildnerness, Make straight the way of the Lord" (John 1:23). Again, when Jesus came to be baptized, John tried to excuse himself, saying he was not even worthy to stoop and untie His shoelaces. He directed his followers to Jesus, saying, "He must increase, but I must decrease" (John 3:30).

Another mark of greatness is courage. True courage is scarce. This is the day of the placid pulpit and the comfortable pew. Christianity slips around in smooth slippers, fearful of giving offense. John the Baptist, on the contrary, was a fearless man who stayed in trouble with the evil rulers of his day. Speaking of John, Jesus asked, "What went ye out into the wilderness to see? A reed shaken with the wind? . . . A man clothed in soft raiment?" (Matthew 11:7-8). Never! John was a rugged man. He was a rock, not a flimsy reed. On one occasion John called some religious leaders a generation of snakes (Matthew 3:7). He bluntly charged them to "bring forth . . . fruits meet for repentance" (Matthew 3:8).

One day John accused King Herod of breaking the law. Pointing his gunlike finger at Herodias, he charged Herod, "It is not lawful for you to have your brother Philip's wife." There is nothing so awesome as the truth.

Humility linked with courage is a mark of greatness, and Jesus singled out John as a great man. The call today is that we who know and love Jesus Christ may be great, with the greatness of God.

> HUMILITY LINKED WITH COURAGE IS A
> MARK OF GREATNESS.

Monday—*John's birth (Luke 1:57-66)*

⁵⁷Now the time had come for Elizabeth to give birth, and she brought forth a son. ⁵⁸And her neighbors and her relatives heard that the Lord had displayed His great mercy toward her; and they were rejoicing with her. ⁵⁹And it came about that on the eighth day they came to circumcise the child, and they were going to call him Zacharias, after his father. ⁶⁰And his mother answered and said, "No indeed; but he shall be called John." ⁶¹And they said to her, "There is no one among your relatives who is called by that name." ⁶²And they made signs to his father, as to what he wanted him called. ⁶³And he asked for a tablet, and wrote as follows, "His name is John." And they were all astonished. ⁶⁴And at once his mouth was opened and his tongue loosed, and he began to speak in praise of God. ⁶⁵And fear came on all those living around them; and all these

matters were being talked about in all the hill country of Judea. 66And all who heard them kept them in mind, saying, "What then will this child turn out to be?" For the hand of the Lord was certainly with him.

Tuesday—*Prayer prophesying John's ministry (Luke 1:67-79)*

67And his father Zacharias was filled with the Holy Spirit, and prophesied, saying;
68"Blessed be the Lord God of Israel,
  For He has visited us and accomplished redemption for His
    people,
69And has raised up a horn of salvation for us
  In the house of David His servant—
70As He spoke by the mouth of His holy prophets from of old—
71Salvation FROM OUR ENEMIES,
  And FROM THE HAND OF ALL WHO HATE US;
72To show mercy toward our fathers,
  And to remember His holy covenant,
73The oath which He swore to Abraham our father,
74To grant us that we being delivered from the hand of our
    enemies,
  Might serve Him without fear,
75In holiness and righteousness before Him all our days.
76And you, child, will be called the prophet of the Most High;
  For you will go on BEFORE THE LORD TO PREPARE HIS WAYS;
77To give to His people the knowledge of salvation
  By the forgiveness of their sins,
78Because of the tender mercy of our God,
  With which the Sunrise from on high shall visit us,
79TO SHINE UPON THOSE WHO SIT IN DARKNESS AND THE SHADOW
    OF DEATH,
  To guide our feet into the way of peace."

Wednesday—*John's ministry of preparation (Mark 1:1-9)*

1The beginning of the gospel of Jesus Christ, the Son of God. 2As it is written in Isaiah the prophet,
  BEHOLD, I SEND MY MESSENGER BEFORE YOUR FACE,
  WHO WILL PREPARE YOUR WAY;
3THE VOICE OF ONE CRYING IN THE WILDERNESS,
  "MAKE READY THE WAY OF THE LORD,
  MAKE HIS PATHS STRAIGHT."

⁴John the Baptist appeared in the wilderness preaching a baptism of repentance for the forgiveness of sins. ⁵And all the country of Judea was going out to him, and all the people of Jerusalem; and they were being baptized by him in the Jordan River, confessing their sins. ⁶And John was clothed with camel's hair and wore a leather belt around his waist, and his diet was locusts and wild honey. ⁷And he was preaching, and saying, "After me comes One who is mightier than I, and I am not even fit to stoop down and untie the thong of His sandals. ⁸I baptized you with water; but He will baptize you with the Holy Spirit." ⁹And it came about in those days that Jesus came from Nazareth in Galilee, and was baptized by John in the Jordan.

Thursday—*John baptizing the Lord Jesus (John 1:21-34)*

²¹And they asked, "What then? Are you Elijah?" And he said, "I am not." "Are you the Prophet?" And he answered, "No." ²²They said then to him, "Who are you, so that we may give an answer to those who sent us? What do you say about yourself?" ²³He said, "I am a voice of one crying in the wilderness, 'MAKE STRAIGHT THE WAY OF THE LORD,' as Isaiah the prophet said." ²⁴Now they had been sent from the Pharisees. ²⁵And they asked him, and said to him, "Why then are you baptizing, if you are not the Christ, nor Elijah, nor the Prophet?" ²⁶John answered them saying, "I baptize in water, but among you stands One whom you do not know. ²⁷It is He who comes after me, the thong of whose sandal I am not worthy to untie." ²⁸These things took place in Bethany beyond the Jordan, where John was baptizing. ²⁹The next day he saw Jesus coming to him, and said, "Behold, the Lamb of God who takes away the sin of the world! ³⁰This is He on behalf of whom I said, 'After me comes a Man who has a higher rank than I, for he existed before me.' ³¹And I did not recognize Him, but in order that He might be manifested to Israel, I came baptizing in water." ³²And John bore witness saying, "I have beheld the Spirit descending as a dove out of heaven; and He remained upon Him. ³³And I did not recognize Him, but He who sent me to baptize in water said to me, 'He upon whom you see the Spirit descending and remaining upon Him, this is the one who baptizes in the Holy Spirit.' ³⁴And I have seen, and have borne witness that this is the Son of God."

Friday—*Jesus' response to John's ministry (Matthew 11:1-14)*

¹And it came about that when Jesus had finished giving instructions to His twelve disciples, He departed from there to teach and preach in their cities. ²Now when John in prison heard of the works of Christ, he sent word by his disciples, ³and said to Him, "Are You the Coming One, or shall we look for someone else?" ⁴And Jesus answered and said to them, "Go and report to John the things which you hear and see: ⁵the BLIND RECEIVE SIGHT and the lame walk, the lepers are cleansed and the deaf hear, and the dead are raised up, and the POOR HAVE THE GOSPEL PREACHED to them. ⁶And blessed is he who keeps from stumbling over Me." ⁷And as these were going away, Jesus began to say to the multitudes concerning John, "What did you go out into the wilderness to look at? A reed shaken by the wind? ⁸But what did you go out to see? A man dressed in soft clothing? Behold, those who wear soft clothing are in kings' palaces. ⁹But why did you go out? To see a prophet? Yes, I tell you, and one who is more than a prophet. ¹⁰This is the one about whom it was written,

'BEHOLD, I SEND MY MESSENGER BEFORE YOUR FACE,
WHO WILL PREPARE YOUR WAY BEFORE YOU.'

¹¹Truly, I say to you, among those born of women there has not arisen anyone greater than John the Baptist; yet he who is least in the kingdom of heaven is greater than he. ¹²And from the days of John the Baptist until now the kingdom of heaven suffers violence, and violent men take it by force. ¹³For all the prophets and the Law prophesied until John. ¹⁴And if you care to accept it, he himself is Elijah, who was to come."

Saturday—*John's honesty costs his life (Matthew 14:1-12)*

¹At that time Herod the tetrarch heard the news about Jesus, ²and said to his servants, "This is John the Baptist; he has risen from the dead; and that is why miraculous powers are at work in him." ³For Herod had seized John, and bound him, and put him in prison on account of Herodias, the wife of his brother Philip. ⁴For John had been saying to him, "It is not lawful for you to have her." ⁵And although he wanted to put him to death, he feared the multitude, because they regarded him as a prophet. ⁶But when Herod's birthday came, the daughter of Herodias danced before them and pleased Herod. ⁷Thereupon

143

he promised with an oath to give her whatever she asked. [8]And having been prompted by her mother, she said, "Give me here on a platter the head of John the Baptist." [9]And although he was grieved, the king commanded it to be given because of his oaths, and because of his dinner guests. [10]And he sent and had John beheaded in the prison. [11]And his head was brought on a platter and given to the girl; and she brought it to her mother. [12]And his disciples came and took away the body and buried it; and they went and reported to Jesus.

24

A Yielded Life

Sunday—*Abram's way (Genesis 16:1-6)*

¹Now Sarai, Abram's wife had borne him no children, and she had an Egyptian maid whose name was Hagar. ²So Sarai said to Abram, "Now behold, the LORD has prevented me from bearing children. Please go in to my maid; perhaps I shall obtain children through her." And Abram listened to the voice of Sarai. ³And after Abram had lived ten years in the land of Canaan, Abram's wife Sarai took Hagar the Egyptian, her maid, and gave her to her husband Abram as his wife. ⁴And he went in to Hagar, and she conceived; and when she saw that she had conceived, her mistress was despised in her sight. ⁵And Sarai said to Abram, "May the wrong done me be upon you. I gave my maid into your arms; but when she saw that she had conceived, I was despised in her sight. May the LORD judge between you and me." ⁶But Abram said to Sarai, "Behold, your maid is in your power; do to her what is good in your sight." So Sarai treated her harshly, and she fled from her presence.

For the apostle Paul, salvation and surrender were simultaneous. Immediately upon believing, he asked, "Lord, what wilt thou have me to do?" (Acts 9:6). Just as Paul wanted only to do God's will, so every Christian should surrender his entire life to God. Paul called upon all Christians to "yield yourselves unto God" (Romans 6:13).

Adolph Deissman suggested that the word *Christian* means "slave of Christ," even as *Caesarian* meant "slave of Caesar." Are we truly servants to the will of our Lord?

In the Old Testament, God promised Abraham that he would be the father of a great nation, with children as numerous as the sands of the sea. But Abraham had no children. Scheming rather than believing God, he fathered a son by Hagar, his wife's slave. It was an act of the flesh, representing man's blundering way rather than God's way. God called upon Abraham to yield, and eventually Abraham surrendered his son Ishmael. Immediately God intervened and performed a miracle. In her old age, Abraham's wife, Sarah, gave birth to Isaac, a child of faith, the vehicle of God's eternal plan.

God calls each Christian to let go of his own solutions to life's problems and accept the way of faith. Do not hang on to anything—yield everything.

It is a mistake to imagine that we can carelessly ramble along in the Christian life. As Samuel Rutherford said, "You will not be carried to heaven lying at ease upon a featherbed." Tertullian said, "He who fears to suffer cannot be His who suffered."

Christ's call was uncompromising and unconventional. His words were so piercing that the hearers tried to kill Him. Too often the Lord of glory is presented only as meek and mild and not high and holy, or as soft and sentimental instead of steadfast and strong. Artists and poets have portrayed Christ with flowing chestnut hair and a feminine face. Some show Him as a mild little fellow who went about breathing sweet benedictions upon everyone. That is a false idea. It is true that He went about doing good, but He was firm, and His words were strin-

146

gent. He offended His disciples, His relatives, and the scribes and Pharisees. On one occasion Jesus said, "Think not that I am come to send peace on earth: I came not to send peace, but a sword" (Matthew 10:34).

"Master," cried one man, "I will follow thee whithersoever thou goest." Jesus answered the enthusiastic offer with a staggering response, "Foxes have holes, and the birds of the air have nests; but the Son of man hath not where to lay his head" (Matthew 8:19-20).

Another cried, "Lord, suffer me first to go and bury my father." The reply struck back as fast and devastating as lightning. "Let the dead bury their dead: but go thou and preach the kingdom of God" (Luke 9:59-60).

A third cried, "Lord, I will follow thee; but let me first go bid them farewell, which are at home at my house." Jesus dealt him a crushing blow: "No man, having put his hand to the plough, and looking back, is fit for the kingdom of God" (Luke 9:61-62).

The Christian life is not easy. Jesus never gained disciples under false pretense. He never hid His scars, but said, "Behold my hands" (John 20:27).

C. T. Studd's motto was, "If Jesus Christ be God and died for me, then no sacrifice can be too great for me to make for Him."

From history's pages we learn of a cowardly young soldier in the army of Alexander the Great. Whenever the battle grew fierce, the young soldier would yield. This timid soldier, also named Alexander, cut the general's pride. One day Alexander the Great addressed him sternly: "Stop being a coward or drop that good name."

The call to all Christians is the same today. With Paul let us say, "Lord, what will You have me to do?" Following Christ is not easy. Yielding to Him will cost us something. Are we willing to pay the price?

DO NOT HANG ON TO ANYTHING—YIELD
EVERYTHING.

Monday—*God's way (Genesis 17:15-21)*

15Then God said to Abraham, "As for Sarai your wife, you shall not call her name Sarai, but Sarah shall be her name. 16And I will bless her, and indeed I will give you a son by her. Then I will bless her, and she shall be a mother of nations; kings of peoples shall come from her." 17Then Abraham fell on his face and laughed, and said in his heart, "Will a child be born to a man one hundred years old? And will Sarah, who is ninety years old, bear a child?" 18And Abraham said to God, "Oh that Ishmael might live before Thee!" 19But God said, "No, but Sarah your wife shall bear you a son, and you shall call his name Isaac; and I will establish My covenant with him for an everlasting covenant for his descendants after him. 20And as for Ishmael, I have heard you; behold, I will bless him, and will make him fruitful, and will multiply him exceedingly. He shall become the father of twelve princes, and I will make him a great nation. 21But My covenant I will establish with Isaac, whom Sarah will bear to you at this season next year."

Tuesday—*Abraham called to surrender (Genesis 22:1-8)*

1Now it came about after these things, that God tested Abraham, and said to him, "Abraham!" And he said, "Here I am." 2And He said, "Take now your son, your only son, whom you love, Isaac, and go to the land of Moriah; and offer him there as a burnt offering on one of the mountains of which I will tell you." 3So Abraham rose early in the morning and saddled his donkey, and took two of his young men with him and Isaac his son; and he split wood for the burnt offering, and arose and went to the place of which God had told him. 4On the third day Abraham raised his eyes and saw the place from a distance. 5And Abraham said to his young men, "Stay here with the donkey, and I and the lad will go yonder; and we will worship and return to you." 6And Abraham took the wood of the burnt offering and laid it on Isaac his son, and he took in his hand the fire and the knife. So the two of them walked on together. 7And Isaac spoke to Abraham his father and said, "My father!" And he said, "Here I am, my son." And he said, "Behold, the fire and the wood, but where is the lamb for the burnt offering?" 8And Abraham said, "God will provide for Himself the lamb for the burnt offering, my son." So the two of them walked on together.

Wednesday—*God's response to Abraham's yielding (Genesis 22:9-18)*

⁹Then they came to the place of which God had told him; and Abraham built the altar there, and arranged the wood, and bound his son Isaac, and laid him on the altar on top of the wood. ¹⁰And Abraham stretched out his hand, and took the knife to slay his son. ¹¹But the angel of the LORD called to him from heaven, and said, "Abraham, Abraham!" And he said, "Here I am." ¹²And he said, "Do not stretch out your hand against the lad, and do nothing to him; for now I know that you fear God, since you have not withheld your son, your only son, from Me." ¹³Then Abraham raised his eyes and looked, and behold, behind him a ram caught in the thicket by his horns; and Abraham went and took the ram, and offered him up for a burnt offering in the place of his son. ¹⁴And Abraham called the name of that place The LORD Will Provide, as it is said to this day, "In the mount of the LORD it will be provided." ¹⁵Then the angel of the LORD called to Abraham a second time from heaven, ¹⁶and said, "By Myself I have sworn," declares the LORD, "because you have done this thing, and have not withheld your son, your only son, ¹⁷indeed I will greatly bless you, and I will greatly multiply your descendants as the stars of the heavens, and as the sand which is on the seashore; and your descendants shall possess the gate of their enemies. ¹⁸And in your descendants all the nations of the earth shall be blessed, because you have obeyed my voice."

Thursday—*Choosing whom you obey (Romans 6:12-18)*

¹²Therefore do not let sin reign in your mortal body that you should obey its lusts, ¹³and do not go on presenting the members of your body to sin as instruments of unrighteousness; but present yourselves to God as those alive from the dead, and your members as instruments of righteousness to God. ¹⁴For sin shall not be master over you, for you are not under law, but under grace. ¹⁵What then? Shall we sin because we are not under law but under grace? May it never be! ¹⁶Do you not know that when you present yourselves to someone as slaves for obedience, you are slaves of the one whom you obey, either of sin resulting in death, or of obedience resulting in righteousness? ¹⁷But thanks be to God that though you were slaves of sin, you became obedient from the heart to that form of teaching to

which you were committed, [18]and having been freed from sin, you became slaves of righteousness.

Friday—*Jesus' call to intense sacrifice (Matthew 10:32-39)*

[32]"Every one therefore who shall confess Me before men, I will also confess him before My Father who is in heaven. [33]But whoever shall deny Me before men, I will also deny him before My Father who is in heaven. [34]Do not think that I came to bring peace on the earth; I did not come to bring peace, but a sword. [35]For I came to SET A MAN AGAINST HIS FATHER, AND A DAUGHTER AGAINST HER MOTHER, AND A DAUGHTER-IN-LAW AGAINST HER MOTHER-IN-LAW; [36]and A MAN'S ENEMIES WILL BE THE MEMBERS OF HIS HOUSEHOLD. [37]He who loves father or mother more than Me is not worthy of Me; and he who loves son or daughter more than Me is not worthy of Me. [38]And he who does not take his cross and follow after Me is not worthy of Me. [39]He who has found his life shall lose it, and he who has lost his life for My sake shall find it."

Saturday—*Because of Christ a call to new life (Romans 11:33 – 12:2)*

[33]Oh, the depth of the riches both of the wisdom and knowledge of God! How unsearchable are His judgments and unfathomable His ways! [34]FOR WHO HAS KNOWN THE MIND OF THE LORD, OR WHO BECAME HIS COUNSELOR? [35]OR WHO HAS FIRST GIVEN TO HIM THAT IT MIGHT BE PAID BACK TO HIM AGAIN? [36]For from Him and through Him and to Him are all things. To Him be the glory forever. Amen. [1]I urge you therefore, brethren, by the mercies of God, to present your bodies a living and holy sacrifice, acceptable to God, which is your spiritual service of worship. [2]And do not be conformed to this world, but be transformed by the renewing of your mind, that you may prove what the will of God is, that which is good and acceptable and perfect.

25

Small Things

Sunday—*Moses' rod (Exodus 4:1-5)*
¹Then Moses answered and said, "What if they will not believe me, or listen to what I say? For they may say, 'The LORD has not appeared to you.'" ²And the LORD said to him, "What is that in your hand?" And he said, "A staff." ³Then He said, "Throw it on the ground." So he threw it on the ground, and it became a serpent; and Moses fled from it. ⁴But the LORD said to Moses, "Stretch out your hand and grasp it by its tail"—so he stretched out his hand and caught it, and it became a staff in his hand— ⁵"that they may believe that the LORD, the God of their fathers, the God of Abraham, the God of Isaac, and the God of Jacob, has appeared to you."

No doubt about it, there is power in bigness—big government, big business, big schools, and even big churches. However, God also enjoys small things. "Who hath despised the day of small things?" (Zechariah 4:10).

In the beginning, God made man from "the dust of the ground" (Genesis 2:7). We were not made from gold or silver, or even diamonds, but dust. Even the word *humanity* comes from the Latin *humus*, meaning "decayed vegetable and animal matter." And that is what we are. With this perspective, it is much easier to give God all the glory.

A little later in Scripture, God called Moses from a burning bush. The Lord could have spoken through a mighty oak tree or even a magnificent cedar, but instead He chose a desert bush. And who can ever forget how God encouraged Moses to go and challenge Egypt with a simple rod (Exodus 4:1-2)? Though it was just a stick, it was the tool God used.

In fact, God often revealed Himself in small things. When He told His people to build a sanctuary, it was not like the ornate temples of the pagans. The tabernacle for the eternal God was made of boards and badgers' skins (Exodus 25).

Judges 4 relates the conflict of Sisera with the people of Israel. God intervened, and Sisera fled by foot all the way to the tent of Jael, the wife of Heber. Exhausted, he asked for water. She gave him milk, and he soon fell into a deep sleep. As he slept, Jael "took a nail of the tent, and took a hammer in her hand, and went softly unto him, and smote the nail into his temples, and fastened it into the ground. . . . So he died" (Judges 4:21). Jael killed him, not with a sword or a golden spear, but with a tent peg. God used a woman and a peg to deliver His people.

All through the Bible, God used small things: dust, a bush, a rod, a jawbone, a sling, and even a boy's lunch. This is the principle that "not many wise men after the flesh, not many mighty, not many noble, are called"

(1 Corinthians 1:26). Why? "That no flesh should glory in his presence" (1:29).

God chooses small things so that everyone will know that all glory is God's alone.

Paul reminds us that "we have this treasure in earthen vessels, that the excellency of the power may be of God, and not of us" (2 Corinthians 4:7).

Most of us feel inadequate, but may I encourage you to yield your smallness to His greatness. God used a small slave girl to bring His message to Naaman the leper. He used a poor widow to save the life of Elijah. Joseph began as a slave boy; he was small enough to be great. Eventually God made him prime minister of Egypt.

John 4 tells how the twelve disciples of Jesus went to a village in Samaria and brought back only lunch (v. 8); whereas the Samaritan woman, a saved prostitute, brought back much more than lunch. "And many of the Samaritans of that city believed on him for the saying of the woman" (v. 39).

Whoever you are, whatever you have, give it to Jesus. He enjoys using small things.

GOD CHOOSES SMALL THINGS SO THAT
EVERYONE WILL KNOW THAT ALL THE
GLORY IS GOD'S ALONE.

Monday—*Aaron's staff used to show God's power*
(Exodus 7:8-13)

8Now the LORD spoke to Moses and Aaron, saying, 9"When Pharaoh speaks to you, saying, 'Work a miracle'; then you shall say to Aaron, 'Take your staff and throw it down before Pharaoh, that it may become a serpent.'" 10So Moses and Aaron came to Pharaoh, and thus they did just as the LORD had commanded; and Aaron threw his staff down before Pharaoh and his servants, and it became a serpent. 11Then Pharaoh also called for the wise men and the sorcerers, and they also, the magicians of Egypt, did the same with their secret arts. 12For each one threw down his staff and they turned into serpents. But Aaron's staff swallowed up their staffs. ¹³Yet Pharaoh's heart was hardened, and he did not listen to them, as the LORD had said.

Tuesday—*A tent peg used to kill a commander* (*Judges 4:17-21*)

¹⁷Now Sisera fled away on foot to the tent of Jael the wife of Heber the Kenite, for there was peace between Jabin the king of Hazor and the house of Heber the Kenite. ¹⁸And Jael went out to meet Sisera, and said to him, "Turn aside, my master, turn aside to me! Do not be afraid." And he turned aside to her into the tent, and she covered him with a rug. ¹⁹And he said to her, "Please give me a little water to drink, for I am thirsty." So she opened a bottle of milk and gave him a drink; then she covered him. ²⁰And he said to her, "Stand in the doorway of the tent, and it shall be if anyone comes and inquires of you, and says, 'Is there anyone here?' that you shall say, 'No.'" ²¹But Jael, Heber's wife, took a tent peg and seized a hammer in her hand, and went secretly to him and drove the peg into his temple, and it went through into the ground; for he was sound asleep and exhausted. So he died.

Wednesday—*A small stone used to fell a giant* (*1 Samuel 17:42-49*)

⁴²When the Philistine looked and saw David, he disdained him; for he was but a youth, and ruddy, with a handsome appearance. ⁴³And the Philistine said to David, "Am I a dog, that you come to me with sticks?" And the Philistine cursed David by his gods. ⁴⁴The Philistine also said to David, "Come to me, and I will give your flesh to the birds of the sky and the beasts of the field. ⁴⁵Then David said to the Philistine, "You come to me with a sword, a spear, and a javelin, but I come to you in the name of the LORD of hosts, the God of the armies of Israel, whom you have taunted. ⁴⁶This day the LORD will deliver you up into my hands, and I will strike you down and remove your head from you. And I will give the dead bodies of the army of the Philistines this day to the birds of the sky and the wild beasts of the earth, that all the earth may know that there is a God in Israel, ⁴⁷and that all this assembly may know that the LORD does not deliver by sword or by spear; for the battle is the

LORD's and He will give you into our hands." ⁴⁸Then it happened when the Philistine rose and came and drew near to meet David, that David ran quickly toward the battle line to meet the Philistine. ⁴⁹And David put his hand into his bag and took from it a stone and slung it, and struck the Philistine on his forehead. And the stone sank into his forehead, so that he fell on his face to the ground.

Thursday—*A small voice heard by Elijah (1 Kings 19:11-18)*

¹¹So He said, "Go forth, and stand on the mountain before the LORD." And behold, the LORD was passing by! And a great and strong wind was rending the mountains and breaking in pieces the rocks before the LORD; but the LORD was not in the wind. And after the wind an earthquake, but the LORD was not in the earthquake. ¹²And after the earthquake a fire, but the LORD was not in the fire; and after the fire a sound of a gentle blowing. ¹³And it came about when Elijah heard it, that he wrapped his face in his mantle, and went out and stood in the entrance of the cave. And behold, a voice came to him and said, "What are you doing here, Elijah?" ¹⁴Then he said, "I have been very zealous for the LORD, the God of hosts; for the sons of Israel have forsaken Thy covenant, torn down Thine altars and killed Thy prophets with the sword. And I alone am left; and they seek my life, to take it away." ¹⁵And the LORD said to him, "Go, return on your way to the wilderness of Damascus, and when you have arrived, you shall anoint Hazael king over Syria; ¹⁶and Jehu the son of Nimshi you shall anoint king over Israel; and Elisha the son of Shaphat of Abel-meholah you shall anoint as prophet in your place. ¹⁷And it shall come about, the one who escapes from the sword of Hazael, Jehu shall put to death, and the one who escapes from the sword of Jehu, Elisha shall put to death. ¹⁸Yet I will leave 7,000 in Israel, all the knees that have not bowed to Baal and every mouth that has not kissed him."

Friday—*A boy's lunch used to feed a multitude (John 6:5-13)*

⁵Jesus therefore lifting up His eyes, and seeing that a great multitude was coming to Him, said to Philip, "Where are we to buy bread, that these may eat?" ⁶And this He was saying to test him; for He Himself knew what He was intending to do. ⁷Philip answered Him, "Two hundred denarii worth of bread is not

155

sufficient for them, for every one to receive a little." ⁸One of His disciples, Andrew, Simon Peter's brother, said to Him, ⁹"There is a lad here, who has five barley loaves, and two fish; but what are these for so many people?" ¹⁰Jesus said, "Have the people sit down." Now there was much grass in the place. So the men sat down, in number about five thousand. ¹¹Jesus therefore took the loaves; and having given thanks, He distributed to those who were seated; likewise also of the fish as much as they wanted. ¹²And when they were filled, He said to His disciples, "Gather up the leftover fragments that nothing may be lost." ¹³And so they gathered them up, and filled twelve baskets with fragments from the five barley loaves, which were left over by those who had eaten.

Saturday—*A widow's small gift most pleasing to God* (Luke 21:1-4)

¹And He looked up and saw the rich putting their gifts into the treasury. ²And He saw a certain poor widow putting in two small copper coins. ³And He said, "Truly I say to you, this poor widow put in more than all of them; ⁴for they all out of their surplus put into the offering; but she out of her poverty put in all that she had to live on."

26

We Need an Awakening

Sunday—*Prayer for revival (Psalm 85:1-7)*
¹O LORD, Thou didst show favor to Thy land;
   Thou didst restore the captivity of Jacob.
²Thou didst forgive the iniquity of Thy people;
   Thou didst cover all their sin.   [Selah.
³Thou didst withdraw all Thy fury;
   Thou didst turn away from Thy burning anger.
⁴Restore us, O God of our salvation,
   And cause Thine indignation toward us to cease.
⁵Wilt Thou be angry with us forever?
   Wilt Thou prolong Thine anger to all generations?
⁶Wilt Thou not Thyself revive us again,
   That Thy people may rejoice in Thee?
⁷Show us Thy lovingkindness, O LORD,
   And grant us Thy salvation.

At times it seems that we are hearing the final gasps of a dying culture. Cities are threatened by corruption and bankruptcy, dark clouds of conflict hover dangerously over the Middle East, and in many places mob rule has replaced common sense and reason.

Unfortunately, the church of Jesus Christ has adopted the spirit of this age and is largely apostate. Situation ethics and the "new morality" have blinded people to God's purposes and redemption. We need a spiritual awakening.

Several years ago Roger Babson, a newspaper journalist, wrote that the test of a nation is the intellectual and spiritual growth of its people. He suggested that money will not save us. Babylon, Persia, Greece, Rome, Spain, and France, he pointed out, all had their turn as the world's richest nation. But their so-called prosperity eventually ruined them. Our nation is now the richest, he said, but it too could decline.

Upsetting, isn't it? But if we honestly face ourselves and our national condition, there is hope, Babson concluded: "Only a sane, spiritual revival which changes the desires of our people will save us." We need a revival!

The word *revival* comes from the Latin re, "again," and *vivo*, "to live." Revival means "to live again."

Revival is a regaining of spiritual consciousness. Those who have been revived find that they love Jesus Christ in a new and significant way. We need to pray for revival in our hearts, our schools, our churches, our nation.

How shall we pray? Through the prophet Hosea, God said, "Break up your fallow ground: for it is time to seek the LORD" (Hosea 10:12). Fallow ground is dry, unproductive ground. We need to pray that we might become productive Christians.

Here are seven steps to revival:

First, *desire to know Jesus Christ better.* Develop a holy dissatisfaction. The contented Christian is a sterile Christian. Paul said in substance, "Jesus arrested me on the

Damascus road. Now I want to lay hold of all I was arrested for."

Second, *pray for a revolutionary change in your life.* Jacob wrestled with God. He would not be denied God's blessing. Throw your entire life into the will of God and seek His best.

Third, *totally repent.* "Create in me a clean heart," David cried (Psalm 51:10). For a year David was out of fellowship with God, but finally he confessed and turned from sin. Then he could sing again, write again, pray again.

Fourth, *make the crooked straight.* If you owe a debt, pay it, or have an understanding with the people you owe. Zacchaeus said, "Lord, the half of my goods I give to the poor; and if I have taken any thing from any man by false accusation, I restore him fourfold" (Luke 19:8).

Fifth, *develop a seriousness of purpose.* Keep off detours. Let nothing deflect the magnetic needle of your callling. Beware lest the things of this world rob your life's purpose.

Sixth, *do not be too busy.* Paul said, "This one thing I do" (Philippians 3:13). The Christian life requires specialists. Too many of us burn energy without drawing nearer to God.

Seventh, *do not rust.* Start sharing your faith. Use your time, talent, and dollars, and expect great things by asking God for faith.

Let us stir up the gift God has planted in us and seek the revival our nation needs!

REVIVAL MEANS "TO LIVE AGAIN."

Monday—*David's confession (Psalm 51:1-6)*
¹Be gracious to me, O God, according to Thy lovingkindness;
According to the greatness of Thy compassion blot out my
    transgressions.
²Wash me thoroughly from my iniquity,

159

And cleanse me from my sin.
³For I know my transgressions,
And my sin is ever before me.
⁴Against Thee, Thee only, I have sinned,
And done what is evil in Thy sight,
So that Thou art justified when Thou dost speak,
And blameless when Thou dost judge.
⁵Behold, I was brought forth in iniquity,
And in sin my mother conceived me.
⁶Behold, Thou dost desire truth in the innermost being,
And in the hidden part Thou wilt make me know wisdom.

Tuesday—*David's repentance (Psalm 51:7-15)*

⁷Purify me with hyssop, and I shall be clean;
Wash me, and I shall be whiter than snow.
⁸Make me to hear joy and gladness,
Let the bones which Thou has broken rejoice.
⁹Hide Thy face from my sins,
And blot out all my iniquities.
¹⁰Create in me a clean heart, O God,
And renew a steadfast spirit within me,
¹¹Do not cast me away from Thy presence,
And do not take Thy Holy Spirit from me.
¹²Restore to me the joy of Thy salvation,
And sustain me with a willing spirit.
¹³Then I will teach transgressors Thy ways,
And sinners will be converted to Thee.
¹⁴Deliver me from bloodguiltiness, O God, Thou God of my
salvation;
Then my tongue will joyfully sing of Thy righteousness.
¹⁵O LORD, open my lips,
That my mouth may declare Thy praise.

Wednesday—*David's plea (Psalm 51:16-19)*

¹⁶For Thou dost not delight in sacrifice, otherwise I would give
it;
Thou art not pleased with burnt offering.
¹⁷The sacrifices of God are a broken spirit;
A broken and a contrite heart, O God, Thou wilt not despise.
¹⁸By Thy favor do good to Zion;
Build the walls of Jerusalem.

¹⁹Then Thou wilt delight in righteous sacrifices,
In burnt offering and whole burnt offering;
Then young bulls will be offered on Thine altar.

Thursday—*Revival under Samuel (1 Samuel 7:1-6)*

¹And the men of Kiriath-jearim came and took the ark of the LORD and brought it into the house of Abinadab on the hill, and consecrated Eleazar his son to keep the ark of the LORD. ²And it came about from the day that the ark remained at Kiriath-jearim that the time was long, for it was twenty years; and all the house of Israel lamented after the LORD. ³Then Samuel spoke to all the house of Israel, saying, "If you return to the LORD with all your heart, remove the foreign gods and the Ashtaroth from among you and direct your hearts to the LORD and serve Him along; and He will deliver you from the hand of the Philistines." ⁴So the sons of Israel removed the Baals and the Ashtaroth and served the LORD alone. ⁵Then Samuel said, "Gather all Israel to Mizpah, and I will pray to the LORD for you." ⁶And they gathered to Mizpah, and drew water and poured it out before the LORD, and fasted on that day, and said there, "We have sinned against the LORD." And Samuel judged the sons of Israel at Mizpah.

Friday—*Habakkuk's prayer for revival (Habakkuk 3:2-6)*

²LORD, I have heard the report about Thee and I fear.
O LORD, revive Thy work in the midst of the years,
In the midst of the years make it known;
In wrath remember mercy.
³God comes from Teman,
And the Holy One from Mount Paran.   [Selah.
His splendor covers the heavens,
And the earth is full of His praise.
⁴His radiance is like the sunlight;
He has rays flashing from His hand,
And there is the hiding of His power.
⁵Before Him goes pestilence,
And plague comes after Him.
⁶He stood and surveyed the earth;
He looked and startled the nations.
Yes, the perpetual mountains were shattered,

161

The ancient hills collapsed.
His ways are everlasting.

Saturday—*A real revival (2 Kings 18:1-6)*

[1]Now it came about in the third year of Hoshea, the son of Elah king of Israel, that Hezekiah the son of Ahaz king of Judah became king. [2]He was twenty-five years old when he became king, and he reigned twenty-nine years in Jerusalem; and his mother's name was Abi the daughter of Zechariah. [3]And He did right in the sight of the LORD, according to all that his father David had done. [4]He removed the high places and broke down the sacred pillars and cut down the Asherah. He also broke in pieces the bronze serpent that Moses had made, for until those days the sons of Israel burned incense to it; and it was called Nehushtan. [5]He trusted in the LORD, the God of Israel; so that after him there was none like him among all the kings of Judah, nor among those who were before him. [6]For he clung to the LORD; he did not depart from following Him, but kept His commandments, which the LORD had commanded Moses.

ABUNDANT LIVING

27

Attitude Makes the Difference

Sunday—*The secret of peace (Philippians 4:4-8)*

⁴Rejoice in the Lord always; again I will say, rejoice! ⁵Let your forbearing spirit be known to all men. The Lord is near. ⁶Be anxious for nothing, but in everything by prayer and supplication with thanksgiving let your requests be made known to God. ⁷And the peace of God, which surpasses all comprehension, shall guard your hearts and your minds in Christ Jesus. ⁸Finally, brethren, whatever is true, whatever is honorable, whatever is right, whatever is pure, whatever is lovely, whatever is of good repute, if there is any excellence and if anything worthy of praise, let your mind dwell on these things.

My Scottish father was a bricklayer. In his late twenties, he experienced a spiritual awakening and became a Christian. He was an extremely hard worker and expected all the men under him to be the same. His men would tease him, "Scotty, don't you know that Rome wasn't built in a day?"

"Yes," he would answer. "I know that. But I wasn't foreman on that job."

My father displayed great faith in the Lord and enthusiasm for all of life. He knew that one's attitude is extremely important.

The apostle Paul also displayed an enthusiastic attitude. Though a prisoner in Rome awaiting martyrdom, he abounded with faith. "Rejoice in the Lord alway" (Philippians 4:4) was his habit.

When we look at ourselves, we can become very discouraged. When we look at the outside world, we can become overwhelmed with its problems. But when we look to the Lord, we are made aware of His power. The secret of an enthusiastic attitude is in recognizing the power of God. We are no match for the situations of life, but God is. For every need we have there is a corresponding fullness in Him.

Feel Paul's spirit and notice his faith as he writes, "If God be for us, who can be against us?" (Romans 8:31); "Thanks be to God, which giveth us the victory through our Lord Jesus Christ" (1 Corinthians 15:57); and "I can do all things through Christ which strengtheneth me" (Philippians 4:13). In fact, the Scriptures teach, "Without faith it is impossible to please [God]" (Hebrews 11:6).

Hundreds of articles and books today advocate self-help methods for attaining success, wealth, and happiness. Much of what they suggest is helpful, but the real formula is not "help yourself," but "yield yourself." As we yield ourselves to Jesus Christ, we avail ourselves of supernatural strength.

The Old Testament tells of twelve messengers who were sent out by Moses to spy out the promised land. Ten brought back discouraging reports and two brought back encouraging reports. The ten, because of their lack of faith, could see only the walled cities and the inhabitants as giants. Unbelief always magnifies problems.

Unbelief also minimizes the answer. They saw themselves like grasshoppers (Numbers 13:33). Usually a negative attitude results in a grasshopper complex.

Unbelief is contagious; soon pandemonium broke loose in the camp of Israel. "And all the congregation lifted up their voice, and cried" (Numbers 14:1).

Joshua and Caleb, on the other hand, possessed an attitude of faith. They saw all the problems, but they also saw the sufficiency of God. They understood that every problem was an opportunity to display divine power. The secret of a believing attitude is found in looking beyond ourselves to an all-sufficient God.

The Greek word for man, *anthropos*, means "the up-looking one." The animal kingdom looks down, but God made man to look up. Fallen man must be born from above. He must look to God to redeem him. When man needs wisdom, he must look up and "ask of God" (James 1:5), because "every good gift and every perfect gift is from above, and cometh down" (James 1:17).

In times of trouble and gloom, we must maintain a heavenly perspective, "For our citizenship is in heaven, from which also we eagerly wait for a Savior, the Lord Jesus Christ" (Philippians 3:20, NASB).* Or, as I often admonish our students, if the outlook is bleak, try the uplook.

THE SECRET OF AN ENTHUSIASTIC ATTITUDE
IS IN RECOGNIZING THE POWER OF GOD.

Monday—*Real humility (Philippians 2:3-11)*

³Do nothing from selfishness or empty conceit, but with humility of mind let each of you regard one another as more

---

New American Standard Bible.

important than himself; ⁴do not merely look out for your own personal interests, but also for the interests of others. ⁵Have this attitude in yourselves which was also in Christ Jesus, ⁶who, although He existed in the form of God, did not regard equality with God a thing to be grasped, ⁷but emptied Himself, taking the form of a bond-servant, and being made in the likeness of man. ⁸And being found in appearance as a man, He humbled Himself by becoming obedient to the point of death, even death on a cross. ⁹Therefore also God highly exalted Him, and bestowed on Him the name which is above every name, ¹⁰that at the name of Jesus every knee should bow, of those who are in heaven, and on earth, and under the earth, ¹¹and that every tongue should confess that Jesus Christ is Lord, to the glory of God the Father.

Tuesday—*A right attitude (Psalm 34:1-8)*

¹I will bless the LORD at all times;
 His praise shall continually be in my mouth.
²My soul shall make its boast in the LORD;
 The humble shall hear it and rejoice.
³O magnify the LORD with me,
 And let us exalt His name together.
⁴I sought the LORD, and He answered me,
 And delivered me from all my fears.
⁵They looked to Him and were radiant,
 And their faces shall never be ashamed.
⁶This poor man cried and the LORD heard him;
 And saved him out of all his troubles.
⁷The angel of the LORD encamps around those who fear Him,
 And rescues them.
⁸O taste and see that the LORD is good;
 How blessed is the man who takes refuge in Him!

Wednesday—*The importance of faith (Hebrews 11:1-6)*

¹Now faith is the assurance of things hoped for, the conviction of things not seen. ²For by it the men of old gained approval. ³By faith we understand that the worlds were prepared by the word of God, so that what is seen was not made out of things which are visible. ⁴By faith Abel offered to God a better sacrifice than Cain, through which he obtained the testimony that he was righteous, God testifying about his gifts, and

through faith, though he is dead, he still speaks. [5]By faith Enoch was taken up so that he should not see death; and he was not found because God took him up; for he obtained the witness that before his being taken up he was pleasing to God. [6]And without faith it is impossible to please Him, for he who comes to God must believe that He is, and that He is a rewarder of those who seek Him.

Thursday—*Faith exemplified (Hebrews 11:39–12:2)*

[39]And all these, having gained approval through their faith, did not receive what was promised, [40]because God had provided something better for us, so that apart from us they should not be made perfect. [1]Therefore, since we have so great a cloud of witnesses surrounding us, let us also lay aside every encumbrance, and the sin which so easily entangles us, and let us run with endurance the race that is set before us, [2]fixing our eyes on Jesus, the author and perfecter of faith, who for the joy set before Him endured the cross, despising the shame, and has sat down at the right hand of the throne of God.

Friday—*Our security (Romans 8:31-39)*

[31]What then shall we say to these things? If God is for us, who is against us? [32]He who did not spare His own Son, but delivered Him up for us all, how will He not also with Him freely give us all things? [33]Who will bring a charge against God's elect? God is the one who justifies; [34]who is the one who condemns? Christ Jesus is He who died, yes, rather who was raised, who is at the right hand of God, who also intercedes for us. [35]Who shall separate us from the love of Christ? Shall tribulation, or distress, or persecution, or famine, or nakedness, or peril, or sword? [36]Just as it is written,

"FOR THY SAKE WE ARE BEING PUT TO DEATH ALL DAY LONG;
WE WERE CONSIDERED AS SHEEP TO BE SLAUGHTERED."

[37]But in all these things we overwhelmingly conquer through Him who loved us. [38]For I am convinced that neither death, nor life, nor angels, nor principalities, nor things present, nor things to come, nor powers, [39]nor height, nor depth, nor any other created thing, shall be able to separate us from the love of God, which is in Christ Jesus our Lord.

Saturday—*Living in the Spirit's fullness (Ephesians 5:15-21)*

[15]Therefore be careful how you walk, not as unwise men, but

as wise, [16]making the most of your time, because the days are evil. [17]So then do not be foolish, but understand what the will of the Lord is. [18]And do not get drunk with wine, for that is dissipation, but be filled with the Spirit, [19]speaking to one another in psalms and hymns and spiritual songs, singing and making melody with your heart to the Lord; [20]always giving thanks for all things in the name of our Lord Jesus Christ to God, even the Father; [21]and be subject to one another in the fear of Christ.

28

Learning to Forget

Sunday—*Something to remember (Psalm 103:1-5)*
¹Bless the LORD, O my soul;
  And all that is within me, bless His holy name.
²Bless the LORD, O my soul,
  And forget none of His benefits;
³Who pardons all your iniquities;
  Who heals all your diseases;
⁴Who redeems your life from the pit;
  Who crowns you with lovingkindness and compassion;
⁵Who satisfies your years with good things,
  So that your youth is renewed like the eagle.

It is just as important to have a good "forgettery" as it is to have a good memory. Many experiences in our lives should be forgotten. The apostle Paul would have been greatly hindered had he been haunted by his past sin. His feelings are clearly expressed in the phrase, "forgetting those things which are behind, and reaching forth unto those things which are before" (Philippians 3:13).

For the most part, we prefer to remember the happy experiences of life. Memory consciously and unconsciously attempts to bury the dark and painful moments. But often trying to forget is not enough.

Recently I spoke with a friend who was defeated by guilt from haunting memories of the past. In attempting to help, I likened her experience to a door wet with red paint. I suggested that in visiting and handling the past, she was smudging everything in the present with the stains of her past.

She wistfully reminded me that learning to forget was far more difficult than quoting a phrase of Scripture. I shared three suggestions that helped her learn to forget and enabled her to experience victory over her past.

First, I suggested, make right everything that needs to be corrected. Face known evil, deal with it, and repent of it. Repentance and restitution aid the forgetting process—one cannot forget wrongs until the wrongs are made right. An accusing conscience keeps one's memory frightfully alive. Upon experiencing God's forgiveness, profit from the lessons and then forget those things that are behind.

Second, in learning how to forget, reverse the process of memory. Remembering is based upon repetition. Repetition is the mother of learning. Do not relive your past sin. Refuse to revive the experience in your memory. Although some people repent and forsake some former sin, the sin is visited in the mind and even occasionally encouraged and enjoyed. This mental activity prohibits success in forgetting. Most experiences you want to forget beg to be forgotten. In learning how to forget, you are really working with nature rather than against it.

Third, displace the thoughts of past sin with the greater thought of God's infinite grace. Contemplation of the cross of Christ and all that His sacrifice for us means is a powerful thought. God's love is greater than everything and anything, no matter how painful and hateful. Best of all, the Bible exhausts the possibilities of language to convey how completely God forgives us. "As far as the east is from the west, so far hath he removed our transgressions from us" (Psalm 103:12). "And thou wilt cast all their sins into the depths of the sea" (Micah 7:19). In fact, the Bible teaches that when God forgives, He also forgets. "I will remember their sin no more" (Jeremiah 31:34). Since God forgives and then forgets, who are we to remember?

> ## REPENTANCE AND RESTITUTION AID THE FORGETTING PROCESS.

Monday—*Something to forget (Psalm 103:6-14)*

⁶The LORD performs righteous deeds,
  And judgments for all who are oppressed.
⁷He made known His ways to Moses,
  His acts to the sons of Israel.
⁸The LORD is compassionate and gracious,
  Slow to anger and abounding in lovingkindness.
⁹He will not always strive with us;
  Nor will He keep His anger forever.
¹⁰He has not dealt with us according to our sins,
  Nor rewarded us according to our iniquities.
¹¹For as high as the heavens are above the earth,
  So great is His lovingkindness toward those who fear Him.
¹²As afar as the east is from the west,
  So far has He removed our transgressions from us.
¹³Just as a father has compassion on his children,
  So the LORD has compassion on those who fear Him.
¹⁴For He Himself knows our frame;
  He is mindful that we are but dust.

172

Tuesday—*A forgiving father (Luke 15:11-32)*

[11]And He said, "A certain man had two sons; [12]and the younger of them said to his father, 'Father, give me the share of the estate that falls to me,' And he divided his wealth between them. [13]And not many days later, the younger son gathered everything together and went on a journey into a distant country, and there he squandered his estate with loose living. [14]Now when he had spent everything, a severe famine occurred in that country, and he began to be in need. [15]And he went and attached himself to one of the citizens of that country, and he sent him into his fields to feed swine. [16]And he was longing to fill his stomach with the pods that the swine were eating, and no one was giving anything to him. [17]But when he came to his senses, he said, 'How many of my father's hired men have more than enough bread, but I am dying here with hunger! [18]I will get up and go to my father, and will say to him, "Father, I have sinned against heaven, and in your sight; [19]I am no longer worthy to be called your son; make me as one of your hired men." [20]And he got up and came to his father. But while he was still a long way off, his father saw him, and felt compassion for him, and ran and embraced him, and kissed him. [21]And the son said to him, 'Father, I have sinned against heaven and in your sight; I am no longer worthy to be called your son.' [22]But the father said to his slaves, 'Quickly bring out the best robe and put it on him, and put a ring on his hand and sandals on his feet; [23]and bring the fattened calf, kill it, and let us eat and be merry; [24]for this son of mine was dead, and has come to life again; he was lost, and has been found.' And they began to be merry. [25]Now his older son was in the field, and when he came and approached the house, he heard music and dancing. [26]And he summoned one of the servants and began inquiring what these things might be. [27]And he said to him, 'Your brother has come, and your father has killed the fattened calf, because he has received him back safe and sound.' [28]But he became angry, and was not willing to go in; and his father came out and began entreating him. [29]But he answered and said to his father, 'Look! For so many years I have been serving you, and I have never neglected a command of yours; and yet you have never given me a kid, that I might be merry with my friends; [30]but when this son of yours came, who has devoured your wealth with harlots, you killed the fattened calf for him.' [31]And he said to him, 'My

child, you have always been with me, and all that is mine is yours. ³²But we had to be merry and rejoice, for this brother of yours was dead and has begun to live, and was lost and has been found.' "

Wednesday—*Assurance of forgiveness (Psalm 32)*

¹How blessed is he whose transgression is forgiven,
  Whose sin is covered!
²How blessed is the man to whom the LORD does not impute
      iniquity,
  And in whose spirit there is no deceit!
³When I kept silent about my sin, my body wasted away
  Through my groaning all day long.
⁴For day and night Thy hand was heavy upon me;
  My vitality was drained away as with the fever-heat of
      summer.   [Selah.
⁵I acknowledged my sin to Thee,
  And my iniquity I did not hide;
  I said, "I will confess my transgressions to the LORD";
  And Thou didst forgive the guilt of my sin.   [Selah.
⁶Therefore, let everyone who is godly pray to Thee in a time
      when Thou mayest be found;
  Surely in a flood of great waters they shall not reach him.
⁷Thou art my hiding place; Thou dost preserve me from
      trouble;
  Thou dost surround me with songs of deliverance.   [Selah.
⁸I will instruct you and teach you in the way which you
      should go;
  I will counsel you with My eye upon you.
⁹Do not be as the horse or as the mule which have no
      understanding;
  Whose trappings include bit and bridle to hold them in
      check,
  Otherwise they will not come near to you.
¹⁰Many are the sorrows of the wicked;
  But he who trusts in the LORD, lovingkindness shall surround
      him.
¹¹Be glad in the LORD and rejoice you righteous ones,
  And shout for joy all you who are upright in heart.

Thursday—*Our wonderful God (Isaiah 55:6-9)*

6Seek the LORD while He may be found;
Call upon Him while He is near.
7Let the wicked forsake his ways,
And the unrighteous man his thoughts;
And let him return to the LORD,
And He will have compassion on him;
And to our God,
For He will abundantly pardon.
8"For My thoughts are not your thoughts,
Neither are your ways My ways," declares the LORD.
9"For as the heavens are higher than the earth,
So are My ways higher than your ways,
And My thoughts than your thoughts."

Friday—*A promise of forgiveness (Ezekiel 33:14-16)*

14But when I say to the wicked, 'You will surely die,' and he turns from his sin and practices justice and righteousness, 15if a wicked man restores a pledge, pays back what he has taken by robbery, walks by the statutes which ensure life without committing iniquity, he will surely live; he shall not die. 16None of his sins that he has committed will be remembered against him. He has practiced justice and righteousness; he will surely live."

Saturday—*An astounding conversion (Luke 19:1-10)*

1And He entered and was passing through Jericho. 2And behold, there was a man called by the name of Zaccheus; and he was a chief tax-gatherer, and he was rich. 3And he was trying to see who Jesus was, and he was unable because of the crowd, for he was small in stature. 4And he ran on ahead and climbed up into a sycamore tree in order to see Him, for He was about to pass through that way. 5And when Jesus came to the place, He looked up and said to him, "Zaccheus, hurry and come down, for today I must stay at your house." 6And he hurried and came down, and received Him gladly. 7And when they saw it, they all began to grumble, saying, "He has gone to be the guest of a man who is a sinner." 8And Zaccheus stopped and said to the Lord, "Behold, Lord, half of my possessions I will give to the poor, and if I have defrauded anyone of anything, I will give back four times as much." 9And Jesus said to him, "Today

175

salvation has come to this house, because he, too, is a son of Abraham. [10]For the Son of Man has come to seek and to save that which was lost."

29

God's Cure for Cares

Sunday—*A prescription for worry-free living (Psalm 37:1-8)*
¹Fret not yourself because of evildoers,
  Be not envious toward wrongdoers.
²For they will wither quickly like the grass,
  And fade like the green herb.
³Trust in the Lord, and do good;
  Dwell in the land and cultivate faithfulness.
⁴Delight yourself in the Lord;
  And He will give you the desires of your heart.
⁵Commit your way to the Lord,
  Trust also in Him, and He will do it.
⁶And He will bring forth your righteousness as the light,
  And your judgment as the noonday.
⁷Rest in the Lord and wait patiently for Him;
  Fret not yourself because of him who prospers in his way,
  Because of the man who carries out wicked schemes.
⁸Cease from anger, and forsake wrath;
  Fret not yourself, it leads only to evildoing.

Recently, a panel of psychologists concluded that forty percent of the things people worry about never happen. Thirty percent of worry is about past events. Twelve percent of an individual's worry is over needless health concerns, ten percent deals with small trifles, and eight percent of what we worry about is related to legitimate concerns. If those statistics are true, we surely waste a lot of worry. George Lyons said, "Worry is the interest paid by those who borrow trouble."

But there is a cure for cares. Psalm 37 pictures David surrounded by his enemies. Although his situation appeared dark and even desperate, he was able to say, "Fret not thyself because of evildoers" (Psalms 37:1).

According to the dictionary, the word *fret* means "to cause to suffer emotional strain; to eat or to gnaw into; to become uneasy, vexed or worried." In Psalm 37, David is saying, "Don't get into perilous heat over things." We would say, "Don't lose your cool. Keep calm and hang loose."

God's cure for cares is given in five ideas from Psalm 37.

First, "trust in the LORD (v. 3). The word translated "trust" throughout the Old Testament means "without care," or literally, "careless." Carelessness in this sense does not imply flippancy, but freedom from cares—like a child who plays confidently, knowing that his parents are nearby and he is safe. It is a positive trust and cooperation with the will of God. It is "casting all your care upon him; for he careth for you" (1 Peter 5:7).

Worry reveals a basic distrust in God. In a sense, worry is a form of atheism, because it denies that God cares and that Christ is praying for us. Worry is an announcement to the world that we do not believe God is big enough and, therefore, we must bear our burdens alone.

Second, "trust in the LORD, and do good" (v. 3). The best cure for worry is hard work on behalf of others. Work is healthy! Worry, not work, kills people.

Third, "delight thyself also in the LORD" (v. 4). David

178

tells us to focus our full attention on the Lord. Literally, "Seek for the delicacies that are to be found in the Lord." Search for all the goodness God has for you. To "delight in the LORD" is to find your joy, excitement, and thrill in Him. Are you wide open to God? Holy delight is a cure for care.

There is more. Fourth, "commit thy way unto the LORD; trust also in him; and he shall bring it to pass" (v. 5). Put Christ in charge of your life; let Him have control. Consciously give Him control of all your opportunities and problems, and He will bring you peace of mind and soul. Remember that prayer is one of God's cures for caving in. "Men ought always to pray, and not to faint" (Luke 18:1).

Mental disorganization is a chief factor in worry. The helter-skelter mind is always overburdened. David is saying, "Stop trying to run your own life. Let the Lord have control. Commit thy way unto the Lord."

Fifth, "rest in the LORD" (v. 7). God is not frustrated or worried. He is King of kings and Lord of lords. He is the Alpha and the Omega and all that there is between. You can safely rest in the Lord because He is fully qualified to care for your cares.

WORRY REVEALS A BASIC DISTRUST IN GOD.

Monday—*The importance of importunity (Luke 18:1-8)*

[1]Now He was telling them a parable to show that at all times they ought to pray and not to lose heart, [2]saying, "There was in a certain city a judge who did not fear God, and did not respect man. [3]And there was a widow in that city, and she kept coming to him, saying, 'Give me legal protection from my opponent.' [4]And for a while he was unwilling; but afterward he said to himself, 'Even though I do not fear God nor respect man, [5]yet because this widow bothers me, I will give her legal protection, lest by continually coming she wear me out.' " [6]And the Lord said, "Hear what the unrighteous judge said; [7]now shall not God bring about justice for His elect, who cry to Him day and night, and will He delay long over them? [8]I tell you that He will

bring about justice for them speedily. However, when the Son of Man comes, will He find faith on the earth?"

Tuesday—*Peace resulting from trust (Isaiah 26:3-4)*
3"The steadfast of mind Thou wilt keep in perfect peace,
Because he trusts in Thee.
4"Trust in the LORD forever,
For in GOD the LORD, we have an everlasting Rock."

Wednesday—*God's protection of His own (Psalm 34:15-22)*
15The eyes of the LORD are toward the righteous,
And His ears are open to their cry.
16The face of the LORD is against evildoers,
To cut off the memory of them from the earth.
17The righteous cry and the LORD hears,
And delivers them out of all their troubles.
18The LORD is near to the brokenhearted,
And saves those who are crushed in spirit.
19Many are the afflictions of the righteous;
But the LORD delivers him out of them all.
20He keeps all his bones;
Not one of them is broken.
21Evil shall slay the wicked;
And those who hate the righteous will be condemned.
22The LORD redeems the soul of His servants;
And none of those who take refuge in Him will be
condemned.

Thursday—*Bold praying exemplified (Ephesians 3:11-21)*
11This was in accordance with the eternal purpose which He carried out in Christ Jesus our Lord, 12in whom we have boldness and confident access through faith in Him. 13Therefore, I ask you not to lose heart at my tribulations on your behalf, for they are your glory. 14For this reason, I bow my knees before the Father, 15from whom every family in heaven and on earth derives its name, 16that He would grant you, according to the riches of His glory, to be strengthened with power through His Spirit in the inner man; 17so that Christ may dwell in your hearts through faith; and that you, being rooted and grounded in love, 18may be able to comprehend with all the saints what is the breadth and length and height and depth, 19and to know the

love of Christ which surpasses knowledge, that you may be
filled up to all the fulness of God. ²⁰Now to Him who is able to
do exceeding abundantly beyond all that we ask or think, according to the power that works within us, ²¹to Him be the
glory in the church and in Christ Jesus to all generations forevor
and ever. Amen.

Friday—*God's omniscience (Psalm 139:1-12)*

¹O Lᴏʀᴅ, Thou hast searched me and known me.
²Thou dost know when I sit down and when I rise up;
  Thou dost understand my thought from afar.
³Thou dost scrutinize my path and my lying down,
  And art intimately acquainted with all my ways.
⁴Even before there is a word on my tongue,
  Behold, O Lᴏʀᴅ, Thou dost know it all.
⁵Thou hast enclosed me behind and before,
  And laid Thy hand upon me.
⁶Such knowledge is too wonderful for me;
  It is too high, I cannot attain to it.
⁷Where can I go from Thy Spirit?
  Or where can I flee from Thy presence?
⁸If I ascend to heaven, Thou art there;
  If I make my bed in Sheol, behold, Thou art there.
⁹If I take the wings of the dawn,
  If I dwell in the remotest part of the sea,
¹⁰Even there Thy hand will lead me,
  And Thy right hand will lay hold of me.
¹¹If I say, "Surely the darkness will overwhelm me,
  And the light around me will be night,"
¹²Even the darkness is not dark to Thee,
  And the night is as bright as the day.
  Darkness and light are alike to Thee.

Saturday—*God's omnipotence (Psalm 139:13-24)*

¹³For Thou didst form my inward parts;
  Thou didst weave me in my mother's womb.
¹⁴I will give thanks to Thee, for I am fearfully and wonderfully
      made;
  Wonderful are Thy works,
  And my soul knows it very well.
¹⁵My frame was not hidden from Thee,
  When I was made in secret,

And skillfully wrought in the depths of the earth.
¹⁶Thine eyes have seen my unformed substance;
  And in Thy book they were all written,
  The days that were ordained for me,
  When as yet there was not one of them.
¹⁷How precious also are Thy thoughts to me, O God!
  How vast is the sum of them!
¹⁸If I should count them, they would outnumber the sand.
  When I awake, I am still with Thee.
¹⁹O that Thou wouldst slay the wicked, O God;
  Depart from me, therefore, men of bloodshed.
²⁰For they speak against Thee wickedly,
  And Thine enemies take Thy name in vain.
²¹Do I not hate those who hate Thee, O LORD?
  And do I not loathe those who rise up against Thee?
²²I hate them with the utmost hatred;
  They have become my enemies.
²³Search me, O God, and know my heart;
  Try me and know my anxious thoughts;
²⁴And see if there be any hurtful way in me,
  And lead me in the everlasting way.

30

Fullness of Joy

Sunday—*Joy in praise (Psalm 95:1-6)*

¹O come, let us sing for joy to the LORD;
  Let us shout joyfully to the rock of our salvation.
²Let us come before His presence with thanksgiving;
  Let us shout joyfully to Him with psalms.
³For the LORD is a great God,
  And a great King above all gods,
⁴In whose hand are the depths of the earth;
  The peaks of the mountains are His also.
⁵The sea is His, for it was He who made it;
  And His hands formed the dry land.
⁶Come, let us worship and bow down;
  Let us kneel before the LORD our Maker.

People in general appear to be suffering from a lack of wholehearted, overflowing joy. Pessimism and gloom hang like smog over the land.

And yet, the words *joy* and *rejoice* are found more than 550 times in the Bible. According to Scripture, authentic joy comes only from being in a right relationship with God. The psalmist wrote, "In thy presence is fulness of joy" (Psalm 16:11).

Counterfeit joy abounds. Current books loudly proclaim the ABCs of wealth, success, and happiness. Repeatedly modern "prophets" encourage us to lift ourselves up to abundance, power, and joy. The great promises of the Bible are often abused and misquoted as a magic formula to guarantee success. Phrases and verses from God's Word are applied indiscriminately to the whole world, although many of them refer only to those who, by an act of faith, have become the children of God.

The Scriptures teach that joy is a product of the knowledge of God. Real joy comes from experiencing God's forgiveness, knowing the reality of His presence, being assured of His victory, and understanding His sovereignty.

The gospels tell how Jesus met and changed a paralytic. "Be of good cheer; thy sins be forgiven thee," Jesus said (Matthew 9:2). The paralytic found joy in God's forgiveness. When evangelist Gypsy Smith was asked the secret of his overflowing joy, he answered, "I've never gotten over the wonder of it all, the wonder of God's love for me." He knew joy because of God's forgiveness.

David, the psalmist, wrote "Blessed [happy] is he whose transgression is forgiven" (Psalm 32:1). Sin kills joy. Later, confessing a great sin, David sobbed. "Restore unto me the joy of thy salvation" (Psalm 51:12). He longed for the joy of knowing God's forgiveness.

To the storm-tossed disciples crossing the sea, Jesus said, "Be of good cheer; it is I; be not afraid" (Matthew 14:27). The disciples discovered the joy of Christ's presence. For centuries, missionaries, as well as other Christians, have claimed the promise, "I am with you alway, even unto the end of the world" (Matthew 28:20). Are you acquainted with the joy of Christ's presence?

A pessimistic friend of mine defines an optimist as a person who has misty optics. And I might agree, were it not for this admonition from Jesus: "Be of good cheer; I have overcome the world" (John 16:33). Two relationships are described in that same verse: "in me ye might have peace" and "in the world ye shall have tribulation." Peace in Christ is God's intention for each believer, even in tribulation.

Acts 5:41 presents the disciples bruised and beaten, yet "rejoicing that they were counted worthy to suffer." They smiled through suffering and even grinned at death. They had joy despite suffering because they were assured of Christ's victory. To the Ephesian elders Paul spoke of his desire, "that I might finish my course with joy" (Acts 20:24). He had joy because he knew victory; and although he knew death was coming, he wanted to finish with the joy of victory.

The infant apostolic church is pictured as "praising God, and having favour with all the people" (Acts 2:47). Even the offering time, according to 2 Corinthians 9:7, was characterized by cheerful giving. The world *cheerful* in this verse can be translated "hilarious." If hilarity described their enthusiasm for the offering, can you imagine their exuberance when they had something really exciting?

Psalm 98 has the whole earth shouting for joy about the sovereignty of God. Faith in God's sovereignty results in holy joy. He is supreme! He is Lord! He shall reign! And miracle of miracles, we, through faith in Jesus Christ, are "labourers together with God" (1 Corinthians 3:9). That should give us real joy.

FAITH IN GOD'S SOVEREIGNTY RESULTS IN
HOLY JOY.

Monday—*Joy in righteousness (Psalm 98)*

¹O sing to the LORD a new song,
   For He has done wonderful things,
   His right hand and His holy arm have gained the victory for
      Him.
²The LORD has made known His salvation;
   He has revealed His righteousness in the sight of the nations.
³He has remembered His lovingkindness and His faithfulness
      to the house of Israel;
   All the ends of the earth have seen the salvation of our God.
⁴Shout joyfully to the LORD, all the earth;
   Break forth and sing for joy and sing praises.
⁵Sing praises to the LORD with the lyre;
   With the lyre and the sound of melody.
⁶With trumpets and the sound of the horn
   Shout joyfully before the King, the LORD.
⁷Let the sea roar and all it contains,
   The world and those who dwell in it.
⁸Let the rivers clap their hands;
   Let the mountains sing together for joy
⁹Before the LORD; for He is coming to judge the earth;
   He will judge the world with righteousness,
   And the peoples with equity.

Tuesday—*Joy in believing (Romans 15:7-13)*

⁷Wherefore, accept one another, just as Christ also accepted
us to the glory of God. ⁸For I say that Christ has become a
servant to the circumcision on behalf of the truth of God to
confirm the promises given to the fathers, ⁹and for the Gentiles
to glorify God for His mercy; as it is written,
"THEREFORE I WILL GIVE PRAISE TO THEE AMONG THE GENTILES,
      AND I WILL SING TO THY NAME."
¹⁰And again he says,
   "REJOICE, O GENTILES, WITH HIS PEOPLE."
¹¹And again,
   "PRAISE THE LORD ALL YOU GENTILES,
   AND LET ALL THE PEOPLES PRAISE HIM."
¹²And again Isaiah says,
   "THERE SHALL COME THE ROOT OF JESSE,
   AND HE WHO ARISES TO RULE OVER THE GENTILES;
   IN HIM SHALL THE GENTILES HOPE."

¹³Now may the God of hope fill you with all joy and peace in believing, that you may abound in hope by the power of the Holy Spirit.

Wednesday—*Joy in the Lord (Isaiah 12:1-6)*

¹Then you will say on that day,
  "I will give thanks to Thee, O Lord;
  For although Thou wast angry with me,
  Thine anger is turned away,
  And Thou dost comfort me,
²Behold, God is my salvation,
  I will trust and not be afraid;
  For the Lord God is my strength and song,
  And He has become my salvation."
³Therefore you will joyously draw water
  From the springs of salvation.
⁴And in that day you will say,
  "Give thanks to the Lord, call on His name.
  Make known His deeds among the peoples;
  Make them remember that His name is exalted."
⁵Praise the Lord in song, for He has done excellent things;
  Let this be known throughout the earth.
⁶Cry aloud and shout for joy, O inhabitant of Zion,
  For great in your midst is the Holy One of Israel.

Thursday—*Joy in giving (2 Corinthians 9:6-15)*

⁶Now this I say, he who sows sparingly shall also reap sparingly; and he who sows bountifully shall also reap bountifully. ⁷Let each one do just as he has purposed in his heart; not grudgingly or under compulsion; for God loves a cheerful giver. ⁸And God is able to make all grace abound to you, that always having all sufficiency in everything, you may have an abundance for every good deed; ⁹as it is written,

  "He scattered abroad, He gave to the poor,
  His righteousness abides forever."

¹⁰Now He who supplies seed to the sower and bread for food, will supply and multiply your seed for sowing and increase the harvest of your righteousness; ¹¹you will be enriched in everything for all liberality, which through us is producing thanksgiving to God. ¹²For the ministry of this service is not only fully supplying the needs of the saints, but is also overflowing

through many thanksgivings to God. [13]Because of the proof given by this ministry they will glorify God for your obedience to your confession of the gospel of Christ, and for the liberality of your contribution to them and to all, [14]while they also, by prayer on your behalf, yearn for you because of the surpassing grace of God in you. [15]Thanks be to God for his indescribable gift!

Friday—*Joy in worship (Psalm 100)*

[1]Shout joyfully to the LORD, all the earth.
[2]Serve the LORD with gladness;
Come before Him with joyful singing.
[3]Know that the LORD Himself is God;
It is He who has made us, and not we ourselves;
We are His people and the sheep of His pasture.
[4]Enter His gates with thanksgiving,
And His courts with praise.
Give thanks to Him; bless His name.
[5]For the LORD is good;
His lovingkindness is everlasting,
And His faithfulness to all generations.

Saturday—*Joy in Salvation (Colossians 1:9-14)*

[9]For this reason also, since the day we heard of it, we have not ceased to pray for you and to ask that you may be filled with the knowledge of His will in all spiritual wisdom and understanding, [10]so that you may walk in a manner worthy of the Lord, to please Him in all respects, bearing fruit in every good work and increasing in the knowledge of God; [11]strengthened with all power, according to His glorious might, for the attaining of all steadfastness and patience, joyously [12]giving thanks to the Father, who has qualified us to share in the inheritance of the saints in light. [13]For He delivered us from the domain of darkness, and transferred us to the kingdom of His beloved Son, [14]in whom we have redemption, the forgiveness of sins.

31

The Importance of Staying Power

Sunday—*Spiritual armor (Ephesians 6:10-17)*

[10]Finally, be strong in the Lord, and in the strength of His might. [11]Put on the full armor of God, that you may be able to stand firm against the schemes of the devil. [12]For our struggle is not against flesh and blood, but against the rulers, against the powers, against the world forces of this darkness, against the spiritual forces of wickedness in the heavenly places. [13]Therefore take up the full armor of God, that you may be able to resist in the evil day, and having done everything, to stand firm. [14]Stand firm therefore, HAVING GIRDED YOUR LOINS WITH TRUTH, and HAVING PUT ON THE BREASTPLATE OF RIGHTEOUSNESS, [15]and having shod YOUR FEET WITH THE PREPARATION OF THE GOSPEL OF PEACE; [16]in addition to all, taking up the shield of faith with which you will be able to extinguish all the flaming missiles of the evil one. [17]And take the helmet of salvation, and the sword of the Spirit, which is the word of God.

There is nothing in this world like old-fashioned dependability. Of the apostolic church, the Scripture says, "They continued stedfastly in the apostles' doctrine" (Acts 2:42). I like that. That excites me! Rain, storm, poverty, or persecution could not stop them. These Christians had *staying power.*

Staying power makes the difference in most of the experiences of life, not only for the missionary and pastor, but for the business person and homemaker as well. It does not require any superior intelligence to quit. Any fool can do that.

A person may have brains, talent, and other helpful traits, but if he does not have *staying power*, he accomplishes very little. In times of adversity, he wilts like a cut flower in the sun. To him the grass usually looks greener somewhere else, although it rarely is. Where we are is usually the place of greatest opportunity.

Many have found great strength and encouragement in the faithfulness of God. Most of us know that He is faithful. We sing, "Great is thy faithfulness" (Lamentations 3:23), and recite, "God is faithful" (1 Corinthians 1:9). It stands to reason that the more we as individuals come to know Him, the more we will possess and reflect His divine qualities, including faithfulness.

The apostle Paul reminds us, "It is required in stewards, that a man be found faithful" (1 Corinthians 4:2). Faithfulness is required, not merely recommended. God does not require us to be successful, but He does require us to be faithful.

Theologian John Calvin was afflicted with rheumatism, intense headaches, and a relatively weak body. Yet he preached, wrote books, and even governed Geneva, Switzerland, for nearly twenty-five years. He possessed an invisible and invincible determination. He was faithful.

We are told that when John Huss was arrested and informed that he would be burned to death for his faith, he purposely practiced holding his hand over fire as he prepared for his final test. He burned himself in preparation. He wanted to be faithful to the end.

Jesus said, "No man, having put his hand to the plough, and looking back, is fit for the kingdom of God" (Luke 9:62).

I once heard Bob Jones, Sr., say, "The greatest ability is dependability." I wonder what we really know about steadfastness and dependability. V. Raymond Edman often warned, "Don't doubt in the dark what God has revealed in the light." It is so easy to let go and give in as we pass through the painful, heartrending experiences of life.

When Christ was on the cross, the crowd cried out, "Save thyself, and come down from the cross" (Mark 15:30). It is human to let go and come down, but it is divine to hang there. And on many sides, we see people doing just that—coming down and quitting. But although it is human and quite natural to quit, it is divine to hang there. Jesus did, and set an example of faithfulness for us.

Repeatedly, we are told to be faithful, to "stand fast in the faith" (1 Corinthians 16:13) and "stand fast in the Lord" (Philippians 4:1), "earnestly contend for the faith" (Jude 3) and "be thou faithful unto death" (Revelation 2:10). Just about anyone can start well, but it is essential to end well. "Therefore, take up the full armor of God, that you may be able to resist in the evil day, and having done everything, to stand firm" (Ephesians 6:13, NASB).

Let us *keep on keeping on.*

IT IS HUMAN TO LET GO AND COME DOWN,
BUT IT IS DIVINE TO HANG THERE.

Monday—*Standing fast (Philippians 1:27-30)*

²⁷Only conduct yourselves in a manner worthy of the gospel of Christ; so that whether I come and see you or remain absent, I may hear of you that you are standing firm in one spirit, with one mind striving together for the faith of the gospel; ²⁸in no

way alarmed by your opponents—which is a sign of destruction for them, but of salvation for you, and that too, from God. ²⁹For to you it has been granted for Christ's sake, not only to believe in Him, but also to suffer for His sake, ³⁰experiencing the same conflict which you saw in me, and now hear to be in me.

Tuesday—*Being faithful (Matthew 24:45-51)*

⁴⁵"Who then is the faithful and sensible slave whom his master put in charge of his household to give them their food at the proper time? ⁴⁶Blessed is that slave whom his master finds so doing when he comes. ⁴⁷Truly I say to you, that he will put him in charge of all his possessions. ⁴⁸But if that evil slave says in his heart, 'My master is not coming for a long time,' ⁴⁹and shall begin to beat his fellow-slaves and eat and drink with drunkards; ⁵⁰the master of that slave will come on a day when he does not expect him and at an hour which he does not know, ⁵¹and shall cut him in pieces and assign him a place with the hypocrites; weeping shall be there and the gnashing of teeth."

Wednesday—*Patient waiting for the Lord (2 Thessalonians 3:1-5)*

¹Finally, brethren, pray for us that the word of the Lord may spread rapidly and be glorified, just as it did also with you; ²and that we may be delivered from perverse and evil men; for not all have faith. ³But the Lord is faithful, and He will strengthen and protect you from the evil one. ⁴And we have confidence in the Lord concerning you, that you are doing and will continue to do what we command. ⁵And may the Lord direct your hearts into the love of God and into the steadfastness of Christ.

Thursday—*David's song of deliverance (2 Samuel 22:20-25)*

²⁰"He also brought me forth into a broad place;
He rescued me, because He delighted in me.
²¹The LORD has rewarded me according to my righteousness;
According to the cleanness of my hands He has recompensed
me.
²²For I have kept the ways of the LORD,
And have not acted wickedly against my God.
²³For all His ordinances were before me;

And as for His statutes, I did not depart from them.
²⁴I was also blameless toward Him,
And I kept myself from my iniquity.
²⁵Therefore the LORD has recompensed me according to my
righteousness,
According to my cleanness before His eyes.

Friday—*Endurance from suffering (1 Peter 1:3-9)*

³Blessed by the God and Father of our Lord Jesus Christ, who according to His great mercy has caused us to be born again to a living hope through the resurrection of Jesus Christ from the dead, ⁴to obtain an inheritance which is imperishable and undefiled and will not fade away, reserved in heaven for you, ⁵who are protected by the power of God through faith for a salvation ready to be revealed in the last time. ⁶In this you greatly rejoice, even though now for a little while, if necessary, you have been distressed by various trials, ⁷that the proof of your faith, being more precious than gold which is perishable, even though tested by fire, may be found to result in praise and glory and honor at the revelation of Jesus Christ; ⁸and though you have not seen Him, you love Him and though you do not see Him now, but believe in Him, you greatly rejoice with joy inexpressible and full of glory, ⁹obtaining as the outcome of your faith the salvation of your souls.

Saturday—*Parable of the talents (Matthew 25:14-30)*

¹⁴"For it is just like a man about to go on a journey, who called his own slaves, and entrusted his possessions to them. ¹⁵And to one he gave five talents, to another, two, and to another, one, each according to his own ability; and he went on his journey. ¹⁶Immediately the one who had received the five talents went and traded with them, and gained five more talents. ¹⁷In the same manner the one who had received the two talents gained two more. ¹⁸But he who received the one talent went away and dug in the ground, and hid his master's money. ¹⁹Now after a long time the master of those slaves came and settled accounts with them. ²⁰And the one who had received the five talents came up and brought five more talents, saying, 'Master, you entrusted five talents to me; see, I have gained five more talents.' ²¹His master said to him 'Well done, good and faithful slave; you were faithful with a few things, I will put

193

you in charge of many things, enter into the joy of your master.' ²²The one also who had received the two talents came up and said, 'Master, you entrusted to me two talents; see, I have gained two more talents.' ²³His master said to him, 'Well done, good and faithful slave; you were faithful with a few things, I will put you in charge of many things; enter into the joy of your master.' ²⁴And the one also who had received the one talent came up and said, 'Master, I knew you to be a hard man, reaping where you did not sow, and gathering where you scattered no seed. ²⁵And I was afraid, and went away and hid your talent in the ground; see, you have what is yours.' ²⁶But his master answered and said to him, 'You wicked, lazy slave, you knew that I reap where I did not sow, and gather where I scattered no seed. ²⁷Then you ought to have put my money in the bank, and on my arrival I would have received my money back with interest. ²⁸Therefore take away the talent from him, and give it to the one who has the ten talents.' ²⁹For to everyone who has shall more be given, and he shall have an abundance; but from the one who does not have, even what he does have shall be taken away. ³⁰And cast out the worthless slave into the outer darkness; in that place there shall be weeping and gnashing of teeth.''

32

How Not to Be Happy

Sunday—*No happiness from power, wisdom, and knowledge (Ecclesiastes 1:12-18)*

¹²I, the Preacher, have been king over Israel in Jerusalem. ¹³And I set my mind to seek and explore by wisdom concerning all that has been done under heaven. It is a grievous task which God has given to the sons of men to be afflicted with. ¹⁴I have seen all the works which have been done under the sun, and behold, all is vanity and striving after wind. ¹⁵What is crooked cannot be straightened, and what is lacking cannot be counted. ¹⁶I said to myself, "Behold, I have magnified and increased wisdom more than all who were over Jerusalem before me; and my mind has observed a wealth of wisdom and knowledge." ¹⁷And I set my mind to know wisdom and to know madness and folly; I realized that this also is striving after wind. ¹⁸Because in much wisdom there is much grief, and increasing knowledge results in increasing pain.

Happiness is one of the chief goals of people. Everyone wants to be happy! The difficulty lies in deciding what happiness really is. What may bring happiness to the body may not bring happiness to the soul. What may give pleasure for the moment may be insignificant in eternity.

As I have studied the Bible, I have found that there are laws that govern a person's happiness. If one is to discover happiness, he cannot plan his life to include only happy times. Happiness, like beauty, is enhanced by contrast. No one would appreciate a Thanksgiving dinner if he ate turkey every day. Daily birthday parties would soon become boring. Happiness is deepened and enriched as it passes through heartache. A nut must be broken before its meat can be eaten. Often the situations that bring us the most happiness have also caused us the most suffering. Happiness is a by-product rather than the goal. Happiness is the bridesmaid, not the bride. It must be the result and not an end in itself! True happiness comes from fulfillment of duty and obedience to God's will.

If someone wrote a book titled *How Not to Be Happy*, it might become a best seller. Many people would buy it just out of curiosity!

Many years ago Solomon wrote such a book. Throughout his life Solomon searched for happiness but failed to find it. Becoming an authority on unhappiness, he wrote about it in the book of Ecclesiastes.

Ecclesiastes is an interesting account of one man's search for happiness. Written by Solomon in his later years, it describes the frustrations and failure he had encountered. He had looked for happiness in the same way men are seeking it today, and his results were just as empty.

He tried the *road of wisdom*. He became a philosopher, scientist, historian, poet, and songwriter. After intense searching, Solomon discovered that all that his knowledge had produced was vanity. In his words, "Much wisdom is much grief; and he that increaseth knowledge increaseth sorrow" (Ecclesiastes 1:18). Solomon did not say that wisdom is wrong, or that it is useless. He simply said that wisdom in itself is empty and unsatisfying.

Solomon also tried the road of wealth. He lived in a gold-plated palace and ate from solid gold dishes. The Scripture says that he "exceeded all the kings of the earth for riches" (1 Kings 10:23). And yet, when he looked at all his work and labor, he found that "all was vanity and vexation of spirit" (Ecclesiastes 2:11).

We find that Solomon also tried the road of pleasure. "I will prove thee with mirth, therefore enjoy pleasure: and, behold, this also is vanity" (Ecclesiastes 2:1). The so-called pleasures of life are all transitory and empty.

Where then, you may ask, is happiness found? Solomon finally found the answer. Happiness is found in a Person. "Remember now thy Creator in the days of thy youth" (Ecclesiastes 12:1) were his words.

That is what the hymn writer Philip Doddridge was speaking of when he wrote, "O happy day that fixed my choice on Thee, my Savior and my God!" Martin Luther realized this same happiness when he placed his faith in Jesus Christ. "I felt born again like a new man," said Luther. "I entered through the open doors into the very paradise of God." Happiness is found in knowing God in the person of Christ.

TRUE HAPPINESS COMES FROM FULFILLMENT OF DUTY AND OBEDIENCE TO GOD'S WILL.

Monday—*No happiness from labor (Ecclesiastes 2:22-26)*

22For what does a man get in all his labor and in his striving with which he labors under the sun? 23Because all his days his task is painful and grievous; even at night his mind does not rest. This too is vanity. 24There is nothing better for a man than to eat and drink and tell himself that his labor is good. This also I have seen, that it is from the hand of God. 25For who can eat and who can have enjoyment without Him? 26For to a person who is good in His sight He has given wisdom and knowledge and joy, while to the sinner He has given the task of gathering

197

and collecting so that He may give to one who is good in God's sight. This too is vanity and striving after wind.

Tuesday—*God greater than man (Ecclesiastes 3:10-14)*

[10]I have seen the task which God has given the sons of men with which to occupy themselves. [11]He has made everything appropriate in its time. He has also set eternity in their heart, yet so that man will not find out the work which God has done from the beginning even to the end. [12]I know that there is nothing better for them than to rejoice and to do good in one's lifetime, [13]moreover, that every man who eats and drinks sees good in all his labor—it is the gift of God. [14]I know that everything God does will remain forever; there is nothing to add to it and there is nothing to take from it, for God has so worked that men should fear Him.

Wednesday—*Life empty without God (Ecclesiastes 12:1-8)*

[1]Remember also your Creator in the days of your youth, before the evil days come and the years draw near when you will say, "I have no delight in them"; [2]before the sun, the light, the moon, and the stars are darkened, and clouds return after the rain; [3]in the day that the watchmen of the house tremble, and mighty men stoop, the grinding ones stand idle because they are few, and those who look through windows grow dim; [4]and the doors on the street are shut as the sound of the grinding mill is low, and one will arise at the sound of the bird, and all the daughters of song will sing softly. [5]Furthermore, men are afraid of a high place and of terrors on the road; the almond tree blossoms, the grasshopper drags himself along, and the caperberry is ineffective. For man goes to his eternal home while mourners go about in the street. [6]Remember Him before the silver cord is broken and the golden bowl is crushed, the pitcher by the well is shattered and the wheel at the cistern is crushed; [7]then the dust will return to the earth as it was, and the spirit will return to God who gave it. [8]"Vanity of vanities," says the Preacher, "all is vanity!"

Thursday—*The fear of the Lord as the beginning of wisdom (Proverbs 9:8-10)*

[8]Do not reprove a scoffer, lest he hate you,
Reprove a wise man, and he will love you.

⁹Give instruction to a wise man, and he will be still wiser,
   Teach a righteous man, and he will increase his learning.
¹⁰The fear of the LORD is the beginning of wisdom,
   And the knowledge of the Holy One is understanding.

Friday—*Evil as foolishness (Proverbs 14:22-27)*

²²Will they not go astray who devise evil?
   But kindness and truth will be to those who devise good.
²³In all labor there is profit,
   But more talk leads only to poverty.
²⁴The crown of the wise is their riches,
   But the folly of fools is foolishness.
²⁵A truthful witness saves lives,
   But he who speaks lies is treacherous.
²⁶In the fear of the LORD there is strong confidence,
   And his children will have refuge.
²⁷The fear of the LORD is a fountain of life,
   That one may avoid the snares of death.

Saturday—*Real happiness from the knowledge of God (Proverbs 15:13-17)*

¹³A joyful heart makes a cheerful face,
   But when the heart is sad, the spirit is broken.
¹⁴The mind of the intelligent seeks knowledge,
   But the mouth of fools feeds on folly.
¹⁵All the days of the afflicted are bad,
   But a cheerful heart has a continual feast.
¹⁶Better is a little with the fear of the LORD,
   Than great treasure and turmoil with it.
¹⁷Better is a dish of vegetables where love is,
   Than a fattened ox and hatred with it.

33

Rejoicing in Recession

Sunday—*Rejoicing in all things (Philippians 4:10-13)*
¹⁰But I rejoiced in the Lord greatly, that now at last you have revived your concern for me; indeed, you were concerned before, but you lacked opportunity. ¹¹Not that I speak from want; for I have learned to be content in whatever circumstances I am. ¹²I know how to get along with humble means, and I also know how to live in prosperity; in any and every circumstance I have learned the secret of being filled and going hungry, both of having abundance and suffering need. ¹³I can do all things through Him who strengthens me.

Some years almost sink us. At times we gasp for breath because of the pressures of life, such as runaway prices, the energy crisis, a shrinking dollar, and general worldwide recession. All of those things place considerable strain upon each of us. The hard places of life make us increasingly aware of the serious responsibility to be wise stewards of our resources. However, in spite of the pressures of life, we can join the Old Testament prophet Habakkuk and affirm, "Yet I will rejoice in the LORD" (Habakkuk 3:18).

Jesus also faced difficult days when He was here on earth. At that time the Roman emperor was the suspicious and cruel Tiberius Caesar. The governor of Judea was Pontius Pilate, the spineless wonder. Wicked Herod was tetrarch of Galilee, and Annas and Caiaphas, dishonest priests, led in religious matters. Yet in the midst of all this hypocrisy, Jesus gave thanks for at least four things.

First, Jesus gave thanks for *physical provisions*. He took a few loaves "and when he had given thanks" (John 6:11), He fed the multitude. So today, in the throes of worldwide need, we too can lift up our voices and give thanks to God for our physical blessings.

Jesus also gave thanks for *answered prayer*. At the grave of Lazarus, "Jesus lifted up his eyes, and said, Father, I thank thee that thou hast heard me" (John 11:41).

Each year the Moody Bible Institute graduates more than three hundred well-prepared young people determined to make a difference in our world by sharing the tried and proven gospel. All of this is possible because of answers to prayer. Have you enjoyed the blessings of answered prayer? Then give thanks to God.

Our Lord also gave thanks for *the revelation of God*. In Matthew 11:25, He said, "I thank thee, O Father, Lord of heaven and earth, because thou hast hid these things from the wise and prudent, and hast revealed them unto babes." We who have come to know Jesus Christ will want to thank God for the revelation of personal salvation. We thank God for the written revelation of Scripture.

But Jesus also gave thanks for *suffering*. At the Last Supper, "He took bread, and gave thanks, and broke it . . . saying, This is my body which is given for you" (Luke 22:19). The Christian experience at times involves difficulty and suffering. Yet thanksgiving is always right and appropriate. There is a purpose in our trials. In fact, James 1:2 encourages us to "count it all joy" when we experience times of turmoil. The Scriptures recommend "thankful joy" rather than "dull resignation." We are to rejoice in recession.

In a very difficult period in world history, Jesus gave thanks and so do we.

THE SCRIPTURES RECOMMEND "THANKFUL JOY" RATHER THAN "DULL RESIGNATION."

Monday—*God's provision (Psalm 104:10-17)*

¹⁰He sends forth springs in the valleys;
They flow between the mountains;
¹¹They give drink to every beast of the field;
The wild donkeys quench their thirst.
¹²Beside them the birds of the heavens dwell;
They lift up their voices among the branches.
¹³He waters the mountains from His upper chambers;
The earth is satisfied with the fruit of His words.
¹⁴He causes the grass to grow for the cattle,
And vegetation for the labor of man,
So that he may bring forth food from the earth,
¹⁵And wine which makes man's heart glad,
So that he may make his face glisten with oil,
And food which sustains man's heart.
¹⁶And trees of the LORD drink their fill,
The cedars of Lebanon which He planted,
¹⁷Where the birds build their nests,
And the stork, whose home is the fir trees.

Tuesday—*Prayer's effectiveness (James 5:16-18)*

¹⁶Therefore, confess your sins to one another, and pray for one another, so that you may be healed. The effective prayer of

a righteous man can accomplish much. ¹⁷Elijah was a man with a nature like ours, and he prayed earnestly that it might not rain; and it did not rain on the earth for three years and six months. ¹⁸And he prayed again, and the sky poured rain, and the earth produced its fruit.

Wednesday—*God's promise of triumph* (2 Corinthians 2:14-17)

¹⁴But thanks be to God, who always leads us in His triumph in Christ, and manifests through us the sweet aroma of the knowledge of Him in every place. ¹⁵For we are a fragrance of Christ to God among those who are being saved and among those who are perishing; ¹⁶to the one an aroma from death to death, to the other an aroma from life to life. And who is adequate for these things? ¹⁷For we are not like many, peddling the word of God, but as from sincerity, but as from God, we speak in Christ in the sight of God.

Thursday—*Victory through trials (2 Corinthians 6:1-10)*

¹And working together with Him, we also urge you not to receive the grace of God in vain— ²for He says,

"AT THE ACCEPTABLE TIME I LISTENED TO YOU,

AND ON THE DAY OF SALVATION I HELPED YOU";

behold, now is "THE ACCEPTABLE TIME," behold, now is "THE DAY OF SALVATION"— ³giving no cause for offense in anything, in order that the ministry be not discredited, ⁴but in everything commending ourselves as servants of God, in much endurance, in afflictions, in hardships, in distresses, ⁵in beatings, in imprisonments, in tumults, in labors, in sleeplessness, in hunger, ⁶in purity, in knowledge, in patience, in kindness, in the Holy Spirit, in genuine love, ⁷in the word of truth, in the power of God; by the weapons of righteousness for the right hand and the left, ⁸by glory and dishonor, by evil report and good report; regarded as deceivers and yet true; ⁹as unknown yet well-known, as dying yet behold, we live; as punished yet not put to death, ¹⁰as sorrowful yet always rejoicing, as poor yet making many rich, as having nothing yet possessing all things.

Friday—*Love for God's Word (Psalm 119:97-104)*

⁹⁷O how I love Thy law!
It is my meditation all the day.

[98]Thy commandments make me wiser than my enemies,
For they are ever mine.
[99]I have more insight than all my teachers,
For Thy testimonies are my meditation.
[100]I understand more than the aged,
Because I have observed Thy precepts.
[101]I have restrained my feet from every evil way,
That I may keep Thy word.
[102]I have not turned aside from Thine ordinances,
For Thou Thyself hast taught me.
[103]How sweet are Thy words to my taste!
Yes, sweeter than honey to my mouth!
[104]From Thy precepts I get understanding;
Therefore I hate every false way.

Saturday—*Suffering for righteousness' sake (1 Peter 3:14-17)*

[14]But even if you should suffer for the sake of righteousness, you are blessed. AND DO NOT FEAR THEIR INTIMIDATION, AND DO NOT BE TROUBLED, [15]but sanctify Christ as Lord in your hearts, always being ready to make a defense to every one who asks you to give an account for the hope that is in you, yet with gentleness and reverence; [16]and keep a good conscience so that in the thing in which you are slandered, those who revile your good behavior in Christ may be put to shame. [17]For it is better, if God should will it so, that you suffer for doing what is right rather than for doing what is wrong.

34

Be Patient

Sunday—*Patience because the Lord is compassionate*
         (James 5:7-11)

⁷Be patient, therefore, brethren, until the coming of the Lord. Behold, the farmer waits for the precious produce of the soil, being patient about it, until it gets the early and late rains. ⁸You too be patient; strengthen your hearts, for the coming of the Lord is at hand. ⁹Do not complain, brethren, against one another, that you yourselves may not be judged; behold, the Judge is standing right at the door. ¹⁰As an example, brethren, of suffering and patience, take the prophets who spoke in the name of the Lord. ¹¹Behold, we count those blessed who endured. You have heard of the endurance of Job and have seen the outcome of the Lord's dealings, that the Lord is full of compassion and is merciful.

Too many of us appear to be always impatient. We are not sure where we are going, but we are already ten minutes late.

Have you ever noticed that many evil things are done in a hurry? Jesus pointedly told Judas, "That thou doest, do quickly" (John 13:27). Satan offered Jesus the kingdoms of the world "if thou wilt fall down and worship me" (Matthew 4:9). Satan was really saying, "Forget the cross. I'll give you a shortcut to the kingdoms of the world—now—in a hurry!"

Impatience is related to selfishness. Our egos clamor for immediate attention. Whether we are waiting for an elevator, service in a restaurant, or the traffic light to change, self calls for instant service.

"Patience overcomes everything," says an ancient proverb. Another says, "The world is his, who has patience." Yet patience is rare in our day.

To the persecuted Christians of the first century, patience was not just commendable, it was indispensable. Because the *outlook* was dark, the apostle James urged them to try the *uplook*. "Be patient," he writes, "unto the coming of the Lord" (James 5:7).

Be patient, Christ is coming. To those scattered, persecuted Christians, the coming of Christ meant unbroken fellowship. All of life is really a series of separations. From the time a child toddles off to grade school, through high school, college, marriage, business, and even in death, we are always saying good-bye. But when the Lord comes, there will be no more good-byes.

These early believers were not only scattered, some were cheated (James 5:4), condemned, deprived of civil rights, and others were even murdered (James 5:6). How they were hindered. Even today many are hindered by fraud, fear, finances, fatigue; sickness, and even uncooperative or antagonistic loved ones and associates. Yet at the coming of the Lord, all hindrances will be banished forever.

Be patient, God is at work. James speaks of the patience

of the farmer as he waits for a harvest (5:7). The farmer plows, plants, cultivates, and then waits for the results.

To us, God is the Master Husbandman and we are His garden (1 Corinthians 3:9), purchased and planted by Him. Always remember, God is at work in our lives and He is not finished with us yet (Philippians 2:13).

Be patient, the Judge is at the door. Even the best judges of this world are partial and finite. But James 5:9 reminds us of a coming day when the all-knowing, everywhere present, infinite Judge will take things in hand. How sad to be groaning against fellow believers when He appears. We must not retaliate or seek revenge, for the Judge is at the door. The same blessed hope that can help us "take it" from an ungodly world can also empower us to get along with fellow believers.

Why should I be patient? First, because "the coming of the Lord draweth nigh" (James 5:8). Second, because God is at work. And third, because "the judge standeth before the door" (5:9).

THE SAME BLESSED HOPE THAT CAN HELP US "TAKE IT" FROM AN UNGODLY WORLD CAN ALSO EMPOWER US TO GET ALONG WITH FELLOW BELIEVERS.

Monday—*Temptation overcome by Jesus' patience (Matthew 4:1-10)*

¹Then Jesus was led up by the Spirit into the wilderness to be tempted by the devil. ²And after He had fasted forty days and forty nights, He then became hungry. ³And the tempter came and said to Him, "If You are the Son of God, command that these stones become bread." ⁴But He answered and said, "It is written, 'MAN SHALL NOT LIVE ON BREAD ALONE, BUT ON EVERY WORD THAT PROCEEDS OUT OF THE MOUTH OF GOD.'" ⁵Then the devil took Him into the holy city; and he stood Him on the pinnacle of the temple, ⁶and said to Him, "If You are the Son of God throw Yourself down; for it is written,

'HE WILL GIVE HIS ANGELS CHARGE CONCERNING YOU;

AND ON THEIR HANDS THEY WILL BEAR YOU UP,
LEST YOU STRIKE YOUR FOOT AGAINST A STONE.'"
⁷Jesus said to him, "On the other hand, it is written, 'YOU SHALL
NOT TEMPT THE LORD YOUR GOD.'" ⁸Again, the devil took Him
to a very high mountain, and showed Him all the kingdoms of
the world, and their glory; ⁹and he said to Him, "All these
things will I give You, if You fall down and worship me."
¹⁰Then Jesus said to him, "Begone, Satan! For it is written, 'YOU
SHALL WORSHIP THE LORD YOUR GOD, AND SERVE HIM ONLY.'"

Tuesday—*God working in you (Philippians 2:12-16)*

¹²So then, my beloved, just as you have always obeyed, not as
in my presence only, but now much more in my absence, work
out your salvation with fear and trembling; ¹³for it is God who
is at work in you, both to will and to work for His good pleasure. ¹⁴Do all things without grumbling or disputing; ¹⁵that you
may prove yourselves to be blameless and innocent, children of
God above reproach in the midst of a crooked and perverse
generation, among whom you appear as lights in the world,
¹⁶holding fast the word of life, so that in the day of Christ I may
have cause to glory because I did not run in vain nor toil in
vain.

Wednesday—*God to finish His work in you*
(Philippians 1:3-6)

³I thank my God in all my remembrance of you, ⁴always
offering prayer with joy in my every prayer for you all, ⁵in view
of your participation in the gospel from the first day until now.
⁶For I am confident of this very thing, that He who began a good
work in you will perfect it until the day of Christ Jesus.

Thursday—*God to bring a harvest of good works*
(Galatians 6:6-10)

⁶And let the one who is taught the word share all good things
with him who teaches. ⁷Do not be deceived, God is not mocked;
for whatever a man sows, this he will also reap. ⁸For the one
who sows to his own flesh shall from the flesh reap corruption,
but the one who sows to the Spirit shall from the Spirit reap
eternal life. ⁹And let us not lose heart in doing good, for in due
time we shall reap if we do not grow weary. ¹⁰So then, while we
have opportunity, let us do good to all men, and especially to
those who are of the household of the faith.

Friday—*Time and good soil needed to bear fruit*
** *(Luke 8:5-15)***

⁵"The sower went out to sow his seed; and as he sowed, some fell beside the road; and it was trampled under foot, and the birds of the air devoured it. ⁶And other seed fell on rocky soil, and as soon as it grew up, it withered away, because it had no moisture. ⁷And other seed fell among the thorns; and the thorns grew up with it, and choked it out. ⁸And other seed fell into the good ground, and grew up, and produced a crop a hundred times as great." As He said these things, He would call out, "He who has ears to hear, let him hear." ⁹And His disciples began questioning Him as to what this parable might be. ¹⁰And He said, "To you it is granted to know the mysteries of the kingdom of God, but to the rest it is in parables; in order that SEEING THEY MAY NOT SEE, AND HEARING THEY MAY NOT UNDERSTAND. ¹¹Now the parable is this: the seed is the word of God. ¹²And those beside the road are those who have heard; then the devil comes and takes away the word from their heart, so that they may not believe and be saved. ¹³And those on the rocky soil are those who, when they hear, receive the word with joy; and these have no firm root; they believe for a while, and in time of temptation fall away. ¹⁴And the seed which fell among the thorns, these are the ones who have heard, and as they go on their way they are choked with worries and riches and pleasures of this life, and bring no fruit to maturity. ¹⁵And the seed in the good ground, these are the ones who have heard the word in an honest and good heart, and hold it fast, and bear fruit with perseverance."

Saturday—*Prayer for patience (Colossians 1:9-12)*

⁹For this reason also, since the day we heard of it, we have not ceased to pray for you and to ask that you may be filled with the knowledge of His will in all spiritual wisdom and understanding, ¹⁰so that you may walk in a manner worthy of the Lord, to please Him in all respects, bearing fruit in every good work and increasing in the knowledge of God; ¹¹strengthened with all power, according to His glorious might, for the attaining of all steadfastness and patience, joyously ¹²giving thanks to the Father, who has qualified us to share in the inheritance of the saints in light.

35

Conquering Our Fears

Sunday—*The promise of deliverance (Psalm 34:1-7)*
¹I will bless the LORD at all times;
His praise shall continually be in my mouth.
²My soul shall make its boast in the LORD;
The humble shall hear it and rejoice.
³O magnify the LORD with me,
And let us exalt His name together.
⁴I sought the LORD, and He answered me,
And delivered me from all my fears.
⁵They looked to Him and were radiant,
And their faces shall never be ashamed.
⁶This poor man cried and the LORD heard him;
And saved him out of all his troubles.
⁷The angel of the LORD encamps around those who fear Him,
And rescues them.

Life should be an exciting adventure; yet for millions of people the adventure is haunted by fear.

What is fear? The dictionary defines it as a "painful emotion marked by alarm or dread or disquiet." Fear began in the Garden of Eden when Adam and Eve disobeyed God. It has shadowed each member of the human race ever since. We fear as babies, we fear as children, and the fears of our youth seem to multiply and hound us through adulthood and into old age.

But not all fear is bad. The Bible repeatedly tells us that the fear of the Lord is the beginning of wisdom. Do you have that kind of fear—a reverent respect and awe for God? Only those who do can expect to know Him and enjoy His blessings.

Faith in God is the key to overcoming disquieting fear. God holds the future. If we fear the future, we do not have faith. If we have faith, we cannot live in fear.

For years David was hounded by King Saul. But God's servant found help: "I sought the LORD, and he heard me, and delivered me from all my fears" (Psalm 34:4). David looked to the Lord and found relief.

Psychologists cite four basic fears. The comforting truth is that God, in His Word, provides the solution to each one.

The fear of want. "What if I lose my job?" you say. "What if I take a cut in salary or get sick and cannot work?" Are these legitimate fears? The Bible says no, because God is the great Provider (Psalm 37:25).

The fear of suffering. Suffering—the pain of body or spirit—may be for the glory of God. It may be for the accomplishing of His purposes, or it may be used to refine our character. Whatever the reason, we can trust the God who permits it, rest on His gracious provision, and leave the outcome totally in His hands.

The fear of failure. We fear failure because we rely on ourselves and not on the Lord. The first chapter of Joshua gives three good rules for success: go forward, trust God, and be guided by the Word of God. And then, God promises, "I will not fail thee" (v. 5).

211

The fear of death. This is the greatest fear of all, but Jesus says, "Because I live, ye shall live also" (John 14:19).

Christ came to deliver you and your loved ones from the fear of death. How? By dying in your place, that you and I might never have to know real death.

God does deliver us from a fear-filled world, and from all our personal fears, but only as we believe Him.

FAITH IN GOD IS THE KEY TO OVERCOMING DISQUIETING FEAR.

Monday—*God to provide (Psalm 37:23-29)*

23The steps of a man are established by the LORD;
And He delights in his way.
24When he falls, he shall not be hurled headlong;
Because the LORD is the One who holds his hand.
25I have been young, and now I am old;
Yet I have not seen the righteous forsaken,
Or his descendants begging bread.
26All day long he is gracious and lends;
And His descendants are a blessing.
27Depart from evil, and do good,
So you will abide forever.
28For the LORD loves justice,
And does not forsake His godly ones;
They are preserved forever;
But the descendants of the wicked will be cut off.
29The righteous will inherit the land,
And dwell in it forever.

Tuesday—*The promise of consolation (2 Corinthians 1:3-7)*

3Blessed be the God and Father of our Lord Jesus Christ, the Father of mercies and God of all comfort; 4who comforts us in all our affliction so that we may be able to comfort those who are in any affliction with the comfort with which we ourselves are comforted by God. 5For just as the sufferings of Christ are ours in abundance, so also our comfort is abundant through Christ. 6But if we are afflicted, it is for your comfort and salva-

212

tion; or if we are comforted, it is for your comfort, which is effective in the patient enduring of the same sufferings which we also suffer; 7and our hope for you is firmly grounded, knowing that as you are sharers of our sufferings, so also you are sharers of our comfort.

Wednesday—*God's deliverance (Psalm 40:1-4)*

1I waited patiently for the LORD;
And He inclined to me, and heard my cry.
2He brought me up out of the pit of destruction, out of the miry clay;
And He set my feet upon a rock making my footsteps firm.
3And He put a new song in my mouth, a song of praise to our God;
Many will see and fear,
And will trust in the LORD.
4How blessed is the man who has made the LORD his trust,
And has not turned to the proud, nor to those who lapse into falsehood.

Thursday—*The promise of success (Joshua 1:3-9)*

3"Every place on which the sole of your foot treads, I have given it to you, just as I spoke to Moses. 4From the wilderness and this Lebanon, even as far as the great river, the river Euphrates, all the land of the Hittites, and as far as the Great Sea toward the setting of the sun, will be your territory. 5No man will be able to stand before you all the days of your life. Just as I have been with Moses, I will be with you; I will not fail you or forsake you. 6Be strong and courageous, for you shall give this people possession of the land which I swore to their fathers to give them. 7Only be strong and very courageous, to be careful to do according to all the law which Moses My servant commanded you; do not turn from it to the right or to the left, so that you may have success wherever you go. 8This book of the law shall not depart from your mouth, but you shall meditate on it day and night, so that you may be careful to do according to all that is written in it; for then you will have success. 9Have I not commanded you? Be strong and courageous! Do not tremble or be dismayed, for the LORD your God is with you wherever you go."

213

Friday—*Heaven assured (John 14:1-3)*

[1]"Let not your heart be troubled; believe in God, believe also in Me. [2]In My Father's house are many dwelling places; if it were not so, I would have told you; for I go to prepare a place for you. [3]And if I go and prepare a place for you, I will come again, and receive you to Myself; that where I am, there you may be also."

Saturday—*Death conquered (1 Corinthians 15:53-58)*

[53]For this perishable must put on the imperishable, and this mortal must put on immortality. [54]But when this perishable will have put on the imperishable, and this mortal will have put on immortality, then will come about the saying that is written, "DEATH IS SWALLOWED UP IN VICTORY. [55]O DEATH, WHERE IS YOUR VICTORY? O DEATH, WHERE IS YOUR STING?" [56]The sting of death is sin, and the power of sin is the law; [57]but thanks be to God, who gives us the victory through our Lord Jesus Christ. [58]Therefore, my beloved brethren, be steadfast, immovable, always abounding in the work of the Lord, knowing that your toil is not in vain in the Lord.

36

Turning on the Power

Sunday—*Life by the Spirit (Galatians 5:15-21)*

[15]But if you bite and devour one another, take care lest you be consumed by one another. [16]But I say, walk by the Spirit, and you will not carry out the desire of the flesh. [17]For the flesh sets its desire against the Spirit, and the Spirit against the flesh; for these are in opposition to one another, so that you may not do the things that you please. [18]But if you are led by the Spirit, you are not under the Law. [19]Now the deeds of the flesh are evident, which are: immorality, impurity, sensuality, [20]idolatry, sorcery, enmities, strife, jealousy, outbursts of anger, disputes, dissensions, factions, [21]envyings, drunkenness, carousings, and things like these, of which I forewarn you just as I have forewarned you that those who practice such things shall not inherit the kingdom of God.

The real thing! That is what people are looking for today. Something genuine—not just talk, but reality.

Some people call our age "the plastic age." It is a time when many things are artificial. Unfortunately, that is often true of people as well as products.

How can we experience reality in our everyday living? Imagine, if you will, a brand-new factory filled with the finest modern equipment—everything that is needed to manufacture quality products.

Then suppose a visitor enters the factory and comments on the beauty of the machines but wonders why the machines are not running. No one is sure, he is told, "Why not oil the machines?" the man suggests. They do. But still nothing happens.

A little later another visitor comes in and comments on the splendid layout of the facilities. But there is no action. "I think you need some drapes and a few pictures on the wall," he says. So these are added. The place looks better, but still none of the equipment moves.

Other suggestions follow one by one—stained glass windows, an organ, even a steeple, but nothing works. The machinery still remains idle.

Finally, someone asks, "Did anyone turn on the power?"

Turn on the power? Of course, that's it! Sure enough, when the master control panels are switched on, the machines begin to roll. Soon the materials are fashioned and processed and the factory begins to produce.

"How simple," you say. You are absolutely right. But what the power was to that factory, the Holy Spirit is in the life of each believer. Just as the factory must have power to produce, so we need the Holy Spirit and the power He gives to live successfully in the Christian life.

Has the power been turned on in your life? Do you long for more spiritual power in your life? Do you wish you had more strength to resist temptation or to effectively share your faith in Jesus Christ with others? Are you filled with the Holy Spirit of God? Is God able to do His super-natural work through you?

What a revolutionary difference there was at Pentecost after the Holy Spirit was given. Men and women were transformed from doubting, stumbling, vacillating fol-lowers into radiant, eloquent proclaimers of the gospel.

A. W. Tozer used to say, "Although every believer has the Holy Spirit, the Holy Spirit does not have every be-liever."

D. L. Moody said, "I believe firmly that the moment our hearts are emptied of pride and selfishness and ambition and everything that is contrary to God's law, the Holy Spirit will fill every corner of our hearts. But if we are full of pride and conceit and ambition and the world, there is no room for the Spirit of God."

There must be an emptying before there can be a filling. Your life may be powerless because you have never given complete control to God's Spirit.

Why not turn on the power in your life today? Give the Holy Spirit of God complete control of your life, and you, too, can know His overwhelming power and leadership.

> THERE MUST BE AN EMPTYING BEFORE
> THERE CAN BE A FILLING.

Monday—*Fruit of the Spirit (Galatians 5:22-26)*

22But the fruit of the Spirit is love, joy, peace, patience, kind-ness, goodness, faithfulness, 23gentleness, self-control; against such things there is no law. 24Now those who belong to Christ Jesus have crucified the flesh with its passions and desires. 25If we live by the Spirit, let us also walk by the Spirit. 26Let us not become boastful, challenging one another, envying one another.

Tuesday—*Power of the Spirit and what it does (Romans 15:13-21)*

13Now may the God of hope fill you with all joy and peace in believing, that you may abound in hope by the power of the

Holy Spirit. ¹⁴And concerning you, my brethren, I myself also am convinced that you yourselves are full of goodness, filled with all knowledge, and able also to admonish one another, ¹⁵But I have written very boldly to you on some points, so as to remind you again, because of the grace that was given me from God, ¹⁶to be a minister of Christ Jesus to the Gentiles, ministering as a priest the gospel of God, that my offering of the Gentiles might become acceptable, sanctified by the Holy Spirit. ¹⁷Therefore in Christ Jesus I have found reason for boasting in things pertaining to God. ¹⁸For I will not presume to speak of anything except what Christ has accomplished through me, resulting in the obedience of the Gentiles by word and deed, ¹⁹in the power of signs and wonders, in the power of the Spirit; so that from Jerusalem and round about as far as Illyricum I have fully preached the gospel of Christ. ²⁰And thus I aspired to preach the gospel, not where Christ was already named, that I might not build upon another man's foundation; ²¹but as it is written,

"They who had no news of Him shall see,
And they who have not heard shall understand."

Wednesday—*The wise Spirit who teaches us* *(1 Corinthians 2:6-16)*

⁶Yet we do speak wisdom among those who are mature; a wisdom, however, not of this age, nor of the rulers of this age, who are passing away; ⁷but we speak God's wisdom in a mystery, the hidden wisdom, which God predestined before the ages to our glory; ⁸the wisdom which none of the rulers of this age has understood; for if they had understood it, they would not have crucified the Lord of glory; ⁹but just as it is written,

"Things which eye has not seen and ear has not heard,
And which have not entered the heart of man,
All that God has prepared for those who love Him."

¹⁰For to us God revealed them through the Spirit; for the Spirit searches all things, even the depths of God. ¹¹For who among men knows the thoughts of a man except the spirit of the man, which is in him? Even so the thoughts of God no one knows except the Spirit of God. ¹²Now we have received, not the spirit of the world, but the Spirit who is from God, that we might know the things freely given to us by God, ¹³which things we also speak, not in words taught by human wisdom, but in those

taught by the Spirit, combining spiritual thoughts with spiritual words. 14But a natural man does not accept the things of the Spirit of God; for they are foolishness to him, and he cannot understand them, because they are spiritually appraised. 15But he who is spiritual appraises all things, yet he himself is appraised by no man. 16For WHO HAS KNOWN THE MIND OF THE LORD, THAT HE SHOULD INSTRUCT HIM? But we have the mind of Christ.

Thursday—*Gifts from the Spirit to the church*
(1 Corinthians 12:3-11)

3Therefore I make known to you, that no one speaking by the Spirit of God says, "Jesus is accursed"; and no one can say, "Jesus is Lord," except by the Holy Spirit. 4Now there are varieties of gifts, but the same Spirit. 5And there are varieties of ministries, and the same Lord. 6And there are varieties of effects, but the same God who works all things in all persons. 7But to each one is given the manifestation of the Spirit for the common good. 8For to one is given the word of wisdom through the Spirit, and to another the word of knowledge according to the same Spirit; 9to another faith by the same Spirit, and to another gifts of healing by the one Spirit, 10and to another the effecting of miracles, and to another prophecy, and to another the distinguishing of spirits, to another various kinds of tongues, and to another the interpretation of tongues. 11But one and the same Spirit works all these things, distributing to each one individually just as He wills.

Friday—*Help in trouble from the Holy Spirit*
(Philippians 1:12-20)

12Now I want you to know, brethren, that my circumstances have turned out for the greater progress of the gospel, 13so that my imprisonment in the cause of Christ has become well-known throughout the whole praetorian guard and to everyone else, 14and that most of the brethren, trusting in the Lord because of my imprisonment, have far more courage to speak the word of God without fear. 15Some, to be sure, are preaching Christ even from envy and strife, but some also from good will; 16the latter do it out of love, knowing that I am appointed for the defense of the gospel; 17the former proclaim Christ out of selfish ambition, rather than from pure motives, thinking to cause me distress in my imprisonment. [18]What then? Only that in every way, whether in pretense or in truth, Christ is proclaimed; and in this I rejoice, yes, and I will rejoice. [19]For I know that this shall turn out for my deliverance through your prayers and the provision of the Spirit of Jesus Christ, [20]according to my earnest expectation and hope, that I shall not be put to shame in anything, but that with all boldness, Christ shall even now, as always, be exalted in my body, whether by life or by death.

Saturday—*Power of joy in the Spirit (1 Thessalonians 1:1-10)*

[1]Paul and Silvanus and Timothy to the church of the Thessalonians in God the Father and the Lord Jesus Christ: Grace to you and peace. [2]We give thanks to God always for all of you, making mention of you in our prayers; [3]constantly bearing in mind your work of faith and labor of love and steadfastness of hope in our Lord Jesus Christ in the presence of our God and Father; [4]knowing, brethren beloved by God, His choice of you, [5]for our gospel did not come to you in word only, but also in power and in the Holy Spirit and with full conviction; just as you know what kind of men we proved to be among you for your sake. [6]You also became imitators of us and of the Lord, having received the word in much tribulation with the joy of the Holy Spirit, [7]so that you became an example to all the believers in Macedonia and in Achaia. [8]For the word of the Lord has sounded forth from you, not only in Macedonia and Achaia, but also in every place your faith toward God has gone forth, so that we have no need to say anything. [9]For they themselves report about us what kind of a reception we had with you, and how you turned to God from idols to serve a living and true God, [10]and to wait for His Son from heaven, whom He raised from the dead, that is Jesus, who delivers us from the wrath to come.

37

How to Love

Sunday—*Great deeds without love*
          (1 Corinthians 12:31–13:3)

31But earnestly desire the greater gifts. And I show you a still more excellent way. 1If I speak with the tongues of men and of angels, but do not have love, I have become a noisy gong or a clanging cymbal. 2And if I have the gift of prophecy, and know all mysteries and all knowledge; and if I have all faith, so as to remove mountains, but do not have love, I am nothing. 3And if I give all my possessions to feed the poor, and if I deliver my body to be burned, but do not have love, it profits me nothing.

First Corinthians 13 tells us that without love, we are nothing. Is there anything less than nothing? A number of people have written to me and asked the practical question, How can I learn to love? Let me briefly share four steps in learning how to love.

Step one is to receive Jesus Christ as your Savior. God is the source of all love, for "God is love" (1 John 4:8). Christ is God's gift of love to us. Without a salvation experience, you will find real love impossible. Jesus said, "Except a man be born again, he cannot see the kingdom of God" (John 3:3); and unless you are born again, your cannot know real love.

Step two in understanding how to love is to experience the power of God's love in your life. Paul told the believers at Rome, "The love of God is shed abroad in our hearts by the Holy Ghost which is given unto us" (Romans 5:5).

Many people make the mistake of struggling to get the fruit of the Spirit without ever yielding themselves to the Holy Spirit Himself. Love is a fruit of the Spirit, and the one who would love must yield himself to the Holy Spirit and let God's love flow through him.

The natural man loves the praise of the people all around him, but the Spirit-filled person yearns for the praise of God. To know real fullness of love you must allow a change in your heart, a change of focus from self to Christ. That change comes from placing God's Holy Spirit in the driver's seat of your life. It results in God's love working in you and out to others through you.

In counseling young people all over the world, I have observed that the primary goals they are seeking are love, joy, and peace. Those are the three greatest pursuits. Isn't it interesting that the Bible tells us in Galatians 5:22, "The fruit of the Spirit is love, joy, peace"? The goals of our young people can be realized by yielding to the Holy Spirit.

Step three is consciously and subconsciously to "follow after [love]" (1 Corinthians 14:1). Pray for an abounding love. Paul wrote, "And this I pray, that your love may abound yet more and more in knowledge and in all judgment" (Philippians 1:9). The word "abound" suggests the sea waves as they roll in, overflowing in every direction. That kind of love gives freely of itself without seeking anything in return. Do you follow after that kind of love?

Step four is to begin to love by faith. You cannot produce real love by yourself. You must trust God to love through you.

Recently, a twenty-two-year-old girl came to me for counsel. As we talked, she poured out a story of hatred and bitterness toward her parents.

After sharing with her from God's Word, I was able to lead her to accept Christ as her personal Savior. Almost immediately she said, "I want to be reconciled with my parents, but how can I love them?"

"By faith," I replied. "Go home and believe that God will give you a new love for your mother and father. He can and He will." And God did.

> YOU MUST TRUST GOD TO LOVE THROUGH YOU.

Monday—*Characteristics of love (1 Corinthians 13:4-7)*
    [4]Love is patient, love is kind, and is not jealous; love does not brag and is not arrogant, [5]does not act unbecomingly; it does not seek its own, is not provoked, does not take into account a wrong suffered, [6]does not rejoice in unrighteousness, but rejoices with the truth; [7]bears all things, believes all things, hopes all things, endures all things.

Tuesday—*Love by sacrifice (1 John 3:16-19)*
    [16]We know love by this, that He laid down His life for us; and we ought to lay down our lives for the brethren. [17]But whoever has the world's goods, and beholds his brother in need and closes his heart against him, how does the love of God abide in him? [18]Little children, let us not love with word or with tongue,

223

but in deed and truth. [19]We shall know by this that we are of the truth, and shall assure our heart before Him.

Wednesday—*Love by abiding in love (1 John 4:16-21)*

[16]And we have come to know and have believed the love which God has for us. God is love, and the one who abides in love abides in God, and God abides in him. [17]By this, love is perfected with us, that we may have confidence in the day of judgment; because as He is, so also are we in this world. [18]There is no fear in love; but perfect love casts out fear, because fear involves punishment, and the one who fears is not perfected in love. [19]We love, because He first loved us. [20]If some one says, "I love God," and hates his brother, he is a liar; for the one who does not love his brother whom he has seen, cannot love God whom he has not seen. [21]And this commandment we have from Him, that the one who loves God should love his brother also.

Thursday—*Love by sharing in other's struggles (Philippians 1:7-11)*

[7]For it is only right for me to feel this way about you all, because I have you in my heart, since both in my imprisonment and in the defense and confirmation of the gospel, you all are partakers of grace with me. [8]For God is my witness, how I long for you all with the affection of Christ Jesus. [9]And this I pray, that your love may abound still more and more in real knowledge and all discernment, [10]so that you may approve the things that are excellent, in order to be sincere and blameless until the day of Christ; [11]having been filled with the fruit of righteousness which comes through Jesus Christ, to the glory and praise of God.

Friday—*Love instead of bad deeds (Leviticus 19:11-18)*

[11]You shall not steal, nor deal falsely, nor lie to one another. [12]And you shall not swear falsely by My name, so as to profane the name of your God; I am the LORD. [13]You shall not oppress your neighbor, nor rob him. The wages of a hired man are not to remain with you all night until morning. [14]You shall not curse a deaf man, nor place a stumbling block before the blind, but you shall revere your God; I am the LORD. [15]You shall do no injustice in judgment; you shall not be partial to the poor nor

defer to the great, but you are to judge your neighbor fairly. ¹⁶You shall not go about as a slanderer among your people, and you are not to act against the life of your neighbor; I am the LORD. ¹⁷You shall not hate your fellow-countryman in your heart; you may surely reprove your neighbor, but shall not incur sin because of him. ¹⁸You shall not take vengeance, nor bear any grudge against the sons of your people, but you shall love your neighbor as yourself; I am the LORD.

Saturday—*God's love reflected in unselfish deeds* *(Luke 7:27-36)*

²⁷"This is the one about whom it is written,

'BEHOLD, I SEND MY MESSENGER BEFORE YOUR FACE,

WHO WILL PREPARE YOUR WAY BEFORE YOU.'

²⁸I say to you, among those born of women, there is no one greater than John; yet he who is least in the kingdom of God is greater than he." ²⁹And when all the people and the tax-gatherers heard this, they acknowledged God's justice, having been baptized with the baptism of John. ³⁰But the Pharisees and the lawyers rejected God's purpose for themselves, not having been baptized by John. ³¹"To what then shall I compare the men of this generation, and what are they like? ³²They are like children who sit in the market place and call to one another; and they say, 'We played the flute for you, and you did not dance; we sang a dirge, and you did not weep.' ³³For John the Baptist has come eating no bread and drinking no wine; and you say, 'He has a demon!' ³⁴The Son of Man has come eating and drinking; and you say, 'Behold, a gluttonous man, and a drunkard, a friend of tax-gatherers and sinners!' ³⁵Yet wisdom is vindicated by all her children." ³⁶Now one of the Pharisees was requesting Him to dine with him. And He entered the Pharisee's house, and reclined at table.

38

What Is Prayer?

Sunday—*Faithful prayer for a need (Luke 18:1-7)*
¹Now He was telling them a parable to show that at all times they ought to pray and not to lose heart, ²saying, "There was in a certain city a judge who did not fear God, and did not respect man. ³And there was a widow in that city, and she kept coming to him, saying, 'Give me legal protection from my opponent.' ⁴And for a while he was unwilling; but afterward he said to himself, 'Even though I do not fear God nor respect man, ⁵yet because this widow bothers me, I will give her legal protection, lest by continually coming she wear me out.' " ⁶And the Lord said, "Hear what the unrighteous judge said; ⁷now shall not God bring about justice for His elect, who cry to Him day and night, and will He delay long over them?"

As I was sitting in my study reviewing the ministry, I asked the question, "What is the greatest need of the church today?" Our primary need is not for better plans. Our basic need is not for more workers or even for more money. Our fundamental need is for Christlike intercessors. Church history shows that divine power and prayer are inseparable. God must wonder at the paucity of our prayer.

A startling statement is made in Isaiah 59:16. The verse pictures our great God as wondering why there is a lack of prayer. "And he saw that there was no man, and wondered that there was no intercessor." Great prominence was given to prayer in the life of Jesus. In the light of His example, we can understand why God should wonder at our prayerlessness.

What is prayer? At times prayer may be a weak gasp while at other times it is worship, adoration, communion, and supplication. The simplest definition of prayer is found in the three-letter word cry. Prayer is a cry. As a newborn child spontaneously cries out, so the believer in Jesus Christ cries out instinctively to the heavenly Father. Paul writes, "Because ye are sons, God hath sent forth the Spirit of his Son into your hearts, crying, Abba, Father" (Galatians 4:6).

Jesus plainly told us that "men ought always to pray, and not to faint" (Luke 18:1). In view of His direct, explicit command, it is understandable that God should wonder at the lack of intercessors.

On one occasion the psalmist said, "I give myself unto prayer" (Psalm 109:4). I wonder if we know anything about giving ourselves to prayer.

Jesus taught that we should pray in humility (Luke 18:9-14). He also instructed us to pray in His name. "Whatsoever ye shall ask in my name, that will I do" (John 14:13). His name represents all that He is. We are also taught to pray in faith (Mark 11:24). In fact, "without faith it is impossible to please him" (Hebrews 11:6).

Prayer is the key that opens the door to God's treasure-house. "Ask, and it shall be given you; seek, and ye shall find; knock, and it shall be opened unto you" (Matthew 7:7). Regardless of one's need, there is abundant fullness in Jesus Christ. In the light of all the great promises of God and in view of the character of God, we can understand why God should wonder at the tragic neglect of prayer.

Prayer is not easy. In fact, it is extremely difficult. Richard Newton once said, "The principal cause of my leanness and unfruitfulness is owing to an unaccountable backwardness to pray. I can write or read or converse or hear with a ready heart; but prayer is more spiritual and inward than any of these, and the more spiritual any duty is the more my carnal heart is apt to start from it."

Martin Luther attributed the success of his ministry to the place of prayer. "I judge that my prayer is more than the devil himself. If it were otherwise I would have fared differently long before this. Yet men will not see and acknowledge the great wonders or miracles God works in my behalf. If I should neglect prayer but a single day, I should lose a great deal of the fire of faith."

Prayer is a gracious privilege; it is a glorious calling. But prayer is also a sacred responsibility. In fact, neglect of prayer is disobedience to God. May each of us in a new way determine to be Christlike intercessors.

> PRAYER IS THE KEY THAT OPENS THE DOOR
> TO GOD'S TREASURE-HOUSE.

Monday—*Right attitude for prayer (Luke 18:9-14)*

9And He also told this parable to certain ones who trusted in themselves that they were righteous, and viewed others with contempt: 10"Two men went up into the temple to pray, one a Pharisee, and the other a tax-gatherer. 11The Pharisee stood and was praying thus to himself, 'God, I thank Thee that I am not like other people, swindlers, unjust, adulterers, or even like this tax-gatherer. 12I fast twice a week; I pay tithes of all that I get.' ¹³But the tax-gatherer, standing some distance away, was even unwilling to lift up his eyes to heaven, but was beating his breast, saying, 'God, bc merciful to me, the sinner!'' ¹⁴I tell you, this man went down to his house justified rather than the other; for every one who exalts himself shall be humbled, but he who humbles himself shall be exalted.''

Tuesday—*Jesus' answer to a cry for help (Luke 18:35-43)*

³⁵And it came about that as He was approaching Jericho, a certain blind man was sitting by the road, begging. ³⁶Now hearing a multitude going by, he began to inquire what this might be. ³⁷And they told him that Jesus of Nazareth was passing by. ³⁸And he called out, saying, "Jesus, Son of David, have mercy on me!" ³⁹And those who led the way were sternly telling him to be quiet; but he kept crying out all the more, "Son of David, have mercy on me!" ⁴⁰And Jesus stopped and commanded that he be brought to Him; and when he had come near, He questioned him, ⁴¹"What do you want Me to do for you?" And he said, "Lord, I want to receive my sight!" ⁴²And Jesus said to him, "Receive your sight; your faith has made you well." ⁴³And immediately he received his sight, and began following Him, glorifying God; and when all the people saw it, they gave praise to God.

Wednesday—*Results from prayer in faith (Mark 11:23-25)*

²³"Truly I say to you, whoever says to this mountain, 'Be taken up and cast into the sea,' and does not doubt in his heart, but believes that what he says is going to happen; it shall be granted him. ²⁴Therefore I say to you, all things for which you pray and ask, believe that you have received them, and they shall be granted you. ²⁵And whenever you stand praying, forgive, if you have anything against anyone; so that your Father also who is in heaven may forgive you your transgressions."

Thursday—*The Father answering His children's requests (Matthew 7:7-11)*

⁷"Ask, and it shall be given to you; seek, and you shall find; knock, and it shall be opened to you. ⁸For every one who asks receives; and he who seeks finds; and to him who knocks it shall be opened. ⁹Or what man is there among you, when his son shall ask him for a loaf, will give him a stone? ¹⁰Or if he

shall ask for a fish, he will not give him a snake, will he? ¹¹If
you then, being evil, know how to give good gifts to your children, how much more shall your Father who is in heaven give
what is good to those who ask Him!"

Friday—*An example of prayer (Luke 10:1-4)*
¹Now after this the Lord appointed seventy others, and sent
them two and two ahead of Him to every city and place where
He himself was going to come. ²And He was saying to them,
"The harvest is plentiful, but the laborers are few; therefore
beseech the Lord of the harvest to send out laborers into His
harvest. ³Go your ways; behold, I sent you out as lambs in the
midst of wolves. ⁴Carry no purse, no bag, no shoes; and greet no
one on the way.

Saturday—*Talking to God in the morning (Psalm 5:1-3)*
¹Give ear to my words, O LORD,
Consider my groaning.
²Heed the sound of my cry for help, my King and my God,
For to Thee do I pray.
³In the morning, O LORD, Thou wilt hear my voice;
In the morning I will order my prayer to Thee and eagerly
watch.

39

Prayer Changes Things

Sunday—*Peace in the midst of danger (Acts 12:1-6)*

¹Now about that time Herod the king laid hands on some who belonged to the church, in order to mistreat them. ²And he had James the brother of John put to death with a sword. ³And when he saw that it pleased the Jews, he proceeded to arrest Peter also. Now it was during the days of the Feast of Unleavened Bread. ⁴And when he had seized him, he put him in prison, delivering him to four squads of soldiers to guard him, intending after the Passover to bring him out before the people. ⁵So Peter was kept in the prison, but prayer for him was being made fervently by the church to God. ⁶And on the very night when Herod was about to bring him forward, Peter was sleeping between two soldiers, bound with two chains; and guards in front of the door were watching over the prison.

"More things are wrought by prayer," said Alfred Lord Tennyson, "than this world dreams of."

That is true. Prayer unlocks the door to God's supply. It is the link that unites our wills with God's will.

Acts 12 illustrates prayer in action. Since the conversion of Saul, the first-century church at Jerusalem had enjoyed relief from persecution. In fact, things were so good that the Christians had become soft; they were spoiled and out of shape.

Then God in His divine plan permitted Herod to kill James, the brother of John. What a shock to the early church! And later when Peter was cast into prison, Luke tells us, "Prayer was made without ceasing by the church unto God for him" (Acts 12:5).

Their prayers became intense and insistent; they did not let up. As heat rises, so does earnest, fervent prayer ascend to God. God heard them, and in answer to their prayers, He performed a miracle the night before Herod intended to kill Peter.

In Acts 12:6 we read that Peter was sleeping between two soldiers in prison—sleeping even though he had been condemned by Herod to be beheaded. Peter trusted toally in God.

Peter's condition was hopeless from the human point of view. He was bound with chains, secured between two soldiers. Guards were by the door, and an iron gate barred the way to his inner cell. He could not escape.

But God takes great difficulties and makes great victories. Circumstances may look impossible, but God is supreme.

The believers were praying without ceasing, and God answered. An angel of the Lord came to Peter, "and a light shined in the prison: and he smote Peter on the side, and raised him up, saying, Arise up quickly. And his chains fell off from his hands" (Acts 12:7).

God's resources are endless. He does not need weapons. He does not need keys to unlock doors. He has legions of angels anxious to do His will. God is able.

232

When Peter arrived at the prayer meeting, a young girl named Rhoda answered his knock. Recognizing Peter's voice, she neglected to let him in but joyfully ran back and broke up the prayer service.

"Peter is waiting outside," she cried.

"Rhoda, you're out of your mind," they said.

But Rhoda insisted. "Peter is there. See for yourself."

When Peter was delivered from prison, the saints were overcome with joy. Prayer has a double effect. It blesses the one prayed for and the one who prays.

Prayer changes things. And prayer changes people! Are you praying? Do you avail yourself of this unlimited resource?

CIRCUMSTANCES MAY LOOK IMPOSSIBLE,
BUT GOD IS SUPREME.

Monday—*Prison doors opened by prayer (Acts 12:7-12)*

7And behold, an angel of the Lord suddenly appeared, and a light shone in the cell; and he struck Peter's side and roused him, saying, "Get up quickly." And his chains fell off his hands. 8And the angel said to him, "Gird yourself and put on your sandals." And he did so. And he said to him, "Wrap your cloak around you and follow me." 9And he went out and continued to follow, and he did not know that what was being done by the angel was real, but thought he was seeing a vision. 10And when they had passed the first and second guard, they came to the iron gate that leads into the city, which opened for them by itself; and they went out and went along one street; and immediately the angel departed from him. 11And when Peter came to himself, he said, "Now I know for sure that the Lord has sent forth His angel and rescued me from the hand of Herod and from all that the Jewish people were expecting." 12And when he realized this, he went to the house of Mary, the mother of John who was also called Mary, where many were gathered together and were praying.

Tuesday—*Prayer meeting interruped by an answer (Acts 12:13-19)*

¹³And when he knocked at the door of the gate, a servant-girl named Rhoda came to answer. ¹⁴And when she recognized Peter's voice, because of her joy she did not open the gate, but ran in and announced that Peter was standing in front of the gate. ¹⁵And they said to her, "You are out of your mind!" But she kept insisting that it was so. And they kept saying, "It is his angel." ¹⁶But Peter continued knocking; and when they had opened, they saw him and were amazed. ¹⁷But motioning to them with his hand to be silent, he described to them how the Lord had led him out of the prison. And he said, "Report these things to James and the brethren." And he departed and went to another place. ¹⁸Now when day came, there was no small disturbance among the soldiers as to what could have become of Peter. ¹⁹And when Herod had searched for him and had not found him, he examined the guards and ordered that they be led away to execution. And he went down from Judea to Caesarea and was spending time there.

Wednesday—*A need for prayer (1 Samuel 1:1-9)*

¹Now there was a certain man from Ramathaim-zophim from the hill country of Ephraim, and his name was Elkanah the son of Jeroham, the son of Elihu, the son of Tohu, the son of Zuph, an Ephraimite. ²And he had two wives: the name of one was Hannah and the name of the other Peninnah; and Peninnah had children, but Hannah had no children. ³Now this man would go up from his city yearly to worship and to sacrifice to the LORD of hosts in Shiloh. And the two sons of Eli, Hophni and Phinehas were priests to the LORD there. ⁴And when the day came that Elkanah sacrificed, he would give portions to Peninnah his wife and to all her sons and her daughters; ⁵but to Hannah he would give a double portion, for he loved Hannah, but the LORD had closed her womb. ⁶Her rival, however, would provoke her bitterly to irritate her, because the LORD had closed her womb. ⁷And it happened year after year, as often as she went up to the house of the LORD, she would provoke her, so she wept and would not eat. ⁸Then Elkanah her husband said to her, "Hannah, why do you weep and why do you not eat and why is your heart sad? Am I not better to you than ten sons?" ⁹Then Hannah rose after eating and drinking in Shiloh. Now Eli

the priest was sitting on the seat by the doorpost of the temple of the LORD.

Thursday—*Prayer from a distressed woman* *(1 Samuel 1:10-18)*

¹⁰And she, greatly distressed, prayed to the LORD and wept bitterly. ¹¹And she made a vow and said, O LORD of hosts, if Thou wilt indeed look on the affliction of Thy maidservant and remember me, and not forget Thy maidservant, but wilt give Thy maidservant a son, then I will give him to the LORD all the days of his life, and a razor shall never come on his head." ¹²Now it came about, as she continued praying before the LORD, that Eli was watching her mouth. ¹³As for Hannah, she was speaking in her heart, only her lips were moving, but her voice was not heard. So Eli thought she was drunk. ¹⁴Then Eli said to her, "How long will you make yourself drunk? Put away your wine from you." ¹⁵But Hannah answered and said, "No, my lord, I am a woman oppressed in spirit; I have drunk neither wine nor strong drink, but I have poured out my soul before the LORD. ¹⁶Do not consider your maidservant as a worthless woman; for I have spoken until now out of my great concern and provocation." ¹⁷Then Eli answered and said, "Go in peace; and may the God of Israel grant your petition that you have asked of Him." ¹⁸And she said, "Let your maidservant find favor in your sight." So the women went her way and ate, and her face was no longer sad.

Friday—*A son given in answer to prayer (1 Samuel 1:19-28)*

¹⁹Then they arose early in the morning and worshiped before the LORD, and returned again to their house in Ramah. And Elkanah had relations with Hannah his wife, and the LORD remembered her. ²⁰And it came about in due time, after Hannah had conceived, that she gave birth to a son; and she named him Samuel, saying, "Because I have asked him of the LORD." ²¹Then the man Elkanah went up with all his household to offer the the LORD the yearly sacrifice and pay his vow. ²²But Hannah did not go up, for she said to her husband, "I will not go up until the child is weaned; then I will bring him, that he may appear before the LORD and stay there forever." ²³And Elkanah her husband said to her, "Do what seems best to you. Remain until you have weaned him; only may the LORD confirm His

word." So the woman remained and nursed her son until she weaned him. ²⁴Now when she had weaned him, she took him up with her, with a three-year-old bull and one ephah of flour and a jug of wine, and brought him to the house of the LORD in Shiloh, although the child was young. ²⁵Then they slaughtered the bull, and brought the boy to Eli. ²⁶And she said, "Oh, my lord! As your soul lives, my lord, I am the woman who stood here beside you, praying to the LORD. ²⁷For this boy I prayed, and the LORD has given me my petition which I asked of Him. ²⁸So I have also dedicated him to the LORD; as long as he lives he is dedicated to the LORD." And he worshiped the LORD there.

Saturday—*Results gained by persistent prayer* *(Luke 11:5-10)*

⁵And He said to them, "Suppose one of you shall have a friend, and shall go to him at midnight, and say to him, 'Friend, lend me three loaves; ⁶for a friend of mine has come to me from a journey, and I have nothing to set before him'; ⁷and from inside he shall answer and say, 'Do not bother me; the door has already been shut and my children and I are in bed; I cannot get up and give you anything.' ⁸I tell you, even though he will not get up and give him anything because he is his friend, yet because of his persistence he will get up and give him as much as he needs. ⁹And I say to you, ask, and it shall be given to you; seek, and you shall find; knock, and it shall be opened to you. ¹⁰For everyone who asks, receives; and he who seeks, finds; and to him who knocks, it shall be opened."

40

Tapping Our Power Source

Sunday—*Humble Christians wanted by God (James 4:5-10)*

⁵Or do you think that the Scripture speaks to no purpose: "He jealously desires the Spirit which He has made to dwell in us"? ⁶But He gives a greater grace. Therefore it says, "GOD IS OPPOSED TO THE PROUD, BUT GIVES GRACE TO THE HUMBLE." ⁷Submit therefore to God. Resist the devil and he will flee from you. ⁸Draw near to God and He will draw near to you. Cleanse your hands, you sinners; and purify your hearts, you double-minded. ⁹Be miserable and mourn and weep: let your laughter be turned into mourning, and your joy to gloom. ¹⁰Humble yourselves in the presence of the Lord, and He will exalt you.

I believe deeply in the power of prayer. Time after time I have asked friends to pray with me about a pressing need or some unusual opportunity, only to be startled by the speed of God's answer.

There are many strong promises in the Bible for prayer partners. God has promised us, "If two of you shall agree on earth as touching any thing that they shall ask, it shall be done for them. . . . where two or three are gathered together in my name, there am I in the midst of them" (Matthew 18:19-20). In the light of promises like those, we can hardly afford to neglect praying together.

Most Christians are aware of the need for prayer with others and that we should pray, but we are not sure how. We find it awkward to pray and to know what to pray for. Here are a few suggestions for all of us:

First, we need to pray with Hosea that God will "break up [our] fallow ground: for it is time to seek the LORD" (Hosea 10:12). Fallow ground is dry, hard, and unproductive soil. Prayer helps us to examine ourselves and see fallow ground in our lives that needs to be broken up. Self-examination on our part is basic to blessing. As long as we are unbroken, unresponsive, and unforgiving, we will be unproductive. As believers in Jesus Christ, we need to pray with Elihu, "If I have done iniquity, I will do no more" (Job 34:32). May we ask God for a genuine spiritual awakening, beginning in our own hearts. To be really effective in prayer, we should be definite.

Second, we need to pray for the full control of the indwelling Holy Spirit in our lives. God, through Zechariah, said, "Not by might, nor by power, but by my spirit, saith the LORD of hosts" (Zechariah 4:6). We need to remember that God's work is just that, His work. He will not be hampered by self-reliant people. Success is not based upon shrewdness or our ability, but on God's ability. Complete reliance upon the Holy Spirit of God is the only way of blessing.

Third, every born-again believer has the serious and solemn responsibility to pray for the leaders of our world. The Bible clearly tells us to pray "for kings, and for all that are in authority" (1 Timothy 2:2).

Daniel 4:17 reminds us that "the most High ruleth in the kingdom of men, and giveth it to whomsoever he will, and setteth up over it the basest of men." Good men and bad men have played their part in history in accordance with God's sovereign purpose. Let us pray for our President, regardless of our agreement or disagreement with his policies or conduct. We should pray that he will be "filled with the knowledge of [God's] will in all wisdom and spiritual understanding" (Colossians 1:9). Let us pray that God will guide our world leaders in those areas that will permit believers to lead "quiet and peaceable [lives] in all godliness and honesty" (1 Timothy 2:2).

Finally, let us pray with Habakkuk, "O LORD, revive thy work in the midst of the years . . . in wrath remember mercy" (Habakkuk 3:2). We need to be revived, don't we? If we seek God together with our fellow believers, He has promised to hear and answer our prayers. Will we claim His promise? Why not find a fellow Christian and pray together for these things this week.

SELF-EXAMINATION ON OUR PART IS BASIC
TO BLESSING.

Monday—*Prayer of confession (Psalm 51)*

[1]Be gracious to me, O God, according to Thy lovingkindness;
  According to the greatness of Thy compassion blot out my
      transgressions.
[2]Wash me thoroughly from my iniquity,
  And cleanse me from my sin.
[3]For I know my transgressions,
  And my sin is ever before me.
[4]Against Thee, Thee only, I have sinned,
  And done what is evil in Thy sight,
  So that Thou art justified when Thou dost speak,
  And blameless when Thou dost judge.
[5]Behold, I was brought forth in iniquity,
  And in sin my mother conceived me.
[6]Behold, Thou dost desire truth in the innermost being,

239

And in the hidden part Thou wilt make me know wisdom.
⁷Purify me with hyssop, and I shall be clean;
Wash me, and I shall be whiter than snow.
⁸Make me to hear joy and gladness,
Let the bones which Thou hast broken rejoice.
⁹Hide Thy face from my sins,
And blot out all my iniquities.
¹⁰Create in me a clean heart, O God,
And renew a steadfast spirit within me.
¹¹Do not cast me away from Thy presence,
And do not take Thy Holy Spirit from me.
¹²Restore to me the joy of Thy salvation,
And sustain me with a willing spirit.
¹³Then I will teach transgressors Thy ways,
And sinners will be converted to Thee.
¹⁴Deliver me from bloodguiltiness, O God, Thou God of my
salvation;
Then my tongue will joyfully sing of Thy righteousness.
¹⁵O LORD, open my lips,
That my mouth may declare Thy praise.
¹⁶For Thou dost not delight in sacrifice, otherwise I would give
it;
Thou are not pleased with burnt offering.
¹⁷The sacrifices of God are a broken spirit;
A broken and a contrite heart, O God, Thou wilt not despise.
¹⁸By Thy favor do good to Zion;
Build the walls of Jerusalem.
¹⁹Then Thou wilt delight in righteous sacrifices,
In burnt offering and whole burnt offering;
Then young bulls will be offered on Thine altar.

Tuesday—*Prayer in secret place (Matthew 6:5-8)*

⁵"And when you pray, you are not to be as the hypocrites; for they love to stand and pray in the synagogues and on the street corners, in order to be seen by men. Truly I say to you, they have their reward in full. ⁶But you, when you pray, GO INTO YOUR INNER ROOM, AND WHEN YOU HAVE SHUT YOUR DOOR, pray to your Father who is in secret, and your Father who sees in secret will repay you. ⁷And when you are praying, do not use meaningless repetition, as the Gentiles do, for they suppose that they will be heard for their many words. ⁸Therefore do not

be like them; for your Father knows what you need, before you ask Him.

Wednesday—*Prayer for our leaders (1 Timothy 2:1-5)*

[1]First of all, then, I urge that entreaties and prayers, petitions and thanksgivings, be made on behalf of all men, [2]for kings and all who are in authority, in order that we may lead a tranquil and quiet life in all godliness and dignity. [3]This is good and acceptable in the sight of God our Savior, [4]who desires all men to be saved and to come to the knowledge of the truth. [5]For there is one God, and one mediator also between God and men, the man Christ Jesus,

Thursday—*Prayer in the Spirit (Ephesians 6:18-20)*

[18]With all prayer and petition pray at all times in the Spirit, and with this in view, be on the alert with all perseverance and petition for all the saints, [19]and pray on my behalf, that utterance may be given to me in the opening of my mouth, to make known with boldness the mystery of the gospel, [20]for which I am an ambassador in chains; that in proclaiming it I may speak boldly, as I ought to speak.

Friday—*When God hears and answers (1 John 5:13-15)*

[13]These things I have written to you who believe in the name of the Son of God, in order that you may know that you have eternal life. [14]And this is the confidence which we have before Him, that, if we ask anything according to His will, He hears us. [15]And if we know that He hears us in whatever we ask, we know that we have the requests which we have asked from Him.

Saturday—*Obedience a key to answered prayer (1 John 3:21-24)*

[21]Beloved, if our heart does not condemn us, we have confidence before God; [22]and whatever we ask we receive from Him, because we keep His commandments and do the things that are pleasing in His sight. [23]And this is His commandment, that we believe in the name of His Son Jesus Christ, and love one another, just as He commanded us. [24]And the one who keeps His commandments abides in Him, and He in him. And we know by this that He abides in us, by the Spirit which He has given us.

EVANGELISM

41

Divine Haste

Sunday—*Haste in telling of the resurrection*
    (Matthew 28:1-8)

¹Now after the Sabbath, as it began to dawn toward the first day of the week. Mary Magdalene and the other Mary came to look at the grave. ²And behold, a severe earthquake had occurred, for an angel of the Lord descended from heaven and came and rolled away the stone and sat upon it. ³And his appearance was like lightning, and his garment as white as snow; ⁴and the guards shook for fear of him, and became like dead men. ⁵And the angel answered and said to the women, "Do not be afraid; for I know that you are looking for Jesus who has been crucified. ⁶He is not here, for He has risen, just as He said. Come, see the place where He was lying. ⁷And go quickly and tell His disciples that He has risen from the dead; and behold, He is going before you into Galilee, there you will see Him; behold, I have told you." ⁸And they departed quickly from the tomb with fear and great joy and ran to report it to His disciples.

We tend to think that God is unconcerned about passing time. We casually quote Peter's words that a thousand years are as a day to Him (2 Peter 3:8) and dismiss the urgency of preaching the gospel. There is evidence in the Scriptures, however, that God is in a hurry.

The father in the parable of the prodigal son pictures God the Father. When the wayward son started home, the father ran to meet him when he was a great way off. He was in a hurry to see his lost son. God is always in a hurry to forgive and restore those who have fallen from fellowship.

In the parable of the great supper, the offended master charged the servants, "Go out quickly into the streets and lanes of the city, and bring in hither the poor, and the maimed, and the halt, and the blind" (Luke 14:21). He was in a hurry to get guests to his supper. God is in a hurry to reach sinners with His Word.

On the resurrection morning, the angel instructed Mary, "Go quickly, and tell his disciples that he is risen from the dead" (Matthew 28:7). God is in a hurry to see that the gospel is preached.

When the Samaritan woman was converted, her testimony inspired many other Samaritans to come to Jesus. Seeing the approaching crowd, Jesus said to His disciples, "Say not ye, There are yet four months, and then cometh harvest? behold, I say unto you, Lift up your eyes, and look on the fields; for they are white already to harvest" (John 4:35). Probably Jesus was referring to the approaching Samaritans as a harvest of souls. The harvest is ripe today, too. We can do one of two things with a harvest: gather it or let it rot. Millions of souls in our world are perishing while we wait, but God is concerned about reaching them.

World evangelization is our primary task. It is not optional but a command from Christ for every believer. We who know the gospel have an obligation to preach it to the world. Salvation is through Jesus Christ alone, and that good news must be given to every creature. To stand idly by and watch the world perish is a great sin.

As believers in Jesus Christ we have all the resources necessary to fulfill our God-given task. We have everything that the apostolic Christian had. Our God is the same. The Holy Spirit indwells and empowers all those who will submit to Him. The Word of God is at our disposal. Prayer power is our sacred privilege. We have all that is necessary, and we fail only because of rebellion and deliberate disobedience.

Evangelization is not the job of a handful of professional "ministers." As believers we are all the ministers of Christ, and His command to spread the gospel is binding on us all. We are His ambassadors (2 Corinthians 5:20), and we make poor ambassadors if our lives do not show His sense of urgency for the lost.

We do not know how much time we have to evangelize, but God does and He reflects a divine haste. How can we fail to share His sense of urgency?

The barker at a circus calls out, "Hurry, hurry, hurry" as he attracts attention to some trivial sideshow. The voice of the triune God calls each of us, not to some passing thrill but to the main issue of time and eternity. The call of God is to evangelize our world now, because the fields are white already.

WE CAN DO ONE OF TWO THINGS WITH A
HARVEST: GATHER IT OR LET IT ROT.

Monday—*Parable of haste in forgiveness (Luke 15:11-24)*

[11]And He said, "A certain man had two sons; [12]and the younger of them said to his father, 'Father, give me the share of the estate that falls to me.' And he divided his wealth between them. [13]And not many days later, the younger son gathered everything together and went on a journey into a distant country, and there he squandered his estate with loose living. [14]Now when he had spent everything, a severe famine occurred in that country, and he began to be in need. [15]And he went and at-

246

tached himself to one of the citizens of that country, and he sent him into his fields to feed swine. [16]And he was longing to fill his stomach with the pods that the swine were eating, and no one was giving anything to him. [17]But when he came to his senses, he said, 'How many of my father's hired men have more than enough bread, but I am dying here with hunger! [18]I will get up and go to my father, and will say to him, "Father, I have sinned against heaven, and in your sight; [19]I am no longer worthy to be called your son; make me as one of your hired men." [20]And he got up and came to his father. But while he was still a long way off, his father saw him, and felt compassion for him, and ran and embraced him, and kissed him. [21]And the son said to him, 'Father, I have sinned against heaven and in your sight; I am no longer worthy to be called your son.' [22]But the father said to his slaves, 'Quickly bring out the best robe and put it on him, and put a ring on his hand and sandals on his feet; [23]and bring the fattened calf, kill it, and let us eat and be merry; [24]for this son of mine was dead, and has come to life again; he was lost, and has been found.' And they began to be merry."

Tuesday—*The task of sharing the Good News (2 Corinthians 5:18-20)*

[18]Now all these things are from God, who reconciled us to Himself through Christ, and gave us the ministry of reconciliation, [19]namely, that God was in Christ reconciling the world to Himself, not counting their trespasses against them, and He has committed to us the word of reconciliation. [20]Therefore, we are ambassadors for Christ, as though God were entreating through us; we beg you on behalf of Christ, be reconciled to God.

Wednesday—*Working for a harvest of souls (John 4:30-38)*

[30]They went out of the city, and were coming to Him. [31]In the meanwhile the disciples were requesting Him, saying, "Rabbi, eat." [32]But He said to them, "I have food to eat that you do not know about." [33]The disciples therefore were saying to one another, "No one brought Him anything to eat, did he?" [34]Jesus said to them, "My food is to do the will of Him who sent Me, and to accomplish His work. [35]Do you not say, 'There are yet four months, and then comes the harvest'? Behold, I say to you,

lift up your eyes, and look on the fields, that they are white for harvest. ³⁶Already he who reaps is receiving wages, and is gathering fruit for life eternal; that he who sows and he who reaps may rejoice together. ³⁷For in this case the saying is true, 'One sows, and another reaps.' ³⁸I sent you to reap that for which you have not labored; others have labored, and you have entered into their labor."

Thursday—*The importance of the Good News to Paul (Philippians 1:12-18)*

¹²Now I want you to know, brethren, that my circumstances have turned out for the greater progress of the gospel, ¹³so that my imprisonment in the cause of Christ has become well-known throughout the whole praetorian guard and to everyone else, ¹⁴and that most of the brethren, trusting in the Lord because of my imprisonment, have far more courage to speak the word of God without fear. ¹⁵Some, to be sure, are preaching Christ even from envy and strife, but some also from good will; ¹⁶the latter do it out of love, knowing that I am appointed for the defense of the gospel; ¹⁷the former proclaim Christ out of selfish ambition, rather than from pure motives, thinking to cause me distress in my imprisonment. ¹⁸What then? Only that in every way, whether in pretense or in truth, Christ is proclaimed; and in this I rejoice, yes, and I will rejoice.

Friday—*The need to hurry to proclaim our riches (Colossians 1:25-29)*

²⁵Of this church I was made a minister according to the stewardship from God bestowed on me for your benefit, that I might fully carry out the preaching of the word of God, ²⁶that is, the mystery which has been hidden from the past ages and generations; but has now been manifested to His saints, ²⁷to whom God willed to make known what is the riches of the glory of this mystery among the Gentiles, which is Christ in you, the hope of glory. ²⁸And we proclaim Him, admonishing every man and teaching every man with all wisdom, that we may present every man complete in Christ. ²⁹And for this purpose also I labor, striving according to His power, which mightily works within me.

**Saturday—*The importance of telling glad tidings*
(Romans 10:11-17)**

¹¹For the Scripture says, "WHOEVER BELIEVES IN HIM WILL NOT BE DISAPPOINTED." ¹²For there is no distinction between Jew and Greek; for the same Lord is Lord of all, abounding in riches for all who call upon Him; ¹³for "WHOEVER WILL CALL UPON THE NAME OF THE LORD WILL BE SAVED." ¹⁴How then shall they call upon Him in whom they have not believed? And how shall they believe in Him whom they have not heard? And how shall they hear without a preacher? ¹⁵And how shall they preach unless they are sent? Just as it is written, "HOW BEAUTIFUL ARE THE FEET OF THOSE WHO BRING GLAD TIDINGS OF GOOD THINGS!" ¹⁶However, they did not all heed the glad tidings; for Isaiah says, "LORD, WHO HAS BELIEVED OUR REPORT?" ¹⁷So faith comes from hearing, and hearing by the word of Christ.

42

Sharing the Gospel

Sunday—*A great preaching campaign (Acts 8:4-8)*
⁴Therefore, those who had been scattered went about preaching the word. ⁵And Philip went down to the city of Samaria and began proclaiming Christ to them. ⁶And the multitudes with one accord were giving attention to what was said by Philip, as they heard and saw the signs which he was performing. ⁷For in the case of many who had unclean spirits, they were coming out of them shouting with a loud voice; and many who had been paralyzed and lame were healed. ⁸And there was much rejoicing in that city.

To Philip, the deacon, God's call must have seemed unusual. "Arise, and go . . . unto Gaza, which is desert" (Acts 8:26).

Philip had just finished an overwhelmingly successful meeting in Samaria, where a great number were baptized in the name of Christ. Some were delivered of unclean spirits, the palsied and lame were healed, and joy abounded in Samaria.

Following this outpouring from the Lord, Philip planned to continue preaching in other Samaritan villages. But God directed him to one man in the desert.

Philip's experience suggests five helpful principles in sharing one's faith.

First, obey the voice of God. God sent His servant Philip from the crowded city to the barren desert, from the masses to a single soul. Common sense dictated otherwise, but the voice of the Lord was clear. Let us always remember that God's ways are not our ways.

Significantly, Philip obeyed. He trusted absolutely that God's orders were right. So it can be with us. We must not hesitate to move forward when the Lord speaks.

Second, recognize that the gospel is for all mankind. As Philip journeyed toward Gaza, he came upon a caravan of soldiers and merchants. In the center he found the treasurer of Ethiopia to whom he was sent to share the Good News.

Since this eunuch had been to Jerusalem to worship, he may have been a Jew who had reached a high place in the government of Ethiopia. However, most Bible students believe that he was a Gentile who had been converted to Judaism. In all probability he was black.

The Body of Jesus Christ is made up of all races. Racism and "classism" are not compatible with true Christianity. Philip had no reservations as he drew near to this man, for he recognized that the gospel is for all mankind.

Third, share your faith with holy enthusiasm. Philip ran to this man. He was Spirit-led, Spirit-filled, and thrilled with the opportunity to speak to the Ethiopian about Jesus Christ. Many of us need that kind of enthusiasm.

Fourth, establish a point of contact. Philip noticed the man was reading the Scriptures, so he took a very direct approach. He simply asked, "Understandest thou what thou readest?" The Ethiopian responded, "How can I, except some man should guide me?" (Acts 8:30-31). Do not be so tactful that you fail to make contact.

Fifth, know the Scriptures. As God's instruments, we must be prepared to guide others in understanding the Bible. The Christian is instructed to study and be ready to rightly divide the Word of truth.

Do you know how to lead a person to Christ? Can you share the meaning of the Scriptures with another?

I am sure that many other questions were asked and answered in this encounter. Evidently Philip led this man right through the whole gospel story.

Then, as they approached a body of water, the man asked, "Here is water; what doth hinder me to be baptized?" (Acts 8:36).

Philip answered, "If thou believest . . . thou mayest" (8:37). The Ethiopian believed. Philip's work was done, and they both went on their way rejoicing.

Are we, like Philip, ready and willing to share our faith in Jesus Christ?

> RACISM AND "CLASSISM" ARE NOT
> COMPATIBLE WITH TRUE CHRISTIANITY.

Monday—*A call to witness (Acts 8:26-29)*

26But an angel of the Lord spoke to Philip saying, "Arise and go south to the road that descends from Jerusalem to Gaza." (This is a desert road.) 27And he arose and went; and behold, there was an Ethiopian eunuch, a court official of Candace, queen of the Ethiopians, who was in charge of all her treasure; and he had come to Jerusalem to worship. 28And he was returning and sitting in his chariot, and was reading the prophet

Isaiah. ²⁹And the Spirit said to Philip, "Go up and join this chariot."

Tuesday—*Philip's obedience (Acts 8:30-35)*

³⁰And when Philip had run up, he heard him reading Isaiah the prophet, and said, "Do you understand what you are reading?" ³¹And he said, "Well, how could I, unless someone guides me?" And he invited Philip to come up and sit with him. ³²Now the passage of Scripture which he was reading was this:

"HE WAS LED AS A SHEEP TO SLAUGHTER;
AND AS A LAMB BEFORE ITS SHEARER IS SILENT,
SO HE DOES NOT OPEN HIS MOUTH.
³³IN HUMILIATION HIS JUDGMENT WAS TAKEN AWAY;
WHO SHALL RELATE HIS GENERATION?
FOR HIS LIFE IS REMOVED FROM THE EARTH."

³⁴And the eunuch answered Philip and said, "Please tell me, of whom does the prophet say this? Of himself, or of someone else?" ³⁵And Philip opened his mouth, and beginning from this Scripture he preached Jesus to him.

Wednesday—*The Ethiopian's conversion (Acts 8:36, 38-39)*

³⁶And as they went along the road they came to some water; and the eunuch said, "Look! Water! What prevents me from being baptized?". . . ³⁸And he ordered the chariot to stop; and they both went down into the water, Philip as well as the eunuch; and he baptized him. ³⁹And when they came up out of the water, the Spirit of the Lord snatched Philip away; and the eunuch saw him no more, but went on his way rejoicing.

Thursday—*Paul's ministry (1 Corinthians 9:16-22)*

¹⁶For if I preach the gospel, I have nothing to boast of, for I am under compulsion; for woe is me if I do not preach the gospel. ¹⁷For if I do this voluntarily, I have a reward; but if against my will, I have a stewardship entrusted to me. ¹⁸What then is my reward? That, when I preach the gospel, I may offer the gospel without charge, so as not to make full use of my right in the gospel. ¹⁹For though I am free from all men, I have made myself a slave to all, that I might win the more. ²⁰And to the Jews I became as a Jew, that I might win Jews; to those who are under the Law, as under the Law, though not being myself under the

Law, that I might win those who are under the Law; ²¹to those who are without law, as without law, though not being without the law of God but under the law of Christ, that I might win those who are without law. ²²To the weak I became weak, that I might win the weak; I have become all things to all men, that I may by all means save some.

Friday—*An evangelistic church (1 Thessalonians 1:1-8)*

¹Paul and Silvanus and Timothy to the church of the Thessalonians in God the Father and the Lord Jesus Christ: Grace to you and peace. ²We give thanks to God always for all of you, making mention of you in our prayers; ³constantly bearing in mind your work of faith and labor of love and steadfastness of hope in our Lord Jesus Christ in the presence of our God and Father; ⁴knowing, brethren beloved by God, His choice of you, ⁵for our gospel did not come to you in word only, but also in power and in the Holy Spirit and with full conviction; just as you know what kind of men we proved to be among you for your sake. ⁶You also became imitators of us and of the Lord, having received the word in much tribulation with the joy of the Holy Spirit, ⁷so that you became an example to all the believers in Macedonia and in Achaia. ⁸For the word of the Lord has sounded forth from you, not only in Macedonia and Achaia, but also in every place your faith toward God has gone forth, so that we have no need to say anything.

Saturday—*How they will hear (Romans 10:8-14)*

⁸But what does it say? "THE WORD IS NEAR YOU, IN YOUR MOUTH AND IN YOUR HEART"—that is, the word of faith which we are preaching, ⁹that if you confess with your mouth Jesus as Lord, and believe in your heart that God raised Him from the dead, you shall be saved; ¹⁰for with the heart man believes, resulting in righteousness, and with the mouth he confesses, resulting in salvation. ¹¹For the Scripture says, "WHOEVER BELIEVES IN HIM WILL NOT BE DISAPPOINTED." ¹²For there is no distinction between Jew and Greek; for the same Lord is Lord of all, abounding in riches for all who call upon Him; ¹³for "WHOEVER WILL CALL UPON THE NAME OF THE LORD WILL BE SAVED." ¹⁴How then shall they call upon Him in whom they have not believed? And how shall they believe in Him whom they have not heard? And how shall they hear without a preacher?

254

43

How I Began Witnessing

Sunday—*How to preach (1 Corinthians 2:1-5)*

[1]And when I came to you, brethren, I did not come with superiority of speech or of wisdom, proclaiming to you the testimony of God. [2]For I determined to know nothing among you except Jesus Christ, and Him crucified. [3]And I was with you in weakness and in fear and in much trembling. [4]And my message and my preaching were not in persuasive words of wisdom, but in demonstration of the Spirit and of power, [5]that your faith should not rest on the wisdom of men, but on the power of God.

I became aware of the call of God in my life on August 16, 1941. A verse of Scripture broke in upon me with such force that I could never be the same. "But be ye doers of the word, and not hearers only, deceiving your own selves" (James 1:22).

Although I was familiar with the claims of the Bible, I failed to obey the very truth I professed to believe. That day I vowed to become a "doer" and forsake my self-deception.

The new birth is the starting point in the adventure of witnessing. No one can successfully witness concerning Jesus Christ until he has been converted. I had received Christ as my Savior, but I was still self-centered and insensitive to the Scripture.

That evening more than three decades ago, I decided to obey the will of God. Although I was an average teenager, I wrote down four goals that have grown more compelling over the passing years.

1. Seek above everything else to bring glory to God.
2. Cultivate, as much as possible, the inner life.
3. Disciple as many people as possible.
4. Win as many people as possible to Jesus Christ.

As I knelt, aglow with first love, I vowed to pursue those goals earnestly.

Immediately I began to share my faith. Most of my school friends were not believers. Paul sat next to me in my high school mechanical drawing class. He was a likable person, and I was concerned about his spiritual condition. How would I begin the conversation? This was my problem.

Following a suggestion given at my home church, I tried using appealing literature to begin a spiritual conversation.

I will never forget my very first try. I gave my friend the booklet *Safety, Certainty, and Enjoyment,* by George Cutting.

"Paul," I said, "here's a booklet that means a lot to me. I'd like you to read it and tell me tomorrow what you think about it." Of course, I was apprehensive. Paul took the booklet and promised to read it.

It was a feeble start, but that is how it was. The next day Paul informed me that he was uncertain about his spiritual condition, but anxious to learn more about Christ. Being shy, I invited Paul to my home after school, where I was able to share answers to his questions.

Witnessing, of course, includes more than merely quoting Scripture. It involves sharing who Jesus is and what Jesus has done; that Jesus Christ is the sinless Son of God who died for the sins of the world, and that He arose from the grave and wants to share in our lives.

Carefully I gave witness, in my limited, stumbling way, to the truth of the gospel. Soon Paul was ready to ask Christ to become his Savior, and in childlike faith he received Jesus Christ. That happy day will always stand out in my memory. Over the years I have seen Paul grow spiritually.

God in His mercy is ready to use any earnest believer as His witness. The best way to begin is to begin, and the best time to begin is now.

NO ONE CAN SUCCESSFULLY WITNESS
CONCERNING JESUS CHRIST UNTIL HE HAS
BEEN CONVERTED.

Monday—*Being ready (1 Peter 3:14-17)*

14But even if you should suffer for the sake of righteousness, you are blessed. AND DO NOT FEAR THEIR INTIMIDATION, AND DO NOT BE TROUBLED, 15but sanctify Christ as Lord in your hearts, always being ready to make a defense to every one who asks you to give an account for the hope that is in you, yet with gentleness and reverence; 16and keep a good conscience so that in the thing in which you are slandered, those who revile your good behavior in Christ may be put to shame. 17For it is better, if God should will it so, that you suffer for doing what is right rather than for doing what is wrong.

Tuesday—*Some words of invitation and warning (Revelation 22:16-21)*

16"I, Jesus, have sent My angel to testify to you these things for the churches. I am the root and the offspring of David, the bright morning star." 17And the Spirit and the bride say, "Come." And let the one who hears say, "Come." And let the one who is thirsty come; let the one who wishes take the water of life without cost. 18I testify to everyone who hears the words of the prophecy of this book: if anyone adds to them, God shall add to him the plagues which are written in this book; 19and if anyone takes away from the words of the book of this prophecy, God shall take away his part from the tree of life and from the holy city, which are written in this book. 20He who testifies to these things says, "Yes, I am coming quickly." Amen. Come, Lord Jesus. 21The grace of the Lord Jesus be with all. Amen.

Wednesday—*Preaching the gospel (Matthew 10:24-27)*

24"A disciple is not above his teacher, nor a slave above his master. 25It is enough for the disciple that he become as his teacher, and the slave as his master. If they have called the head of the house Beelzebul, how much more the members of his household! 26Therefore do not fear them, for there is nothing covered that will not be revealed, and hidden that will not be known. 27What I tell you in the darkness, speak in the light; and what you hear whispered in your ear, proclaim upon the housetops."

Thursday—*The Great Commission (Matthew 28:16-20)*

16But the eleven disciples proceeded to Galilee, to the mountain which Jesus had designated. 17And when they saw Him, they worshiped Him; but some were doubtful. 18And Jesus came up and spoke to them, saying, "All authority has been given to Me in heaven and on earth. 19Go therefore and make disciples of all the nations, baptizing them in the name of the Father and the Son and the Holy Spirit, 20teaching them to observe all that I commanded you; and lo, I am with you always, even to the end of the age."

Friday—*The message (1 Corinthians 15:1-4)*

1Now I make known to you, brethren, the gospel which I preached to you, which also you received, in which also you stand, ²by which also you are saved, if you hold fast the word which I preached to you, unless you believed in vain. ³For I delivered to you as of first importance what I also received, that Christ died for our sins according to the Scriptures, ⁴and that He was buried, and that He was raised on the third day according to the Scriptures.

Saturday—*Assurance of eternal life (1 John 5:9-13)*

⁹If we receive the witness of men, the witness of God is greater; for the witness of God is this, that He has borne witness concerning His Son. ¹⁰The one who believes in the Son of God has the witness in himself; the one who does not believe God has made Him a liar, because he has not believed in the witness that God has borne concerning His Son. ¹¹And the witness is this, that God has given us eternal life, and this life is in His Son. ¹²He who has the Son has the life; he who does not have the Son of God does not have the life. ¹³These things I have written to you who believe in the name of the Son of God, in order that you may know that you have eternal life.

44

If My People

Sunday—*A king's prayer for God's healing*
**   *(2 Chronicles 6:28-31, 36-39)***

[28]"If there is famine in the land, if there is pestilence, if there is blight or mildew, if there is locust or grasshopper, if their enemies besiege them in the land of their cities, whatever plague or whatever sickness there is. [29]whatever prayer or supplication is made by any man or by all Thy people Israel, each knowing his own affliction and his own pain, and spreading his hands toward this house, [30]then hear Thou from heaven Thy dwelling place, and forgive, and render to each according to all his ways, whose heart Thou knowest for Thou alone dost know the hearts of the sons of men, [31]that they may fear Thee, to walk in Thy ways as long as they live in the land which Thou hast given to our fathers. . . . [36]When they sin against Thee (for there is no man who does not sin) and Thou art angry with them and dost deliver them to an enemy, so that they take them away captive to a land far off or near, [37]if they take thought in the land where they are taken captive, and repent and make supplication to Thee in the land of their captivity, saying, 'We have sinned, we have committed iniquity, and have acted wickedly'; [38]if they return to Thee with all their heart and with all their soul in the land of their captivity, where they have been taken captive, and pray toward their land which Thou hast given to their fathers, and the city which Thou hast chosen, and toward the house which I have built for Thy name, [39]then hear from heaven, from Thy dwelling place, their prayer and supplications, and maintain their cause, and forgive Thy people who have sinned against Thee.

Everywhere we turn today we hear that our world is coming apart, that our global village is about to disintegrate. A national leader recently wrote, "Our world is finished; I'm giving it up." Some ask, "Is there any hope? Who can bring us together? What can be done to heal our world?"

In the Word of God we have a divine prescription for today's crisis. The Lord said to Solomon, "If my people, which are called by my name, shall humble themselves, and pray, and seek my face, and turn from their wicked ways; then will I hear from heaven, and will forgive their sin, and will heal their land" (2 Chronicles 7:14).

Think for a few moments about the phrase "If my people." If we as a nation are to enjoy God's blessing, it must start with men and women who know and love Jesus Christ. Where does revival begin? It begins with "my people." It begins with those who have been born of the Spirit of God. Have you received Jesus Christ? If so, you are God's man or woman; you are a member of God's great family.

It is wonderful to be God's child, wonderful to be in God's family. We sing, "Blest be the tie that binds." We also speak about the communion of saints. We believe in a brotherhood, too. As Christians we do enjoy special communion; there is a brotherhood, a tie that binds us together in fellowship. We come into that brotherhood through the shed blood of Jesus Christ when we are born again of the Holy Spirit. What a family this is! We are brothers and sisters in God's family forever.

First, we are God's people because He is our Creator. Second, we are God's people because He is our Redeemer. He shed His blood and purchased us, so we are His people. But not only is He our Creator and Redeemer; He is our Sanctifier as well. He sets us apart as His peculiar people to accomplish His supreme purpose, which is world evangelization. We are to bring glory to Him and be witnesses to our world concerning His salvation.

God told Jonah to go to Nineveh and minister His word,

but Jonah said no. Jonah was prejudiced against the Gentiles. He did not care for the people of Nineveh, and he rebelled and went the opposite direction.

The greatest obstacle to the saving of Nineveh was not the people of Nineveh, but God's man, Jonah. It was not the corruption of the people of Nineveh, not the taverns and the prostitutes of Nineveh, not the pool halls of Nineveh, not the graft-ridden police force of Nineveh. The biggest obstacle to the salvation of Nineveh was a pious, prejudiced man named Jonah.

Jonah was the key to the salvation of the people of Nineveh. When he repented of his prejudice and rebellion and obeyed the simple word of God, the people of Nineveh repented. Jonah was the key.

We have a similar situation in our land today. The gospel is the only salvation for our world, and we Christians have been commanded by God to preach it. Our reluctance to give the message to our world is sin.

"If my people." We are His people. He has promised to heal our land if we are committed to Him. Shall we live on in unconcern and disobedience? Or will we humble ourselves, pray, seek His face, turn from our sin, and serve Him in obedience? We have the key to our world's predicament. Revival begins with us. Will we commit ourselves to Him?

WE HAVE THE KEY TO OUR WORLD'S
PREDICAMENT.

Monday—*God's answer—a principle for national healing* *(2 Chronicles 7:12-18)*

[12]Then the LORD appeared to Solomon at night and said to him, "I have heard your prayer, and have chosen this place for Myself as a house of sacrifice. [13]If I shut up the heavens so that there is no rain, or if I command the locust to devour the land, or if I send pestilence among My people, [14]and My people who are called by My name humble themselves and pray, and seek

My face and turn from their wicked ways, then I will hear from heaven, will forgive their sin, and will heal their land. ¹⁵Now My eyes shall be open and My ears attentive to the prayer offered in this place. ¹⁶For now I have chosen and consecrated this house that My name may be there forever, and My eyes and My heart will be there perpetually. ¹⁷And as for you, if you walk before Me as your father David walked even to do according to all that I have commanded you and will keep My statutes and My ordinances, ¹⁸then I will establish your royal throne as I covenanted with your father David, saying, 'You shall not lack a man to be ruler in Israel.'

Tuesday—*Abraham's intercession to save a city* *(Genesis 18:20-33)*

²⁰And the LORD said, "The outcry of Sodom and Gomorrah is indeed great, and their sin is exceedingly grave. ²¹I will go down now, and see if they have done entirely according to its outcry, which has come to Me; and if not, I will know." ²²Then the men turned away from there and went toward Sodom, while Abraham was still standing before the LORD. ²³And Abraham came near and said, "Wilt Thou indeed sweep away the righteous with the wicked? ²⁴Suppose there are fifty righteous within the city; wilt Thou indeed sweep it away and not spare the place for the sake of the fifty righteous who are in it? ²⁵Far be it from Thee to do such a thing, to slay the righteous with the wicked, so that the righteous and the wicked are treated alike. Far be it from Thee! Shall not the Judge of all the earth deal justly?" ²⁶So the LORD said, "If I find in Sodom fifty righteous within the city, then I will spare the whole place on their account." ²⁷And Abraham answered and said, "Now behold, I have ventured to speak to the Lord, although I am but dust and ashes. ²⁸Suppose the fifty righteous are lacking five, wilt Thou destroy the whole city because of Five?" And He said, "I will not destroy it if I find forty-five there." ²⁹And he spoke to Him yet again and said, "Suppose forty are found there?" And He said, "I will not do it on account of the forty." ³⁰Then he said, "Oh may the Lord not be angry, and I shall speak; suppose thirty are found there?" And He said, "I will not do it if I find thirty there." ³¹And he said, "Now behold, I have ventured to speak to the Lord; suppose twenty are found there?" And He said "I will not destroy it on account of the twenty." ³²Then he

said, "Oh may the Lord not be angry, and I shall speak only this once; suppose ten are found there?" And He said, "I will not destroy it on account of the ten." ³³And as soon as He had finished speaking to Abraham the LORD departed; and Abraham returned to his place.

Wednesday—*Jonah's running from God's call (Jonah 1:1-9)*

¹The word of the LORD came to Jonah the son of Amittai saying, ²"Arise, go to Nineveh the great city, and cry against it, for their wickedness has come up before Me." ³But Jonah rose up to flee to Tarshish from the presence of the LORD. So he went down to Joppa, found a ship; which was going to Tarshish, paid the fare, and went down into it to go with them to Tarshish from the presence of the LORD. ⁴And the LORD hurled a great wind on the sea and there was a great storm on the sea so that the ship was about to break up. ⁵Then the sailors became afraid, and every man cried to his god, and they threw the cargo which was in the ship into the sea to lighten it for them. But Jonah had gone below into the hold of the ship, lain down, and fallen sound asleep. ⁶So the captain approached him and said, "How is it that you are sleeping? Get up, call on your god. Perhaps your god will be concerned about us so that we will not perish." ⁷And each man said to his mate, "Come, let us cast lots so we may learn on whose account this calamity has struck us." So they cast lots and the lot fell on Jonah. ⁸Then they said to him, "Tell us, now! On whose account has this calamity struck us? What is your occupation? And where do you come from? What is your country? From what people are you?" ⁹And he said to them, "I am a Hebrew, and I fear the LORD God of heaven who made the sea and the dry land."

Thursday—*God's second call (Jonah 3:1-3)*

¹Now the word of the LORD came to Jonah the second time, saying, ²"Arise, go to Nineveh the great city and proclaim to it the proclamation which I am going to tell you." ³So Jonah arose and went to Nineveh according to the word of the LORD. Now Nineveh was an exceedingly great city, a three days' walk.

Friday—*Why Jonah had fled (Jonah 4:1-4)*

¹But it greatly displeased Jonah, and he became angry. ²And he prayed to the LORD and said, "Please LORD, was not this

what I said while I was still in my own country? Therefore, in order to forestall this I fled to Tarshish for I knew that Thou art a gracious and compassionate God, slow to anger and abundant in lovingkindness, and one who relents concerning calamity. ³Therefore now, O LORD, please take my life from me, for death is better to me than life." ⁴And the LORD said, "Do you have good reason to be angry?"

Saturday—*God's mercy on nations (Jonah 4:5-11)*

⁵Then Jonah went out from the city and sat east of it. There he made a shelter for himself and sat under it in the shade until he could see what would happen in the city. ⁶So the LORD God appointed a plant and it grew up over Jonah to be a shade over his head to deliver him from his discomfort. And Jonah was extremely happy about the plant. ⁷But God appointed a worm when dawn came the next day, and it attacked the plant and it withered. ⁸And it came about when the sun came up that God appointed a scorching east wind, and the sun beat down on Jonah's head so that he became faint and begged with all his soul to die, saying, "Death is better to me than life." ⁹Then God said to Jonah, "Do you have good reason to be angry about the plant?" And he said, "I have good reason to be angry, even to death." ¹⁰Then the LORD said, "You had compassion on the plant for which you did not work, and which you did not cause to grow, which came up overnight and perished overnight. ¹¹And should I not have compassion on Nineveh, the great city in which there are more than 120,000 persons who do not know the difference between their right and left hand, as well as many animals?"

45

A Passion for Souls

Sunday—*Paul's compassion (Romans 9:1-5)*

¹I am telling the truth in Christ, I am not lying, my conscience bearing me witness in the Holy Spirit, ²that I have great sorrow and unceasing grief in my heart. ³For I could wish that I myself were accursed, separated from Christ for the sake of my brethren, my kinsmen according to the flesh, ⁴who are Israelites, to whom belongs the adoption as sons and the glory and the covenants and the giving of the Law and the temple service and the promises, ⁵whose are the fathers, and from whom is the Christ according to the flesh, who is over all, God blessed forever. Amen.

Study the lives of great men of God and you will notice that certain themes stand out in their ministries.

Charles G. Finney was intensely concerned with human responsibility. Count Nicholas Zinzendorf, writing in hymns, sermons, and pamphlets, seems to say, "I have one passion—Christ." George Whitefield preached so often on "Ye must be born again" that he was criticized. When asked why he used that text so much, he would answer, "Because you must be born again!" Jonathan Edwards's emphasis was judgment. Billy Sunday's was "Be sure your sin will find you out." Gypsy Smith's great theme was the beauty of Jesus.

D. L. Moody also had a theme—God's love. In fact, "God is love" was printed on each light in the old Moody Church.

A sermon on love touched Moody so deeply he could not keep back the tears. His personal study of God's love as revealed in the Bible led him to the place where he said, "I just couldn't help loving people."

But all those men, and every man whom God uses mightily as he used them, have one thing in common—a passion for souls. It is their fervent desire to see men come to Christ.

The apostle Paul likewise knew a great burden for the lost. "I say the truth in Christ," he said in Romans 9:1. "I lie not, my conscience also bearing me witness in the Holy Ghost."

He was saying, "What I have is real. It is in dead earnest. I care about the lost." Then he added, "My conscience confirms it by the Holy Spirit."

We know what it is to be troubled about such things as stealing, lying, and immoral acts, but are we troubled about the lost? Paul had a conscience about people perishing without Christ.

The apostle's burden was no now-and-then concern. "I have . . . continual sorrow," he said (v. 2). And of Ephesus he said, "By the space of three years I ceased not to warn every one night and day with tears" (Acts 20:31).

The same was true of our Lord. He looked on the multitude and "was moved with compassion." God loves people and so must we.

The word *compassion* is made up of two words. *Passion* means "to suffer" and *com* means "with"; so the compound simply means "to suffer with." Do you know what it is to suffer with those around you?

John Henry Jowett in his book *A Passion for Souls* notes, "The gospel of a broken heart demands the ministry of a bleeding heart." He adds, "We can never heal the needs that we do not feel."

Paul went even further; he had a redemptive passion. "I could wish ... myself ... accursed .. for my brethren," he said in Romans 9:3.

What did he mean? Simply that he would have surrendered his own salvation if, by so doing, his kinsmen could have been saved.

That is redemptive passion—the kind that moved Scotsman John Knox to agonize, "Give me Scotland or I die!"

It is the kind of deep passion Rachel felt because she was barren. Embarrassed and ashamed, she cried out to her husband, Jacob, "Give me children, or else I die!" (Genesis 30:1).

When you and I get that concerned for the lost around us, God will give us spiritual children.

GOD LOVES PEOPLE AND SO MUST WE.

Monday—*Christ's compassion (Matthew 9:35-38)*

35And Jesus was going about all the cities and the villages, teaching in their synagogues, and proclaiming the gospel of the kingdom, and healing every kind of disease and every kind of sickness. 36And seeing the multitudes, He felt compassion for them, because they were distressed and downcast like sheep without a shepherd. 37Then He said to His disciples, "The harvest is plentiful, but the workers are few. 38Therefore beseech the Lord of the harvest to send out workers into His harvest."

Tuesday—*The lost sheep (Matthew 18:11-14)*

11["For the Son of Man has come to save that which was lost.] 12What do you think? If any man has a hundred sheep, and one of them has gone astray, does he not leave the ninety-nine on the mountains and go and search for the one that is straying? 13And if it turns out that he finds it, truly I say to you, he rejoices over it more than over the ninety-nine which have not gone astray. 14Thus it is not the will of your Father who is in heaven that one of these little ones perish."

Wednesday—*The multitudes fed by Jesus (Mark 8:1-9)*

1In those days again, when there was a great multitude and they had nothing to eat, He summoned His disciples and said to them, 2"I feel compassion for the multitude because they have remained with Me now three days, and have nothing to eat; 3and if I send them away fasting to their home, they will faint on the way; and some of them have come from a distance." 4And His disciples answered Him, "Where will anyone be able to find enough to satisfy these men with bread here in the wilderness?" 5And He was asking them, "How many loaves do you have?" And they said, "Seven." 6And He directed the multitude to sit down on the ground; and taking the seven loaves, He gave thanks and broke them, and began giving them to His disciples to serve to them, and they served them to the multitude. 7They also had a few small fish; and after He had blessed them, He ordered these to be served as well. 8And they ate and were satisfied; and they picked up seven full baskets of what was left over of the broken pieces. 9And about four thousand were there; and He sent them away.

Thursday—*Peace with God (Romans 5:1-5)*

1Therefore having been justified by faith, we have peace with God through our Lord Jesus Christ, 2through whom also we have obtained our introduction by faith into this grave in which we stand; and we exult in hope of the glory of God. 3And not only this, but we also exult in our tribulations; knowing that tribulation brings about perseverance; 4and perseverance, proven character; and proven character, hope; 5and hope does not disappoint; because the love of God has been poured out within our hearts through the Holy Spirit who was given to us.

Friday—*God's love for us (Romans 5:6-11)*

⁶For while we were still helpless, at the right time Christ died for the ungodly. ⁷For one will hardly die for a righteous man; though perhaps for the good man someone would dare even to die. ⁸But God demonstrates His own love toward us, in that while we were yet sinners, Christ died for us. ⁹Much more then, having now been justified by His blood, we shall be saved from the wrath of God through Him. ¹⁰For if while we were enemies, we were reconciled to God through the death of His Son, much more, having been reconciled, we shall be saved by His life. ¹¹And not only this, but we also exult in God through our Lord Jesus Christ, through whom we have not received the reconciliation.

Saturday—*Christ's redemption (Romans 5:12-21)*

¹²Therefore, just as through one man sin entered into the world, and death through sin, and so death spread to all men, because all sinned— ¹³for until the Law sin was in the world; but sin is not imputed when there is no law. ¹⁴Nevertheless death reigned from Adam until Moses, even over those who had not sinned in the likeness of Adam's offense, who is a type of Him who was to come. ¹⁵But the free gift is not like the transgression. For if by the transgression of the one the many died, much more did the grace of God and the gift by the grace of the one Man, Jesus Christ, abound to the many. ¹⁶And the gift is not like that which came through the one who sinned; for on the one hand the judgment arose from one transgression resulting in condemnation, but on the other hand the free gift arose from many transgressions resulting in justification. ¹⁷For if by the transgression of the one, death reigned through the one, much more those who receive the abundance of grace and of the gift of righteousness will reign in life through the One, Jesus Christ. ¹⁸So then as through one transgression there resulted condemnation to all men; even so through one act of righteousness there resulted justification of life to all men. ¹⁹For as through the one man's disobedience the many were made sinners, even so through the obedience of the One the many will be made righteous. ²⁰And the Law came in that the transgression might increase; but where sin increased, grace abounded all the more, ²¹that, as sin reigned in death, even so grace might reign through righteousness to eternal life through Jesus Christ our Lord.

46

Let's Tell the World

Sunday—*Paul's early upbringing (Acts 26:1-8)*

[1]And Agrippa said to Paul, "You are permitted to speak for yourself." Then Paul stretched out his hand and proceeded to make his defense: [2]"In regard to all the things of which I am accused by the Jews, I consider myself fortunate, King Agrippa, that I am about to make my defense before you today; [3]especially because you are an expert in all customs and questions among the Jews; therefore I beg you to listen to me patiently. [4]So then, all Jews know my manner of life from my youth up, which from the beginning was spent among my own nation and at Jerusalem; [5]since they have known about me for a long time previously, if they are willing to testify, that I lived as a Pharisee according to the strictest sect of our religion. [6]And now I am standing trial for the hope of the promise made by God to our fathers; [7]the promise to which our twelve tribes hope to attain, as they earnestly serve God night and day. And for this hope, O King, I am being accused by Jews. [8]Why is it considered incredible among you people if God does raise the dead?"

It is a high and holy privilege to be a child of God. To be ashamed of Christ is a sad experience, which really implies error, thoughtlessness, and failure on our part. It dishonors Christ and brings personal defeat.

Some new Christians try to be secret believers, but that is a mistake. Just imagine Dr. Jonas Salk keeping the Salk vaccine a secret! That would have been criminal. He knew that he had a responsibility to share his discovery with the world, and he did. Our knowledge of salvation places us in debt to the whole world. Silence on our part is sinful because we owe the world a witness.

Both Nicodemus and Joseph of Arimathea tried to be secret disciples. It took the death of Christ to bring them to the place of openly acknowledging their association with Him. The Scripture states, "And after this Joseph of Arimathea, being a disciple of Jesus, but secretly for fear of the Jews, besought Pilate that he might take away the body of Jesus" (John 19:38).

Someone might ask, "Do I have to confess Christ openly?" I ask, "How can you help it?" Do not let the fear of others rob you of the joy of open allegiance to Jesus Christ.

We could easily understand if Christ were ashamed of sinful creatures. But for men and women to be ashamed of Christ is unthinkable. Joseph Grigg has written:

> Ashamed of Jesus! that dear Friend
> On whom my hopes of heaven depend!
> No; when I blush, be this my shame,
> That I no more revere His name.

Ashamed of Christ? Never! Repeatedly we are encouraged to confess Christ openly and not be ashamed. In fact, Jesus said, "Whosoever therefore shall be ashamed of me and of my words in this adulterous and sinful generation; of him also shall the Son of man be ashamed, when he cometh in the glory of his Father with the holy angels" (Mark 8:38).

Failure to acknowledge Christ often results in careless living, whereas a public confession puts us on record before our fellowman as well as before God. The very fact that others know of our decision often helps to guard against temptation.

R. A. Torrey said, "If you make a great deal of Christ, He will make a great deal of you; but if you make but little of Christ, Christ will make but little of you."

Your decision to receive Jesus Christ has provoked a real, happy, lasting change. Seek to tell someone intelligently and lovingly about Jesus Christ this week.

SILENCE ON OUR PART IS SINFUL BECAUSE
WE OWE THE WORLD A WITNESS.

Monday—*Paul's zeal against Christians (Acts 26:9-11)*

9"So then, I thought to myself that I had to do many things hostile to the name of Jesus of Nazareth. 10And this is just what I did in Jerusalem; not only did I lock up many of the saints in prisons, having received authority from the chief priests, but also when they were being put to death I cast my vote against them. 11And as I punished them often in all the synagogues, I tried to force them to blaspheme; and being furiously enraged at them, I kept pursuing them even to foreign cities."

Tuesday—*The vision that changed Paul (Acts 26:12-20)*

12While thus engaged as I was journeying to Damascus with the authority and commission of the chief priests, 13at midday, O King, I saw on the way a light from heaven, brighter than the sun, shining all around me and those who were journeying with me. 14And when we had all fallen to the ground, I heard a voice saying to me in the Hebrew dialect, 'Saul, Saul, why are you persecuting me? It is hard for you to kick against the goads.' 15And I said, 'Who art Thou, Lord?' And the Lord said, 'I am Jesus whom you are persecuting. 16But arise, and stand on your feet; for this purpose I have appeared to you, to appoint you a minister and a witness not only to the things which you have seen, but also to the things in which I will appear to you; 17delivering you from the Jewish people and from the Gentiles, to whom I am sending you, 18to open their eyes so that they may turn from darkness to light and from the dominion of

273

Satan to God, in order that they may receive forgiveness of sins and an inheritance among those who have been sanctified by faith in Me.' [19]Consequently, King Agrippa, I did not prove disobedient to the heavenly vision, [20]but kept declaring both to those of Damascus first, and also at Jerusalem and then throughout all the region of Judea, and even to the Gentiles, that they should repent and turn to God, performing deeds appropriate to repentance."

Wednesday—*The gospel proclaimed to the king* (Acts 26:21-26)

[21]"For this reason some Jews seized me in the temple and tried to put me to death. [22]And so, having obtained help from God, I stand to this day testifying both to small and great, stating nothing but what the Prophets and Moses said was going to take place; [23]that the Christ was to suffer, and that by reason of His resurrection from the dead He should be the first to proclaim light both to the Jewish people and to the Gentiles." [24]And while Paul was saying this in his defense, Festus said in a loud voice, "Paul, you are out of your mind! Your great learning is driving you mad." [25]But Paul said, "I am not out of my mind, most excellent Festus, but I utter words of sober truth. [26]For the king knows about these matters, and I speak to him also with confidence, since I am persuaded that none of these things escape his notice; for this has not been done in a corner."

Thursday—*Invitation to believe (Acts 26:27-32)*

[27]"King Agrippa, do you believe the Prophets? I know that you do." [28]And Agrippa replied to Paul, "In a short time you will persuade me to become a Christian." [29]And Paul said, "I would to God, that whether in a short or long time, not only you, but also all who hear me this day, might become such as I am, except for these chains." [30]And the king arose and the governor and Bernice, and those who were sitting with them, [31]and when they had drawn aside, they began talking to one another, saying, "This man is not doing anything worthy of death or imprisonment." [32]And Agrippa said to Festus, "This man might have been set free if he had not appealed to Caesar."

Friday—*Why Paul preached eagerly (Romans 1:14-17)*

[14]I am under obligation both to Greeks and to barbarians, both to the wise and to the foolish. [15]Thus, for my part, I am eager to preach the gospel to you also who are in Rome. [16]For I am not ashamed of the gospel, for it is the power of God for salvation to every one who believes, to the Jew first and also to the Greek. [17]For in it the righteousness of God is revealed from faith to faith; as it is written, "BUT THE RIGHTEOUS man SHALL LIVE BY FAITH."

Saturday—*The cost of being ashamed (Mark 8:34-38)*

[34]And He summoned the multitude with His disciples, and said to them, "If anyone wishes to come after Me, let him deny himself, and take up his cross, and follow Me. [35]For whoever wishes to save his life shall lose it; and whoever loses his life for My sake and the gospel's shall save it. [36]For what does it profit a man to gain the whole world, and forfeit his soul? [37]For what shall a man give in exchange for his soul? [38]For whoever is ashamed of Me and My words in this adulterous and sinful generation, the Son of Man will also be ashamed of him when He comes in the glory of His Father with the holy angels."

47

Have Me Excused

Sunday—*No excuse (Romans 1:18-22)*

¹⁸For the wrath of God is revealed from heaven against all ungodliness and unrighteousness of men, who suppress the truth in unrighteousness, ¹⁹because that which is known about God is evident within them; for God made it evident to them. ²⁰For since the creation of the world His invisible attributes, His eternal power and divine nature, have been clearly seen, being understood through what has been made, so that they are without excuse. ²¹For even though they knew God, they did not honor Him as God, or give thanks; but they became futile in their speculations, and their foolish heart was darkened. ²²Professing to be wise, they became fools.

"The man who is good for excuses," said wise Benjamin Franklin, "is good for little else." Yet making excuses is a way of life for many people.

The dictionary defines an excuse as an attempt "to regard or judge with indulgence . . . to pardon or forgive one's actions."

There is a great difference between a reason and an excuse. Reasons are usually sincere, but an excuse is a rationalization. A reason involves reality, but an excuse is an invention or, at best, a frail, sick reason.

When God questioned Adam and Eve about their sin, they offered excuses but failed to give the real reasons for their disobedience. Adam answered, "The woman whom thou gavest to be with me, she gave me of the tree" (Genesis 3:12). Eve excused herself by responding, "The serpent beguiled me, and I did eat" (Genesis 3:13).

The real reason for their sin had nothing to do with those empty excuses. Scripture gives three reasons for their disobedience. The fruit "was good for food . . . pleasant to the eyes, and . . . desired to make one wise" (Genesis 3:6).

Sometimes we offer excuses for not witnessing because we are timid. Moses did that. "I am not eloquent . . . I am slow of speech" (Exodus 4:10). Moses seemed to say, "My mouth gets dry, my tongue won't move, I can't speak." Most of us have questioned our abilities, only to receive divine assurance that God is able.

In Luke 14, Jesus told a story of a man who planned a large dinner party and invited many guests. But just before the dinner they changed their minds and backed out.

"And they all with one consent began to make excuse. The first said . . . I have bought a piece of ground, and I must needs go and see it: I pray thee have me excused. And another said, I have bought five yoke of oxen, and I go to prove them: I pray thee have me excused. And another said, I have married a wife, and therefore I cannot come" (Luke 14:18-20).

These people had already consented to come to this

special occasion, but all three excused themselves and failed to attend.

The first one said, "I have bought a piece of ground, and I must needs go and see it." If he had been a good businessman, he would have looked at the land before he bought it. Furthermore, he had already purchased the land, and it would still be there after the dinner. His answer was nothing more than an excuse.

The second man excused himself because he had purchased five yoke of oxen and had wanted to go prove them. Why hadn't he proved his animals before the dinner or, for that matter, why couldn't they wait? His was just another excuse.

But the third man's excuse was the most ridiculous of all. "I have married a wife and cannot come." He had promised ahead of time that he would attend. Why couldn't he have brought his wife with him?

People generally do what they want to do. Excuses satisfy only the people who make them.

Alexander Pope characterized excuses much more severely. "An excuse," he wrote, "is more terrible than a lie, for an excuse is a lie guarded." He who *excuses* himself really *accuses* himself.

But, of course, our primary concern is what God thinks of excuses. As the master of the feast was angry when his guests spurned him, so God is grieved when we spurn Him and excuse ourselves.

REASONS ARE USUALLY SINCERE, BUT AN
EXCUSE IS A RATIONALIZATION.

Monday—*Adam's and Eve's excuses (Genesis 3:9-13)*

⁹Then the Lᴏʀᴅ God called to the man, and said to him, "Where are you?" ¹⁰And he said, "I heard the sound of Thee in the garden, and I was afraid because I was naked; so I hid myself." ¹¹And He said, "Who told you that you were naked? Have you eaten from the tree of which I commanded you not to

278

eat?" ¹²And the man said, "The woman whom Thou gavest to be with me, she gave me from the tree, and I ate." ¹³Then the LORD God said to the woman, "What is this you have done?" And the woman said, "The serpent deceived men, and I ate."

Tuesday—*Saul's excuse (1 Samuel 13:9-14)*

⁹So Saul said, "Bring to me the burnt offering and the peace offerings." And he offered the burnt offering. ¹⁰And it came about as soon as he finished offering the burnt offering, that behold, Samuel came; and Saul went out to meet him and to greet him. ¹¹But Samuel said, "What have you done?" And Saul said, "Because I saw that the people were scattering from me, and that you did not come within the appointed days, and that the Philistines were assembling at Michmash, ¹²therefore I said, 'Now the Philistines will come down against me at Gilgal, and I have not asked the favor of the LORD.' So I forced myself and offered the burnt offering." ¹³And Samuel said to Saul, "You have acted foolishly; you have not kept the commandment of the LORD your God, which He commanded you, for now the LORD would have established your kingdom over Israel forever. ¹⁴But now your kingdom shall not endure. The LORD has sought out for Himself a man after His own heart, and the LORD had appointed him as ruler over His people, because you have not kept what the LORD commanded you."

Wednesday—*Naaman's excuses deflated (2 Kings 5:10-14)*

¹⁰And Elisha sent a messenger to him, saying, "Go and wash in the Jordan seven times, and your flesh shall be restored to you and you shall be clean." ¹¹But Naaman was furious and went away and said, "Behold, I thought, 'He will surely come out to me, and stand and call on the name of the LORD his God, and wave his hand over the place, and cure the leper.' ¹²Are not Abanah and Pharpar, the rivers of Damascus, better than all the waters of Israel? Could I not wash in them and be clean?" So he turned and went away in a rage. ¹³Then his servants came near and spoke to him and said, "My father, had the prophet told you to do some great thing, would you not have done it? How much more then, when he says to you, 'Wash, and be clean'?" ¹⁴So he went down and dipped himself seven times in the Jordan, according to the word of the man of God; and his flesh was restored like the flesh of a little child, and he was clean.

Thursday—*God's answer to Jeremiah's excuses*
     (Jeremiah 1:4-10)

[4]Now the word of the LORD came to me saying,
[5]"Before I formed you in the womb I knew you,
  And before you were born I consecrated you;
  I have appointed you a prophet to the nations."
[6]Then I said, "Alas, Lord GOD!
  Behold, I do not know how to speak,
  Because I am a youth."
[7]But the LORD said to me,
  "Do not say, 'I am a youth,'
  Because everywhere I send you, you shall go,
  And all that I command you, you shall speak.
[8]Do not be afraid of them,
  For I am with you to deliver you," declares the LORD.
[9]The the LORD stretched out His hand and touched my mouth,
          and the LORD said to me,
  Behold, I have put My words in your mouth.
[10]See, I have appointed you this day over the nations and over
          the kingdoms,
  To pluck up and to break down,
  To destroy and to overthrow,
  To build and to plant."

Friday—*Some poor excuses (Luke 9:59-62)*

[59]And He said to another, "Follow Me." But he said, "Permit me first to go and bury my father." [60]But He said to him, "Allow the dead to bury their own dead; but as for you, go and proclaim everywhere the kingdom of God." [61]And another also said, "I will follow You, Lord; but first permit me to say goodbye to those at home." [62]But Jesus said to him, "No one, after puttting his hand to the plow and looking back, is fit for the kingdom of God."

Saturday—*The parable of the guests (Luke 14:18-20)*

[18]"But they all alike began to make excuses. The first one said to him, 'I have bought a piece of land and I need to go out and look at it; please consider me excused.' [19]And another one said, 'I have bought five yoke of oxen, and I am going to try them out; please consider me excused.' [20]And another one said, 'I have married a wife, and for that reason I cannot come.'"

LIFE IN THIS
WORLD

48

The Pleasure Boom

Sunday—*Jesus' invitation to rest (Matthew 11:28-30)*

28"Come to Me, all who are weary and heavy-laden, and I will give you rest. 29Take My yoke upon you, and learn from Me, for I am gentle and humble in heart; and YOU SHALL FIND REST FOR YOUR SOULS. 30For My yoke is easy, and My load is light."

Our world rocks from a pleasure explosion.

According to *U. S. News and World Report,* Americans will spend an estimated 105 billion dollars on pleasure activities this year. Our pleasure spending has increased almost one hundred percent during the past seven years.

This preoccupation with pleasure takes on many different forms. A Department of the Interior survey shows that seventy-five percent of the U. S. population age nine or older is involved in some form of outdoor recreation. Campers purchase more than $500 million worth of tent trailers and camping vehicles each year.

Each year tennis enthusiasts spend some $50 million on equipment and accessories. Twelve million golfers vie for playing time on ten thousand courses. Bicycle and snowmobile manufacturers must push to meet the increasing demands of the public. Over $50 billion worth of recreation equipment and services will be purchased this year. America is hard at play!

Now, of course, I do not condemn pleasure. My wife and I thoroughly enjoy moments of relaxation. We all do! The Christian life is not a sad or morbid experience. It is alive and exciting!

As we study God's Word, we find three specific kinds of pleasure—sinful pleasure, legitimate pleasure, and eternal pleasure.

For forty years Moses indulged in the wisdom and wealth of Egypt. All the opportunities of that great nation were his. But he turned his back on it all, "choosing rather to suffer affliction with the people of God, than to enjoy the pleasures of sin for a season" (Hebrews 11:25).

Moses refused to become addicted to the pleasures that were all around him. Let us be honest. Sin provides enjoyment. Satan is not such a fool as to fish without bait.

All pleasures, of course, are not sinful. God intends for His children to enjoy many legitimate pleasures. Paul wrote to Timothy that it is the "Living God, who giveth us richly all things to enjoy" (1 Timothy 6:17).

Each of us must make time for legitimate pleasure.

Even as a bow kept under constant tension loses its resilience, so it is with us.

On one occasion Jesus told His disciples, "Come . . . apart into a desert place, and rest a while: for there were many coming and going, and they had no leisure so much as to eat" (Mark 6:31). That sounds just like today.

However, legitimate pleasure can be abused. Paul warned the Christians in Rome, "Make not provision for the flesh, to fulfil the lusts thereof" (Romans 13:14). Sometimes a simple thing like a boat or an automobile develops into an idol. An innocent hobby can become an obsession. Paul is saying, "Don't let your search for pleasure control your life."

Here are two tests to evaluate our pleasure:

First, do these pleasures encourage Christian development? "All things are lawful unto me, but all things are not expedient" (1 Corinthians 6:12). "Expedient" means profitable. Many activities may be legitimate, but do they help me to glorify my Lord and Savior Jesus Christ?

Second, do these pleasures endanger Christian maturity? "All things are lawful for me," said Paul, "but I will not be brought under the power of any" (1 Corinthians 6:12b). Seemingly innocent pleasures can choke out our spiritual lives.

God's Word talks about another kind of pleasure: eternal pleasure, lasting pleasure, pleasures forevermore. David said, "Thou wilt shew me the path of life: in thy presence is fulness of joy; at thy right hand there are pleasures for evermore" (Psalm 16:11). Are we seeking those eternal pleasures?

SATAN IS NOT SUCH A FOOL AS TO FISH
WITHOUT BAIT.

Monday—*Choices determined by remembering the Lord
(1 Corinthians 6:12-17)*

[12]All things are lawful for me, but not all things are profitable. All things are lawful for me, but I will not be mastered by

284

anything. ¹³Food is for the stomach, and the stomach is for food; but God will do away with both of them. Yet the body is not for immorality, but for the Lord; and the Lord is for the body. ¹⁴Now God has not only raised the Lord, but will also raise us up through His power. ¹⁵Do you not know that your bodies are members of Christ? Shall I then take away the members of Christ and make them members of a harlot? May it never be! ¹⁶Or do you not know that the one who joins himself to a harlot is one body with her? For He says, "THE TWO WILL BE-COME ONE FLESH." ¹⁷But the one who joins himself to the Lord is one spirit with Him.

Tuesday—*Moses' refusal of sin's pleasures (Hebrews 11:24-26)*

²⁴By faith Moses, when he had grown up, refused to be called the son of Pharaoh's daughter; ²⁵choosing rather to endure ill-treatment with the people of God, than to enjoy the passing pleasures of sin; ²⁶considering the reproach of Christ greater riches than the treasures of Egypt; for he was looking to the reward.

Wednesday—*Forsaking evil; time is short (Romans 13:11-14)*

¹¹And this do, knowing the time, that it is already the hour for you to awaken from sleep; for now salvation is nearer to us than when we believed. ¹²The night is almost gone, and the day is at hand. Let us therefore lay aside the deeds of darkness and put on the armor of light. ¹³Let us behave properly as in the day, not in carousing and drunkenness, not in sexual promiscuity and sensuality, not in strife and jealousy. ¹⁴But put on the Lord Jesus Christ, and make no provision for the flesh in regard to its lusts.

Thursday—*Enjoying God's presence (Psalm 16:7-11)*

⁷I will bless the LORD who has counseled me;
   Indeed, my mind instructs me in the night.
⁸I have set the LORD continually before me;
   Because He is at my right hand, I will not be shaken.
⁹Therefore my heart is glad, and my glory rejoices;
   My flesh also will dwell securely.
¹⁰For Thou wilt not abandon my soul to Sheol;
   Neither wilt Thou allow Thy Holy One to undergo decay.
¹¹Thou wilt make known to me the path of life;

In Thy presence is fulness of joy;
In Thy right hand there are pleasures forever.

Friday—*Jesus' difficulty in finding rest (Mark 6:30-36)*

[30]And the apostles gathered together with Jesus; and they reported to Him all that they had done and taught. [31]And He said to them, "Come away by yourselves to a lonely place and rest a while." (For there were many people coming and going, and they did not even have time to eat.) [32]And they went away in the boat to a lonely place by themselves. [33]And the people saw them going, and many recognized them, and they ran there together on foot from all the cities, and got there ahead of them. [34]And disembarking, He saw a great multitude, and He felt compassion for them because they were like sheep without a shepherd; and He began to teach them many things. [35]And when it was already quite late, His disciples came up to Him and began saying, "The place is desolate and it is already quite late; [36]send them away so that they may go into the surrounding countryside and villages and buy themselves something to eat."

Saturday—*Jesus meeting others' needs; turning to prayer (Mark 6:37-46)*

[37]But He answered and said to them, "You give them something to eat!" And they said to Him, "Shall we go and spend two hundred denarii on bread and give them something to eat?" [38]And He said to them, "How many loaves do you have? Go look!" And when they found out, they said, "Five and two fish." [39]And He commanded them all to recline by groups on the green grass. [40]And they reclined in companies of hundreds and of fifties. [41]And He took the five loaves and the two fish, and looking up toward heaven, He blessed the food and broke the loaves and He kept giving them to the disciples to set before them; and He divided up the two fish among them all. [42]And they all ate and were satisfied. [43]And they picked up twelve full baskets of the broken pieces, and also of the fish. [44]And there were five thousand men who ate the loaves. [45]And immediately He made His disciples get into the boat and go ahead of Him to the other side of Bethsaida, while He Himself was sending the multitude away. [46]And after bidding them farewell, He departed to the mountain to pray.

49

A Mother's Influence

Sunday—*Timothy's heritage of faith (2 Timothy 1:1-5)*

¹Paul, an apostle of Christ Jesus by the will of God, according to the promise of life in Christ Jesus, ²to Timothy, my beloved son: Grace, mercy and peace from God the Father and Christ Jesus our Lord. ³I thank God, whom I serve with a clear conscience the way my forefathers did, as I constantly remember you in my prayers night and day, ⁴longing to see you, even as I recall your tears, so that I may be filled with joy. ⁵For I am mindful of the sincere faith within you, which first dwelt in your grandmother Lois, and your mother Eunice, and I am sure that it is in you as well.

Mothers influence their children in many ways. Paul recognized that fact when he said to Timothy, "When I call to remembrance the unfeigned faith that is in thee, which dwelt first in thy grandmother Lois, and thy mother Eunice; and I am persuaded that in thee also" (2 Timothy 1:5). Paul seems to be saying that Timothy had two generations pushing him in the right direction.

Napoleon once said, "Let France have good mothers and she will have good sons." Lord Bacon's mother was a woman of superior mind and deep devotion to God. The mother of Nero was greedy, lustful, and a murderess. Both men reflected their mother's attitudes.

The mother of John Wesley, founder of Methodism, was intellectually alert and extremely well organized. She taught her children at an early age to fear the rod and cry softly. Just about everything in her children's lives was regulated, from speech to play and work. She believed in conquering the will of the child early and started each child reading the Bible through at age five. Her influence produced fruit in the lives of all her children.

An older mother tried to explain her daughter's tragic failure in marriage and ultimate suicide. She said, "Pastor, apples do not fall far from the trees." The mother knew her own life had influenced her daughter.

Never in the history of this world has there been a greater need for godly mothers than now. One of our nation's leaders a few years ago spoke before the Senate committee investigating crime in interstate commerce. He said, "The home is the first great training school in behavior or misbehavior, and parents serve as the first teachers for the inspirational education of youth. In the home, the child learns that others besides himself have rights which he must respect.

"Here the spadework is laid for instilling in the child those values which will cause him to develop into an upright, law-abiding, wholesome citizen. He must learn respect for others, respect for property, courtesy, truthfulness and reliability. He must learn not only to manage his own affairs but also to share in the responsibility for the affairs of the community. He must be taught to understand the necessity of obeying the laws of God."

Dr. Charles Payson said, "What if God should place a diamond in your hand and tell you to inscribe on it a sentence which should be read at the Last Day and shown there as an index of your thoughts and feelings! What care, what caution would you exercise in the selection!"

That is what God has done. He has placed before us the immortal minds of our children, less perishable than the diamond, on which we are inscribing every day and every hour by our instruction, by our spirit, by our example, something that will remain and be exhibited for or against us at the Judgement Day!

The memory of a happy, Christlike home is the best legacy anyone can leave to his children.

> ## APPLES DO NOT FALL FAR FROM THE TREES.

Monday—*Qualities of a godly mother (Proverbs 31:25-31)*

25Strength and dignity are her clothing,
  And she smiles at the future.
26She opens her mouth in wisdom,
  And the teaching of kindness is on her tongue.
27She looks well to the ways of her household,
  And does not eat the bread of idleness.
28Her children rise up and bless her;
  Her husband also, and he praises her, saying:
29"Many daughters have done nobly,
  But you excel them all."
30Charm is deceitful and beauty is vain,
  But a woman who fears the LORD, she shall be praised.
31Give her the product of her hands,
  And let her works praise her in the gates.

Tuesday—*Jochebed's love for her baby boy (Exodus 2:1-10)*

1Now a man from the house of Levi went and married a

289

daughter of Levi. ²And the woman conceived and bore a son; and when she saw that he was beautiful, she hid him for three months. ³But when she could hide him no longer, she got him a wicker basket and covered it over with tar and pitch. Then she put the child into it, and set it among the reeds by the bank of the Nile. ⁴And his sister stood at a distance to find out what would happen to him. ⁵Then the daughter of Pharaoh came down to bathe at the Nile, with her maidens walking alongside the Nile; and she saw the basket among the reeds and sent her maid, and she brought it to her. ⁶When she opened it, she saw the child, and behold, the boy was crying. And she had pity on him and said, "This is one of the Hebrews' children." ⁷Then his sister said to Pharaoh's daughter. "Shall I go and call a nurse for you from the Hebrew women, that she may nurse the child for you?" ⁸And Pharaoh's daughter said to her, "Go ahead." So the girl went and called the child's mother. ⁹Then Pharaoh's daughter said to her, "Take this child away and nurse him for me and I shall give you your wages." So the woman took the child and nursed him. ¹⁰And the child grew, and she brought him to Pharaoh's daughter, and he became her son. And she named him Moses, and said, "Because I drew him out of the water."

Wednesday—*Hannah's care for her son, God's servant* *(1 Samuel 2:18-21)*

¹⁸Now Samuel was ministering before the LORD, as a boy wearing a linen ephod. ¹⁹And his mother would make him a little robe and bring it to him from year to year when she would come up with her husband to offer the yearly sacrifice. ²⁰Then Eli would bless Elkanah and his wife and say, "May the LORD give you children from this woman in place of the one she dedicated to the LORD." And they went to their own home. ²¹And the LORD visited Hannah; and she conceived and gave birth to three sons and two daughters. And the boy Samuel grew before the LORD.

Thursday—*One godly mother-to-be to another (Luke 1:41-45)*

⁴¹And it came about that when Elizabeth heard Mary's greeting, the baby leaped in her womb; and Elizabeth was filled with the Holy Spirit. ⁴²And she cried out with a loud voice, and said, "Blessed among women are you, and blessed is the fruit of

your womb! ⁴³And how has it happened to me, that the mother of my Lord should come to me? ⁴⁴For behold, when the sound of your greeting reached my ears, the baby leaped in my womb for joy. ⁴⁵And blessed is she who believed that there would be a fulfillment of what had been spoken to her by the Lord."

Friday—*Godly examples from older women (Titus 2:3-5)*

³Older women likewise are to be reverent in their behavior, not malicious gossips, nor enslaved to much wine, teaching what is good, ⁴that they may encourage the young women to love their husbands, to love their children, ⁵to be sensible, pure, workers at home, kind, being subject to their own husbands, that the word of God may not be dishonored.

Saturday—*Comfort like a mother's (Isaiah 66:10-14)*

¹⁰"Be joyful with Jerusalem and rejoice for her, all you who
    love her;
Be exceedingly glad with her, all you who mourn over her;
¹¹That you may nurse and be satisfied with her comforting
    breasts;
That you may suck and be delighted with her bountiful
    bosom."
¹²For thus says the LORD, "Behold I extend peace to her like a
    river,
And the glory of the nations like an overflowing stream;
And you shall be nursed, you shall be carried on the hip and
    fondled on the knees.
¹³As one whom his mother comforts, so I will comfort you;
And you shall be comforted in Jerusalem."
¹⁴Then you shall see this, and your heart shall be glad,
And your bones shall flourish like the new grass;
And the hand of the LORD shall be made known to His
    servants,
But He shall be indignant toward His enemies.

50

The Sins of the Parents

Sunday—*Family suffering for parents' sin (Joshua 7:20-26)*
²⁰So Achan answered Joshua and said, "Truly, I have sinned against the LORD, the God of Israel, and this is what I did; ²¹when I saw among the spoil a beautiful mantle from Shinar and two hundred shekels of silver and a bar of gold fifty shekels in weight, then I coveted them and took them; and behold, they are concealed in the earth inside my tent with the silver underneath it." ²²So Joshua sent messengers, and they ran to the tent; and behold, it was concealed in his tent with the silver underneath it. ²³And they took them from inside the tent and brought them to Joshua and to all the sons of Israel, and they poured them out before the LORD. ²⁴Then Joshua and all Israel with him, took Achan the son of Zerah, the silver, the mantle, the bar of gold, his sons, his daughters, his oxen, his donkeys, his sheep, his tent and all that belonged to him; and they brought them up to the valley of Achor. ²⁵And Joshua said, "Why have you troubled us? The LORD will trouble you this day." And all Israel stoned them with stones; and they burned them with fire after they had stoned them with stones. ²⁶And they raised over him a great heap of stones that stands to this day, and the LORD turned from the fierceness of His anger. Therefore the name of that place has been called the Valley of Achor to this day.

What is happening to the family? Is marriage on the way out? Those questions are being asked more and more as divorce rates soar and broken homes multiply.

Although our nation today enjoys its highest standard of living ever, there are increasing signs that the divine institution of the home is in critical condition. Dr. Appel of the University of Pennsylvania psychology department contends that the American family is in a state of serious crisis. He suggests three reasons why this condition exists.

First, he states that the family is fragmented. It does not hold together any longer than circumstances compel it to do so. *Newsweek* editor Richard Boeth maintains that it is futile to believe there can be any reversal of this trend. "It is novel and bizarre of us latter-day Westernoids," says Boeth, "to imagine that we can make something tolerable of marriage. It doesn't seem to have occurred to any earlier era that this was even possible. The Greeks railed against marriage and the Romans mocked and perverted it." Is he right? The Word of God suggests otherwise.

Dr. Appel gives a second reason for this crisis in the home: The average family is rootless. Since the end of World War II, America has been on the move. Twenty percent of the population change their places of residence annually. American industry today is demanding people who will move. One-third of all families with husbands under thirty-five move each year.

Third, Dr. Appel states that there is a lack of communication between family members today, resulting in a loss of intimacy and oneness. In many homes the husband, wife, and children all come and go as they please, often failing even to check in. In at atmosphere such as this, real communication is impossible, and the family structure breaks down.

As the children of Israel pitched their tents around Mount Sinai, God gave them His immutable Law. In explaining the first commandment, Exodus 20:5 states, "I the LORD thy God am a jealous God, visiting the iniquity of the fathers upon the children unto the third and fourth generation of them that hate me."

Moses was so impressed by that statement that he repeated it in Exodus 34:7 and again in Deuteronomy 5:9. Those words were terrifying then, and they are terrifying now. Our children to the third and fourth generations reap the result of our sins.

A Chinese proverb states, "In a broken nest there are few whole eggs." Sadly, thousands of emotionally disturbed children are the products of shattered marriages. It behooves every parent to do everything possible to avoid a broken home.

The first step in the establishment of a happy and successful home is to build it upon the foundation of the Word of God. God instructed the Israelites to devote themselves to the Scriptures, to teach and instruct their children in the precepts of Jehovah.

"And thou shalt teach them diligently unto thy children, and shalt talk of them when thou sittest in thine house, and when thou walkest by the way, and when thou liest down, and when thou risest up" (Deuteronomy 6:7).

That is the way it should be in every home. The reading of God's Word and family prayer are essentials that must not be overlooked. Then the parents must set an example for their children to follow.

IN A BROKEN NEST THERE ARE FEW WHOLE EGGS.

What are our homes like? Are they anchored to the rock of God's Word or are they drifting on the sea of uncertainty? Are we setting an example for our children to follow? Are we teaching them the Scriptures? Are we leading them into spiritual maturity?

Monday—*Making the Bible a way of life*
   (Deuteronomy 6:4-9)

⁴"Hear, O Israel! The LORD is our God, the LORD is one! ⁵And

you shall love the LORD your God with all your heart and with all your soul and with all your might. ⁶And these words, which I am commanding you today, shall be on your heart; ⁷and you shall teach them diligently to your sons and shall talk of them when you sit in your house and when you walk by the way and when you lie down and when you rise up. ⁸And you shall bind them as a sign on your hand and they shall be as frontals on your forehead. ⁹And you shall write them on the doorposts of your house and on your gates.

Tuesday—*Curses and blessings (Deuteronomy 5:9-10; Psalm 103:17-18)*

⁹"You shall not worship them or serve them; for I, the LORD your God, am a jealous God, visiting the iniquity of the fathers on the children, and on the third and the fourth generations of those who hate Me, ¹⁰but showing lovingkindness to thousands, to those who love Me and keep My commandments. . . .

¹⁷But the lovingkindness of the LORD is from everlasting to
      everlasting on those who fear Him,
   And His righteousness to children's children,
¹⁸To those who keep His covenant,
   And who remember His precepts to do them.

Wednesday—*Parents asking God's direction (Judges 13:8-18)*

⁸Then Manoah entreated the LORD and said, "O Lord, please let the man of God whom Thou hast sent come to us again that he may teach us what to do for the boy who is to be born." ⁹And God listened to the voice of Manoah; and the angel of God came again to the woman as she was sitting in the field, but Manoah her husband was not with her. ¹⁰So the woman ran quickly and told her husband, "Behold, the man who came the other day has appeared to me." ¹¹Then Manoah arose and followed his wife, and when he came to the man he said to him, "Are you the man who spoke to the woman?" And he said, "I am." ¹²And Manoah said, "Now when your words come to pass, what shall be the boy's mode of life and his vocation?" ¹³So the angel of the LORD said to Manoah, "Let the woman pay attention to all that I said. ¹⁴"She should not eat anything that comes from the vine nor drink wine or strong drink, nor eat any unclean thing; let her observe all that I commanded." ¹⁵Then Manoah said to the angel of the LORD, "Please let us detain you so that we may

prepare a kid for you." ¹⁶And the angel of the LORD said to Manoah, "Though you detain me, I will not eat your food, but if you prepare a burnt offering, then offer it to the LORD." For Manoah did not know that he was the angel of the LORD. ¹⁷And Manoah said to the angel of the LORD, "What is your name, so that when your words come to pass, we may honor you?" ¹⁸But the angel of the LORD said to him, "Why do you ask my name, seeing it is wonderful?"

Thursday—*Blessing of the family the Lord builds (Psalm 127)*

¹Unless the LORD builds the house,
They labor in vain who build it;
Unless the LORD guards the city,
The watchman keeps awake in vain.
²It is vain for you to rise up early,
To retire late,
To eat the bread of painful labors;
For He gives to His beloved even in his sleep.
³Behold, children are a gift of the LORD;
The fruit of the womb is a reward.
⁴Like arrows in the hand of a warrior,
So are the children of one's youth.
⁵How blessed is the man whose quiver is full of them;
They shall not be ashamed,
When they speak with their enemies in the gate.

Friday—*Wise parents bringing their children to Jesus (Mark 10:13-16)*

¹³And they began bringing children to Him, so that He might touch them; and the disciples rebuked them. ¹⁴But when Jesus saw this, He was indignant and said to them, "Permit the children to come to Me; do not hinder them; for the kingdom of God belongs to such as these. ¹⁵Truly I say to you, whoever does not receive the kingdom of God like a child shall not enter it at all." ¹⁶And he took them in His arms and began blessing them, laying His hands upon them.

Saturday—*Teaching children to obey God (Psalm 78:1-8)*

¹Listen, O my people, to my instruction;
Incline your ears to the words of my mouth.
²I will open my mouth in a parable;

I will utter dark sayings of old,
³Which we have heard and known,
And our fathers have told us.
⁴We will not conceal them from their children,
But tell to the generation to come the praises of the LORD,
And His strength and His wondrous works that He has done.
⁵For He established a testimony in Jacob,
And appointed a law in Israel,
Which He commanded our fathers,
That they should teach them to their children;
⁶That the generation to come might know, even the children
yet to be born,
That they may arise and tell them to their children,
⁷That they should put their confidence in God,
And not forget the works of God,
But keep His commandments,
⁸And not be like their fathers,
A stubborn and rebellious generation,
A generation that did not prepare its heart,
And whose spirit was not faithful to God.

51

What Makes a Nation Great?

Sunday—*Greatness from service (Matthew 20:25-28)*

25But Jesus called them to Himself, and said, "You know that the rulers of the Gentiles lord it over them, and their great men exercise authority over them. 26It is not so among you, but whoever wishes to become great among you shall be your servant, 27and whoever wishes to be first among you shall be your slave; 28just as the Son of Man did not come to be served, but to serve, and to give His life a ransom for many."

One of our great historians, Arnold Toynbee, speaks of nineteen civilizations that have existed since man began to form governments. Of the nineteen, only five still remain. Ours is one of the five.

When our nation was very young, a famous French political philosopher, Alexis de Tocqueville, visited to learn what magic quality had enabled a handful of people to defeat the mighty British Empire.

He looked for greatness in our harbors and rivers, our fertile fields and boundless forests, our mines and natural resources. He studied our schools, our Congress, and our Constitution, without finding the secret of our strength. It was not until he went into the churches of America and heard the pulpits "aflame with righteousness" that he found the secret of our greatness. He returned to France and wrote this warning: "America is great because America is good, and if America ever ceases to be good, America will cease to be great."

There is no doubt that God has blessed America. Yet we also agree that greatness is not measured in silver and gold, rivers and forests, or even muscles and missiles.

Greatness is an inner quality. It is found in what we are, not in what we have. Greatness is a quality of the heart, mind, and soul. We agree with de Tocqueville that "goodness and greatness" are inseparable. Let me suggest three ways to attain greatness in our nation.

First, we must resolve to serve our fellow citizens in humility. Recently *Time* magazine used over thirty pages to explore the subject of leadership. Renowned leaders attempted to define the essence of leadership. I was surprised that no one suggested the biblical definition of humble service. "Whosoever will be great among you, let him be your [servant]" (Matthew 20:26).

Old-fashioned concern for others is a quality that makes a nation great. Our Lord gave us the example when He "laid aside his garments; and took a towel . . . and began to wash the disciples' feet" (John 13:4-5). May we as citizens resolve to render humble service to one another.

Second, we should resolve to be totally honest and courageous. For many years, Dr. Madison Sarratt taught mathematics at Vanderbilt University. Prior to giving exams, he would say something like this, "Today I am giving two examinations—one in trigonometry and the other in honesty. I hope you will pass them both. If you must fail one, fail trigonometry. There are many good people in the world who can't pass trigonometry, but there are no good people who cannot pass the examination of honesty."

Each year it costs us collectively $40 billion to take care of white-collar crooks who embezzle from banks and corporations. It costs the nation's hotels and motels $500 million a year for petty stealing.

Third, we must acknowledge God as sovereign. No nation or person can be hardened and proud against God and expect to prosper. National prosperity, like personal prosperity, is contingent on righteousness. "Righteousness exalteth a nation," said Solomon, "but sin is a reproach to any people" (Proverbs 14:34). Our nation needs to return to God and to righteousness.

In the past few years, our nation has shown a frightening tendency to accept and even institutionalize sin. We seem to be going the way of Sodom and Gomorrah. Are we losing our greatness? Can the trend be reversed? It can if we will return to God.

Righteousness, courage, integrity, honesty, and humility—those are the things that make a nation great.

OLD-FASHIONED CONCERN FOR OTHERS IS A QUALITY THAT MAKES A NATION GREAT.

Monday—*The importance of honesty (2 Corinthians 8:18-24)*

[18]And we have sent along with him the brother whose fame in the things of the gospel has spread through all the churches;

¹⁹and not only this, but he has also been appointed by the churches to travel with us in this gracious work, which is being administered by us for the glory of the Lord Himself, and to show our readiness, ²⁰taking precaution that no one should discredit us in our administration of this generous gift; ²¹for we have regard for what is honorable, not only in the sight of the Lord, but also in the sight of men. ²²And we have sent with them our brother, whom we have often tested and found diligent in many things, but now even more diligent, because of his great confidence in you. ²³As for Titus, he is my partner and fellow-worker among you; as for our brethren, they are messengers of the churches, a glory to Christ. ²⁴Therefore openly before the churches show them the proof of your love and of our reason for boasting about you.

Tuesday—*Living properly as a citizen*
(1 Thessalonians 4:9-12)

⁹Now as to the love of the brethren, you have no need for any one to write to you, for you yourselves are taught by God to love one another; ¹⁰for indeed you do practice it toward all the brethren who are in all Macedonia. But we urge you, brethren, to excel still more, ¹¹and to make it your ambition to lead a quiet life and attend to your own business and work with your hands, just as we commanded you; ¹²so that you may behave properly toward outsiders and not be in any need.

Wednesday—*Citizenship prized by Paul (Acts 16:35-39)*

³⁵Now when day came, the chief magistrates sent their policemen, saying, "Release those men." ³⁶And the jailer reported these words to Paul, saying, "The chief magistrates have sent to release you. Now therefore come out and go in peace." ³⁷But Paul said to them, "They have beaten us in public without trial, men who are Romans, and have thrown us into prison; and now are they sending us away secretly? No indeed! But let them come themselves and bring us out." ³⁸And the policemen reported these words to the chief magistrates. And they were afraid when they heard that they were Romans, ³⁹and they came and appealed to them, and when they had brought them out, they kept begging them to leave the city.

Thursday—*Good deeds as proof of sterling character*
**   *(James 3:13-17)***
¹³Who among you is wise and understanding? Let him show by his good behavior his deeds in the gentleness of wisdom. ¹⁴But if you have bitter jealousy and selfish ambition in your heart, do not be arrogant and so lie against the truth. ¹⁵This wisdom is not that which comes down from above, but is earthly, natural, demonic. ¹⁶For where jealousy and selfish ambition exist, there is disorder and every evil thing. ¹⁷But the wisdom from above is first pure, then peaceable, gentle, reasonable, full of mercy and good fruits, unwavering, without hypocrisy.

Friday—*The Lord as sovereign over all (Psalm 103:19-22)*
¹⁹The LORD has established His throne in the heavens;
  And His sovereignty rules over all.
²⁰Bless the LORD, you His angels,
  Mighty in strength, who perform His word,
  Obeying the voice of His word!
²¹Bless the LORD, all you His hosts,
  You who serve Him, doing His will.
²²Bless the LORD, all you works of His,
  In all places of His dominion;
  Bless the LORD, O my soul!

Saturday—*The way to national greatness*
**   *(Proverbs 14:33-35)***
³³Wisdom rests in the heart of one who has understanding,
  But in the bosom of fools it is made known.
³⁴Righteousness exalts a nation,
  But sin is a disgrace to any people.
³⁵The king's favor is toward a servant who acts wisely,
  But his anger is toward Him who acts shamefully.

52

America, Right or Wrong?

Sunday—*Commandment to obey authorities (Romans 13:1-4)*

¹Let every person be in subjection to the governing authorities. for there is no authority except from God, and those which exist are established by God. ²Therefore he who resists authority has opposed the ordinance of God; and they who have opposed will receive condemnation upon themselves. ³For rulers are not a cause of fear for good behavior, but for evil. Do you want to have no fear of authority? Do what is good, and you will have praise from the same; ⁴for it is a minister of God to you for good. But if you do what is evil, be afraid; for it does not bear the sword for nothing; for it is a minister of God, an avenger who brings wrath upon the one who practices evil.

America—what is wrong and what is right with it? Despite the immense problems that plague our land, we do have much for which to be thankful. God has blessed America!

The Bible tells us that as Christians we are to honor those who are in places of authority. The Bible also teaches that we are to be the finest citizens possible. Paul wrote, "Let every soul be subject unto the higher powers. For there is no power but of God: the powers that be are ordained of God. Whosoever therefore resisteth the power, resisteth the ordinance of God" (Romans 13:1-2). That is direct and easy to understand.

Our allegiance is to God first, but we also have a clear responsibility to uphold those who rule over us. We are to be subject to civil authority.

As responsible citizens, we do not blindly approve every action of government. We are aware of our national failures. We do not wish to sweep our sins under the rug. When America is right, we support her. When America is wrong, we still love her—and do our best to correct her.

Looking at the past, we see that America has been a nation that has honored God. When the *Mayflower* landed at Plymouth in November 1620, the Pilgrims made an agreement called the Mayflower Compact. In that official pact, God was acknowledged and given His rightful place. A look at the present, however, finds America quite removed from her religious foundations.

Professor Richard Hofstader of Columbia University has said, "We are living in a culture that is secular. Religion does not play the role that it used to play. This is particularly true for people under forty years of age in this society. When a strong religious bond is missing, there are few things that can hold the culture together."

It has been said that the key to a nation's greatness is the combined character of all of its people. Unfortunately, our collective character is not too good. We desperately need a spiritual awakening.

But then, not all is wrong. America has much for which

to be thankful. The United States has passed more social legislation and enacted more laws providing individual liberty than any other nation in world history. Through the decades she has opened her heart to the poor of the world. She has given generously to every nation, even her enemies, in time of emergency. Because of her belief in freedom of speech, she has not hidden her scars. All that she does is an open book for everyone to see.

Yes, we love America. We love her rocks and rills, her woods and templed hills, her rock-ribbed shores and booming cities. We love her people. May we resolve anew, as believers in Jesus Christ, to be "the salt of the earth" for America and the world.

WHEN AMERICA IS WRONG, WE STILL LOVE HER AND DO OUR BEST TO CORRECT HER.

Monday—*Paying taxes, giving allegiance (Romans 13:5-7)*

5Wherefore it is necessary to be in subjection, not only because of wrath, but also for conscience' sake. 6For because of this you also pay taxes, for rulers are servants of God, devoting themselves to this very thing. 7Render to all what is due them: tax to whom tax is due; custom to whom custom; fear to whom fear; honor to whom honor.

Tuesday—*Wise behavior before leaders (1 Peter 2:13-17)*

13Submit yourselves for the Lord's sake to every human institution: whether to a king as the one in authority; 14or to governors as sent by him for the punishment of evildoers and the praise of those who do right. 15For such is the will of God that by doing right you may silence the ignorance of foolish men. 16Act as free men, and do not use your freedom as a covering for evil, but use it as bondslaves of God. 17Honor all men; love the brotherhood, fear God, honor the king.

Wednesday—*Jesus' teaching on respect of authorities*
(Luke 20:20-26)

20And they watched Him, and sent spies who pretended to be

righteous, in order that they might catch Him in some statement, so as to deliver Him up to the rule and the authority of the governor. 21And they questioned Him, saying, "Teacher, we know that You speak and teach correctly, and You are not partial to any, but teach the way of God in truth. 22Is it lawful for us to pay taxes to Caesar, or not?" 23But He detected their trickery and said to them, 24"Show Me a denarius. Whose head and inscription does it have?" And they said, "Caesar's." 25And He said to them, "Then render to Caesar the things that are Caesar's, and to God the things that are God's." 26And they were unable to catch Him in a saying in the presence of the people; and marveling at His answer, they became silent.

Thursday—*Taxes paid by Jesus and Peter* (Matthew 17:24-27)

24And when they had come to Capernaum, those who collected the two-drachma tax came to Peter, and said, "Does your teacher not pay the two-drachma tax?" 25He said, "Yes." And when he came into the house, Jesus spoke to him first, saying, "What do you think, Simon? From whom do the kings of the earth collect customs or poll-tax, from their sons or from strangers?" 26And upon his saying, "From strangers," Jesus said to him, "Consequently the sons are exempt. 27But, lest we give them offense, go to the sea, and throw in a hook, and take the first fish that comes up; and when you open its mouth, you will find a stater; take that and give it to them for you and Me."

Friday—*God, the supreme governor (Acts 5:17-29)*

17But the high priest rose up, along with all his associates (that is the sect of the Sadducees), and they were filled with jealousy; 18and they laid hands on the apostles, and put them in a public jail. 19But an angel of the Lord during the night opened the gates of the prison, and taking them out he said, 20"Go your way, stand and speak to the people in the temple the whole message of this Life." 21And upon hearing this, they entered into the temple about daybreak, and began to teach. Now when the high priest and his associates had come, they called the Council together, and all the Senate of the sons of Israel, and sent orders to the prison house for them to be brought. 22But the officers who came did not find them in the prison; and they returned, and reported back, 23saying, "We found the prison-house locked quite securely and the guards standing at the doors; but when we had opened up, we found no one inside." ²⁴Now when the captain of the temple guard and the chief priests heard these words, they were greatly perplexed about them as to what would come of this. ²⁵But someone came and reported to them, "Behold, the men whom you put in prison are standing in the temple and teaching the people!" ²⁶Then the captain went along with the officers and proceeded to bring them back without violence; (for they were afraid of the people, lest they should be stoned). ²⁷And when they had brought them, they stood them before the Council. And the high priest questioned them, ²⁸saying, "We gave you strict orders not to continue teaching in this name, and behold, you have filled Jerusalem with your teaching, and intend to bring this man's blood upon us." ²⁹But Peter and the apostles answered and said, "We must obey God rather than men."

Saturday—*Our heavenly citizenship (Philippians 3:17-21)*

¹⁷Brethren, join in following my example, and observe those who walk according to the pattern you have in us. ¹⁸For many walk, of whom I often told you, and now tell you even weeping, that they are enemies of the cross of Christ, ¹⁹whose end is destruction, whose god is their appetite, and whose glory is in their shame, who set their minds on earthly things. ²⁰For our citizenship is in heaven, from which also we eagerly wait for a Savior, the Lord Jesus Christ; ²¹who will transform the body of our humble state into conformity with the body of His glory, by the exertion of the power that He has even to subject all things to Himself.

Moody Press, a ministry of the Moody Bible Institute, is designed for education, evangelization, and edification. If we may assist you in knowing more about Christ and the Christian life, please write us without obligation: Moody Press, c/o MLM, Chicago, Illinois 60610.